The Losses of Nations

Nations

Deadweight Politics
versus
Public Rent Dividends

Fred Harrison
Editor

OTHILA

First published in 1998 by
Othila Press Ltd.,
58a Abingdon Road,
London, W8 6AP, UK

British Library CIP Data
A catalogue record of this book
is available from the British Library

ISBN
1 901647 16 1 (hardback)
1 901647 15 3 (paperback)

Printed and bound in
the United Kingdom by
MFP Design & Print,
Manchester

Contents

Tables, Boxes, Figures and Graphs

Need-to-Know Knowledge
for
Presidents & Prime Ministers

The Market, Taxation, & the Public Rent Dividend

The Jobless Growth Crisis Governments are driving the mightiest economies into the ground. There is no mystery about the process. The cause is government itself. It controls the tax system, which is the primary dynamic underlying the economic crisis.

The effect is summarized in Table A: the leading industrial economies are gliding towards a halt, **driven into the ground by governments that claim to represent the best interests of their citizens**.

The flattening of growth to the rate of increase of population is dangerous. It slides society into a stationary state.

Zero real growth threatens a deterioration in living standards of devastating proportions.

Table A
Unemployment & Growth
in Industrial Counties : %

	Unemployment		Per Capita GDP Growth	
	1965/75	1976/95	1965/75	1976/95
EC	2.8	9.4	3.4	1.7
Scandinavia	2.0	4.8	3.4	1.5
US & Canada	5.0	8.0	2.8	1.5
Japan	1.3	2.4	6.0	3.0
Australia	2.3	7.7	2.3	1.2

SOURCE: Daveri & Tabellini 1997: 42, drawing on OECD National Accounts.

Taxation on people and their savings undermines the ability to work and to set aside sufficient income to invest in the future. This is *not* a crisis of capitalism (the vulgar marxist thesis). It is a crisis of governance - a long, drawn-out challenge to the viability of the liberal democratic system which is no less potentially fatal now that the communist creed has been set aside as a curiosity of history.

Governments blame the "high cost" of employing people on trade unions. In fact, people are priced out of work by government taxation. This has two distinct effects, depending on whether people are unionized (such as in Germany and France) or weakened in the workplace (USA, UK).

- **Highly unionized economies**: taxes on employees are displaced on to employers. This results in unemployment. The lower profits of firms leads to the substitution of capital for labor, causing a drop in the returns to investment; which, in time, encourages people to reduce their savings. Thus, high unemployment is associated with low growth.
- **Weak employee institutions**: taxes are absorbed by employees, reducing their take-home pay. Because the cost of employing people does not rise, the immediate effect on unemployment or the ratio of capital to labor is not the same as in highly organized labor markets.

But in both cases trends are the in the same direction: downwards for growth, upwards for unemployment.

A study of 14 countries with varying grades of employee power concluded that "in all countries, unemployment and labor taxes are strongly positively correlated over time. Correlation tends to be stronger for the countries in continental Europe.... The rise in labor tax rates over time....is associated with a decline in growth and investment" (Daveri and Tabellini 1997: 18-19).

Governments have sole responsibility for revenue-raising policies. They cannot displace responsibility for the jobless growth crisis onto others. Not, that is, if they have the option of a practical policy that does *not* damage people's ability to work, save and invest for the future.

There is such a policy. It provides the only solution to the crisis. Everyone wins. Its adoption would, for the first time, liberate people to make free choices about the quality of the lives they wish to enjoy. The solution flows naturally from corrections to the primary source of jobless growth: taxation.

Fiscal Fatigue   Nation-states enter the new millennium hamstrung by the fiscal crisis. Governments have hit the limit of their capacity to try and solve social and economic problems by redistributing income through coercive taxation. That strategy did not work and the ballot box has driven home the lesson that people are not willing to pay more.

And yet, deeply entrenched social problems demand resources. Some of these problems would be alleviated by new economic growth. But governments are constantly reminded by the stock markets that new growth is seriously constrained by bottlenecks that threaten to further destabilize the economy. Inflation jeopardizes growth; so, paradoxically, governments resort to policies that restrain growth. They impose a ceiling on opportunity. **There is no vision of, or strategy for, virtuous growth**: stable and sustainable development of wealth creation and social development.

The primary economic problems and many social challenges are associated with a single flaw in the foundation of the economy. This flaw is to be found in the character of taxation. Public finance has evolved into an abusive system which destroys the capacity of the economy to meet everyone's needs. This is achieved by denying people their basic right to work.

A solution is available for statesmen who have the vision to perceive the fundamental reform that offers virtuous growth. To evaluate the necessity for this reform, however, a historical perspective is necessary. This makes sense of what appear to be insoluble problems such as unemployment and poverty-level wages, and encourages the scientific solutions that simultaneously offer both economic efficiency and social justice.

These objectives were never part of the origins of the tax system that we have inherited. As the director of the International Monetary Fund's Fiscal Affairs Department put it: "The tax systems that have come into existence, both in their levels and in their structures, are more the result of political and administrative considerations and of historical developments than of the rational prescriptions of economists" (Tanzi 1995: 4).

Democratic governments do have it in their power to abolish unemployment and poverty-level wages. This could be accomplished through market-led changes in the incentives to work and produce wealth.

The primary constraint on work and wealth is not to be found in the conventional explanation: inflexible labor markets. Historically, the latter are just one of the institutional responses to the changing character of public finance. The straightjacket that distorts people's motivations and work-related processes - from factory-floor organization of employees to the use of secret off-shore bank accounts - is the tax system. This straightjacket is the product of an obsolete philosophy of property rights which is designed to defeat the ambitions of people in a free society.

Tax-driven unemployment   Unemployment was one of the characteristic hallmarks of the 20th century. By the 1980s, governments accepted defeat: they abandoned the struggle to ensure that every able-bodied person could work to earn his or her living.

Periods of full employment have generally been the by-product of the devastation of war: people were needed to restore the infrastructure of their bombed economies. In time, however, levels of near-zero unemployment were eroded as the industrial economies returned to "normality".

Despite the strong rates of economic growth in the 1980s, unemployment continued on an upward trend. In 1996, almost 36 million people were without jobs in the 23 OECD countries. That was 6 million more than in the mid 1980s and almost 25 million more than in the previous decade. The OECD has calculated unemployment on a structural basis; unemployment that is not purely cyclical, which provides a more accurate comparison between countries over time. Table B provides the data for the richest seven (G7) countries.

Table B
G7: Structural unemployment
(per cent of total labor force)

	1990	1996
Canada	9.0	8.5
France	9.3	9.7
Germany	6.9	9.6
Italy	9.7	10.6
Japan	2.5	2.7
UK	8.4	7.0
USA	5.8	5.6

Source: S. Blondal & S. Scarpetta (1997:9)

If existing models of how the economy works were valid, governments would be able to assemble the rules to liberate every person so that he or she could work without hindrance, to earn wages that were sufficient to meet all needs over the family life-cycle. But because employment is not a sustainable characteristic of the so-called free market economy, we have to conclude (after all this time, and after all the sincere efforts by generations of statesmen) that the existing rules impose artificial limits on people's freedom. Somewhere in the system there is a flaw that governments and their economic advisers have failed to eliminate. Responsibility is conventionally attributed to a wide range of issues. Insufficient attention is paid to the warning, first issued 200 years ago by the classical economists, that **taxes destroy the capacity of people to work and produce wealth**.

Smoke-and-mirrors conceal the truth about taxation. This emerges when we note the following fact. Much of what people think they pay out of their wages or the income from their savings does not come from them at all. **A large part of tax revenue that is imposed on labor and capital is actually paid out of the rent of land and natural resources**.

The classical economists took the trouble to explain the process. In essence, much of what appears to be taxation on wages and the interest received from savings is passed on to others, through higher prices, until it eventually falls on the net income of the community. That net income is what economists call the economic rent of land and natural resources.

A crystal clear understanding of this process is crucial for good government. It is barely noted in the economic textbooks which presume to offer intelligent advice to governments. This has bequeathed a legacy of ignorance which inflicts a grievous limitation on policy-makers. It is not surprising, therefore, that when economists offer advice on how to modify the tax system, they fail to promote the optimum result: economic efficiency combined with social justice.

In fact, as the world community of nations struggles towards the harmonization of policies on taxation, they are unwittingly consolidating the underlying conditions that disrupt production; and are pushing the global economy towards crises even greater than those that blighted the 20th century (Ch3).

The global economy could bring enormous gains in private and public welfare. These are possible only if governments factor into their policies what we shall call The Absorption Effect of economic progress. As prosperity grows, so does the net income of the economy. And this income can be used either to enhance everybody's welfare, or (as happens now) as a weapon to disrupt people's lives.

Understanding that fundamental process is crucial if citizens are to democratize public finance. The alternative is to struggle on with a tax system from a bygone age, which was created in the interests of a minority whose motivation was purely self-centered, contrary to the private interests of everyone else and in disregard of the community's interest.

Deadloss taxation Economists as a class have been negligent in failing to highlight the ideal fiscal system. That they have failed to quantify the negative costs of taxation, therefore, is not surprising. The IMF's tax expert, Vito Tanzi (1995: 4), has argued that "The magnitudes of these effects remain controversial. Empirical evidence has not been able to provide results that were beyond challenge". An informed public debate must begin by providing people at least with order-of-magnitude estimates of the losses which are inflicted on them. Only then will they be able to decide whether it matters if the scale of losses is smaller by 50% or bigger by 100%. In fact, every year, the wealth lost to nations is so large as to override all scholastic concerns for precision (Ch. 6). Losses there are, of enormous quantities sufficient to finance current social needs and environmental clean-up programs many times over. Acting rationally, people might decide that they would prefer to shift towards the structure of public finance that removes these costs and liberates them to work and create the wealth they want. But at no time in the last two centuries have economists troubled to calculate - and publish for the public's benefit - a comprehensible account of the losses imposed by taxation. The destructive character of taxation is horrifying.

● The United States loses over $1 trillion every year. This estimate is derived from the calculations of Martin Feldstein, a leading specialist in the field of taxation, a former Chairman of the President's Council of Economic Advisers who is professor of economics at Harvard University.

That $1 trillion is the measure of the goods and services that would be produced by the people of the USA if government abandoned the destructive taxation in favor of virtuous public finance.

New calculations deepen the taxpayers' understanding of the loss of wealth that is attributable to taxation. Table C reports the value that would have been enjoyed by citizens in the G7 countries *if a rational public finance had been in place*. The gain for the seven countries would have been of the order of $6.8 trillion (£4,357 billion).

Table C
G7: Gain in Output and *Per Capita* Income
under the Public Rent Policy (1993)

	NDP $ bn	NDP *per capita* $
USA	1,602	6,902
Canada	275	9,142
France	879	15,166
Germany	1,018	12,406
Italy	815	14,128
Japan	1,535	12,284
UK	716	12,133
Total	*6,840*	

Source: Derived from Table 6:I (page 147, below)

On the basis of the assumptions used in the model (Ch.6, Appendix), the UK's Net Domestic Product (NDP) in 1993 would have been larger by £456 bn, and *per capita* incomes would have been greater by £7,728.

The loss of this wealth is the legacy of mismanagement by governments of all political shades.

Because of the variable quality of data available, and because of disagreement among economists over some of the empirical issues, other analysts will adjust the calculations downwards (or upwards). A consensus will emerge around estimates of the losses, but we can be certain of one conclusion even now: the scale of the material losses inflicted by taxation has been unimaginably large.

- **The loss to the wealth of nations is a measure of the indictment of governments that abandoned the best interests of all their citizens to retain a tax system that preserved the anti-democratic privileges of the few.**

The indictment is not limited to considerations of hard cash. The social and psychological deprivation inflicted on people has been enormous, and needless.

- **The inability to adopt fair finance - recommended at the beginning of the 20th century by statesmen (like Winston Churchill) and prominent economists in the USA, Germany and Britain - was and remains the crisis of governance.**

Given the scale of these losses, governments are not entitled to claim that society cannot afford to finance the social services that are the legitimate responsibility of the public sector. **At the end of President Bill Clinton's two administrations, the people of the United States would lose the equivalent of a full year's output of goods and services.** Wealth gone forever, lost in a dead zone beyond people's reach. It could have been used to eradicate the social and environmental problems that blight people's lives.

Net Income as Public Value The solution is for the guardians of the public welfare to move towards a system of charging people directly for the public and environmental services from which they benefit. This would immediately liberate people and the economy **and generate sufficient revenue to finance all legitimate public sector obligations.**

- In the modern economy about one third of a nation's income constitutes the net (or "surplus") income. This is the income that has traditionally been reserved as public revenue. It is, in fact, publicly-created value.

This reform would abolish taxation on people's wages and the income from their savings. In its place, people would agree to pay rent to the community for the use of land and natural resources. This model of public finance is at the heart of the policy of restricting charges to the principle that people should pay for the benefits that they receive.

Every viable community generates sufficient public value to pay for the services which individuals could not provide for themselves.

That income is net of what people need to pay for the reproduction of their families (the *wages of labor*) and the production of wealth (the *interest and dividends on capital*). When these two costs of living and working have been met, the remaining flow of income is the material base on which the public sector has traditionally been built.

Tax-related economic crises become endemic when public spending exceeds the net income recovered by the community for its social services.

Historically, there were two main reasons for the emergence of tax-driven friction in the economy.

(1) The earliest civilizations failed to develop a philosophy of land that respected the territorial rights of others. And even if they had done, they remained vulnerable to the aggressive expansion of other peoples. External threat to the territorial integrity of the community required a commitment of considerable resources to military defense. This resulted in expensive wars. The outcome was indebtedness, both for the State and for citizens

(2) A growing part of net income was siphoned into private pockets. Thus, governments were driven to exploiting the wages of labor and the profits from people's savings.

Today, the misappropriation of public revenue is not regarded as immoral. And the passage of time has bestowed a sheen of legitimacy on the ensuing resort of governments to attack people's privately-earned income. A parallel social process was slavery, which was not outlawed until the 19th century.

Historically, the private appropriation of public value has been the stuff of high politics, the basis of some of the greatest dramas. The struggle to control this income has ebbed and flowed with the epochs (in fact, that struggle defines much of Western civilization). The private pursuit of the public value found its complete expression in government capitulation to landowners in the post-feudal stage of cultural evolution. Thus was embedded the values of exploitation into the modern value-for-money system of production.

The greatest challenge facing democratic society is not just to try and balance

BOX 1
The Hong Kong Paradigm

ECONOMISTS point to the prosperity of Hong Kong as a model of what can be achieved by the market. The IMF, for example, reports that Hong Kong is the world leader in the growth of productivity: over 4% per annum on average between 1970 and 1989. This eclipsed France, Italy and Japan (between 2 and 2.5%), the UK (1.5%) and the US (0.5%).

What the IMF describes as "a critical ingredient" in Hong Kong's policy framework "has been a prudent fiscal policy aimed at keeping government small, avoiding deficits, and not pursuing counter-cyclical stabilization policies. By and large... the fiscal stance should be broadly neutral. Budgetary strategy has been guided by four broad principles: to maintain a simple and stable tax system with low tax rates; keep current spending in line with GDP growth; provide funding for key infrastructure products; and maintain an adequate level of fiscal reserves" (Husain 1997:5).

The colony's policy was shaped by Lord Aberdeen, the Foreign Secretary who dispatched his instructions on 4 January 1843:

"The principle source from which revenue is to be looked for is the Land; and if by the liberality of the Commercial regulations enforced in the Island, foreigners as well as British Subjects are tempted to establish themselves on it, and thus to make it a great mercantile Entrepot, with very limited dimensions, Her Majesty's Government conceived that they would be fully justified in securing to the Crown all the benefits to be expected from the increased value which such a state of things would confer upon Land. Her Majesty's Government would therefore caution you against the permanent alienation of any portion of the land, and they would prefer that Parties should hold land under Leases from the Crown, the terms of which might be sufficiently long to warrant the holders in building upon their allotments."

Lord Aberdeen suggested: "It would probably be advantageous also that the portions of land should be let by auction" (Welsh 1997: 149).

Land auctions were to feature not only as a major source of finance for the colony's infrastructure and administration, but also to serve as a barometer of the health of the economy ("Property Prices In Hong Kong May Fall Again", *Wall Street Journal Europe*, Jan 14, 1998). Hong Kong is now judged to be top of the free economies in the world: *see page 119.*

the public books. It is to restore a principled basis to the distribution of the wealth. This entails re-laying the foundations of public finance.

The Public Rent Dividend Much of what appears as taxation on the income from people's wages and savings is, in fact, ultimately drawn out of the net income (Ch. 1). This is an inescapable law of economics. But in that case, why go to the trouble of transforming the structure of public finance if the shifting process ultimately displaces much of current tax revenue onto the rent of land anyway? The indirect capture of the public value that is called "rent" imposes enormous disincentives on people's willingness and ability to work and save. The reform would generate large material benefits that are beyond the reach of current economic activity. These benefits are locked into the dead zone. Until, that is, we use the key that unlocks the wealth that would enrich us all. This additional wealth is the dividend that would flow when we rebase public finance directly on the rent of land and natural resources. (*See Box 1*)

This proposal is within the realms of political realism. For example, the government elected in Britain on May 1, 1997, explicitly set out to modernize the nation. Prime Minister Tony Blair issued a public warning to the officials and democratically-elected politicians of local government that he would show them "zero tolerance of failure". That standard applies equally to central government, which could not function without revenue. The manner in which revenue is raised, then, is a test of the performance of the Blair government. Since the election of New Labour the people of Britain have been losing over £10 billion every month - a deadweight loss that has to be attributed directly to the inefficiencies of central government's tax system.

● Using conservative estimates, and assumptions based on the impact of taxation in the USA, the annual loss of output in Britain exceeds £115 billion. That is the additional revenue - the goods and services that people would produce if they were liberated from taxation - that would be available if government modernized its revenue system.

It is clear, then, that there are sound financial reasons for charging people directly for the natural resources and public services from which they benefit. One outcome would be honest and open government that serves the people rather than, as now, an embarrassed government that deploys considerable resources into defending the inefficiencies of public administration.

● The Blair government claims that it does not have the money to undertake expenditures such as £5.7 bn to repair the nation's schools. Urgent repairs go by default, for want of a drop in the ocean of wealth that is willfully lost every year by the preservation of taxes on labor.

- The costs of collecting taxes are higher than they would be under the rent-based system of finance by a ratio of 15:1 (according to data for the US [Netzer 1997: 30]). This is inefficiency that the Blair government would not tolerate from local government politicians, and is a logical reason for reviewing the philosophy of government finance.
- People's attitude towards public finance would be transformed. They correctly perceive taxes to be inefficient; disproportionate to the services that they receive, as individuals; and not fair.

Beyond such material benefits, however, the transformation of public finance is a precondition for a free society. The treatment of the rent of land and natural resources as public revenue is the only policy that places every citizen on an equal footing:

- Only then do people enjoy democracy, individual responsibility - and stake their claim to all their rights as citizens (Ch. 5).
- Only then do we convert the idealism of equality into economic reality.
- Only then do people derive the self esteem which is their psychological need and right, a pre-condition not only of the healthy individual but also of the healthy community.

The rhetoric of tax efficiency   The damage inflicted on people's rights is conceded by the way in which governments *finesse* the tax system. Governments are urged to spread the tax burden more widely, to reduce the existing rates of taxation. In the G7 countries this has led to a contrasting spread of tactics (Table D, overleaf), with the UK the worst offender for its use of indirect taxes to conceal the impact from people.

Taxation-by-stealth compromises the democratic process. Indirect taxes are 43% of the total in Britain; this compares with 26% (Japan) and 28% (USA). Economists - and politicians - rationalize the use of indirect taxation as the means to spread the burden and therefore ease the pain. These rationalizations are designed to mislead people into not realizing just how much money they are paying to government. So one of the principles on which democracy is supposed to be founded - the transparency of behavior by politicians - is abused by the ruses employed in the raising of revenue.

Justice is also a victim. From the data on direct taxes, we see that corporations are systematically favored against households. The reason is due solely to the fact that the owners can shift capital beyond the reach of governments, whereas

Table D
Taxes & Social Security Contributions % of total: G7 countries (1993)

	Direct taxes paid by Households	Corporations	Indirect taxes	Taxes on capital	Social Security contributions
UK[1]	29.4	7.4	43.0	0.6	18.6
USA	35.0	9.4	28.6	0.9	26.1
CANADA	39.3	8.9	39.0	1.0	11.9
FRANCE	16.3	4.7	33.4	0.9	44.7
GERMANY	24.2	3.9	31.8	0.3	39.8
ITALY	29.7	8.2	30.0	0.2	31.9
JAPAN	24.9	14.2	26.5	2.1	32.3

[1] Total includes 1% from Community Charge.
Source: OECD data, in ONS (1996: Table 10.72, p.137)

families are generally tied by kinship and psychology to their root neighborhoods (until they become so desperate that they are forced to migrate in search of work in a new country). For this, **people are penalized by a taxation that adds to the stresses of employment that lead to work and income related illnesses and even deaths.**

Governments regularly promise to "reform" the tax system to deliver "efficiency". This is a promise that, with the best will in the world, they cannot keep. Their proposals are restricted to changes within the existing philosophy of finance. This means that they are engaged in a surreal quest for benefits that are beyond their reach.

The rhetoric of tax "fairness"   The word *fairness* is routinely used in relation to tax policy. This concept is so rarely defined that people cannot be blamed for suspecting that the word is designed more to conceal than shed light on action by governments. When attempts are made to define it, the consequence is a root-and-branch condemnation of conventional taxation.

Examination of the use of the word helps to identify the direction in which reform ought to move. (*See Box 2*) A practical opportunity has been afforded by the British government's 1998 budget, which is supposed to be re-based on a philosophy of fairness. The elements were outlined in a pre-budget discussion document. This offered a definition which set a standard which is impossible to achieve under the existing tax regime. It defines the principles of fairness in this way:

> These are to encourage work, savings, investment and fairness. Fairness means that the tax system evolves in ways which benefit the many, not just the few, and by ensuring that it is seen to be fair (Treasury 1997a: 57).

WHEN DID YOU LAST hear a government announce that it was going to cause unemployment by raising taxes on wages?

Governments destroy jobs and wealth through their chosen instruments for raising money, but this is not how unemployment is explained. It is necessary to decode the linguistic "spins" from economists and politicians, if the economic crisis is to be solved democratically.

First, recognize that there is a perpetual struggle over the distribution of the nation's income. Clarification of the words exposes the underlying dynamics.

- Labor markets with strong unions are called "non-competitive". Why? Because unions can protect the real value of wages against the tax attacks from governments that discriminate in favor of incomes going to capital and land. From the employees' viewpoint, this is a *competitive* market: capable of challenging the power exercised by owners of capital and land.
- Weak unionization is called a "competitive" market, in which employees are vulnerable. They would say that theirs was a *non-competitive* market, vis-à-vis the capital and land markets.

In seeking solutions to tax-induced unemployment and poverty, economists talk about identifying "the optimal structure of taxation across alternative tax bases such as capital, labor or consumption" (Daveri & Tabellini 1997: 35). But the optimal tax policy lies *outside* these categories. Economists confused themselves by conflating *land* - which is a distinctive factor of production (Gaffney 1994a) - with man-made *capital*.

In economics, reality and language often do not converge; which is why the words have to be decoded, if motives are to be analyzed and effective solutions defined.

The tax system inherited by the people of Britain - the model for many other countries - defeats all these aspirations. Taxes on labor deter people from working. Taxes on savings deter people from investing. Marginal adjustments in tax rates and the closing of loopholes does nothing to moderate people's perception of taxation as unfair; they merely deepen the discontent.

The definition offers no criterion for determining whether taxes should fall on income that is earned or unearned. The concept of people paying "a fair share" (Treasury 1997a: 61) is not defined beyond noting that Parliament is the arbiter of this fairness. The definition says nothing about the rules that should determine either how much an individual should pay or how much government may take, in total, from the wealth creators.

Nor does the definition help us to determine the legitimacy of avoiding the payment of taxes. The British government says that "there is a limit to what can be regarded as acceptable behavior in minimizing tax bills", but offers no principle for determining the nature of that limit beyond what parliament intended. (*Ibid*: 62).

In sum, this attempt to re-shape taxation on the strength of fairness offers no new guide beyond the arbitrary will of Parliament. The British government

- does not yet appreciate that public finance offers the comprehensive solution to the distribution of income in the private sector;
- does not yet recognize that a rational approach to public finance would liberate people to work under conditions that would remove the need for legislation on minimum wages;
- does not yet accept that features like inheritance taxation offends its declared principle of being fair to future generations.

It did begin to struggle with tax policies that address the environmental crisis, but these are likely to fall short of action proportionate to the scale of the problems, because of the absence of a coherent fiscal philosophy.

Public finance and Property rights   A public finance rebased on the rent of land and natural resources would generate profound changes in public attitudes. Such a transformation is needed in the labor market. Historically, trade unions emerged to defend the interests of vulnerable employees. The social forces that created the pool of landless laborers were responsible for the imbalance in bargaining power which favored urban employers. At the beginning of the 19th century, poverty-level wages were the "market" rate. That rate had nothing to do with the market as a social process; everything to do with the dispossession of people who tilled the land. They were displaced from the countryside, and had nothing but their labor on which to survive. The felt need for solidarity among employees, who had no means of power other than through the organized control over their services, resulted in the development of unions.

Today, that vulnerability still exists. The underlying reasons have not been moderated by the passage of time or events. The conflict-based approach to negotiating wages is not the desirable method, but it is the stark reality for landless workforces that need to exercise countervailing power. This has led to rigidities in the labor market and destructive behavior (through the use of the strike weapon) which damages everyone's interests. A rational alternative is available.

Current analysis, however, is compromised by the partial understanding of the origins of the problem. Thus, the International Monetary Fund (IMF), in its annual world economic forecast published in 1997, claimed that the root cause of structural unemployment in Europe was "elaborate job and income protection arrangements that raise the cost of labor and discourage job creation". **The IMF fails to explain that taxes raise the cost of employing labor and discourage entrepreneurs from creating new jobs**. Government is responsible for the primary distortion in the market for jobs; for governments have the law-making power to determine the character of taxation.

A rational public finance would become the heart of a new relationship between government and people. This would entail a redefinition of property rights which would remove the ambiguities that are currently associated with phrases like "the right to work". It would also remove the animosity now directed at governments, transforming people's attitude towards the public sector into the perception of an equal partner in the wealth-creating process. **The equal share of every citizen to the net income that he or she helps to create becomes the stake held in society. Without this tangible benefit, attempts to define the "stakeholder society" will be fruitless.**

Self-financing Investment   Under the conventional tax regime, growth that promises the creation of more jobs tends to send stock markets into a state of anxiety. From bitter experience, investors know the disruptive consequences of "bottlenecks". But under the new economics raising the level of output by improving efficiency would not run the risk of hitting bottlenecks that cause a general rise in prices (inflation). The increased output would satisfy the demand side of the economy; and the increased supply would bear down on prices, which is the most effective counter-inflationary strategy.

The spare capacity that is untapped has been measured in Britain, where industry is inefficient compared to the United States. According to the Confederation of British Industry:

> If we were to raise average UK manufacturing performance to average US levels through the adoption of 'best practice', this would generate an additional £60 bn contribution to GDP (CBI 1997).

Corporate performance is affected by a variety of factors. One of them is the tax regime that affects incentives to invest in fixed capital, and in research and development. The tax regime faced by UK entrepreneurs is more hostile than the one in the USA. This would explain, in part, why world-class British corporations are not as productive as their US counterparts.

Better quality data from the national income accounts would enable governments to measure the losses in the land market. Anecdotal losses are alluded to in the financial press, but without systematic quantification of the costs to the community. For example, in 1995 the vacancy rate of buildings in

New York was 30%. Whole buildings stood empty. What was the loss of jobs and income as a result of this routine phenomenon of the "over-built" property market?

Such losses are connected to the character of taxation by a chain that sometimes has many links; which is one reason why the causation is not generally understood. One example is the direct tax-related waste stemming from shortcomings in information. This has been identified by economists in the realm of investment in public infrastructure. To achieve efficiency, economists say that the expenditure of the public's money ought to be undertaken only when the losses induced by taxation are covered by the new investment. On the basis of this rule, "many projects accepted by government agencies in recent years on the basis of cost-benefit ratios exceeding unity might have been rejected if the additional effects of distortionary taxes had been taken into account. The cost-benefit standard should be more stringent" (Ballard *et. al.* 1985: 128).

The implication of such a rule, were government to comply with it, is serious. It would mean that socially-necessary investment projects would be prejudiced by the bias in the tax structure. A project that could pay for itself (*including* the rent of the land that is used) - but not for the costs of the tax burden - would be disallowed, even though people were willing to pay for the input of labor, capital and land that must be invested for the project to deliver the desired service. **Projects would be disallowed because they were not sufficiently super-efficient to over-ride the artificial burden of costs imposed by taxation.**

This means government has to ignore tax-driven losses if it is to invest in socially-desirable projects; but it cannot pick between the best of those social projects without an accurate financial evaluation of which projects are the least damaging to the economy and society. National income statistics are a disgrace. We present a critique of the US accounts, but similar strictures apply to every government's statistical treatment of rational incomes.

As a result of the proposed reforms
- resources would be transparently and accurately allocated to the projects needed by the community;
- investment of the public's money, if the projects were correctly selected, would be self-financing ventures that add to the wealth of the nation; rather than, as frequently happens now, massive drains on resources that people desperately need to provide themselves with minimum decent standards of life.

Virtuous growth   Abolishing poverty would be an easy accomplishment. The world enjoys a $25 trillion economy. Because of the common character of the tax system, the world is under-producing by something like $8 trillion every year. And yet, according to the United Nations, it would take just $80 bn (£50 bn) to finance an anti-poverty program that could provide access to basic social services and support for the poverty-stricken (UN 1997). According to the UN report's main author, Dr Richard Jolly, "It is an ethical scandal that we do not provide the basics of education and health for everyone in a world with a $25 trillion economy" (Elliott and Brittain 1997).

The "trickle-down" theory that has influenced contemporary economic policy-making - reduce taxes on the high-income earners and the benefits will percolate down to the poorest segments of society - was thoroughly tested during the 1980s. It failed.

The problem was not with the tax rates, but the character of the tax system itself.

The United Nations argues that the cost of eradicating poverty is just 1% of the world's income. But the permanent, inter-generational solution is not to transfer other people's earned incomes. **The fiscal crisis demonstrates that income redistribution was not the solution to the poverty and unemployment of the 19th century. A new philosophy is needed for the 21st century**. The welfare state creed is no longer viable to meet the needs of the sick and the aged; and it does not provide the philosophical basis for defining solutions for the third millennium.

The proposed fiscal reform would immediately create the conditions for virtuous growth. The increase in productivity and general prosperity, and the removal of tax-led obstacles to work, would provide people with choices that are not currently available to them. One of these choices is to work fewer hours a week while maintaining their standard of living. Another choice would be to change the pattern of consumption, to nurture more spiritual ways of living. Such possibilities would be for people to determine on a personal and democratic basis: no attempt is made here to prescribe the kind of life that people ought to adopt for themselves.

But some changes would be necessary. The primary one would be the elimination of the **capital** value of land and natural resources as a tradable asset. People will be told that government was confiscating one of their most valuable assets.

Even today many people see the value of their assets savaged when their investments in stocks and shares fall victim to the boom/bust cycle. The value of money which they had saved for pensions is wiped out overnight, as happened in the global stock market crashes of 1987 and 1997. When this happens, there is no *quid pro quo* for the loss of asset value. Example: the stockholders who invested in the Gucci Group hoped that by saving money to help the shoemakers manufacture products for high income consumers they would be able to walk their way to prosperity. Gucci shares were worth $80 in late 1996. Land speculation in Thailand was at its peak, ready to collapse and drag the rest of the Thai economy down with it. Among the victims of the global crisis were the investors in Gucci, whose assets were halved in value to $39.75 on the Amsterdam stock exchange in late November 1997.

Under the proposed reforms land would cease to be a tradable asset. The market process would continue to determine the reallocation of land and the level of chargeable rents. If the rent of land and natural resources is paid to government, it could not be capitalized into a selling price. The compensating benefits would offset this effect.

- The land user's earned incomes become more valuable through the elimination of taxes on take-home wages and salaries, and the dividends from savings.
- The quality of public services increases; what is sometimes called the Social Wage.
- The size of the economy expands, providing more revenue with which to undertake the social and environmental programs that people require.

The sustainable economy The bottleneck in political ideology will not be broken unless there is a democratic debate about the character of the society in which people want to live. The present study does not examine the environmental benefits of the proposed fiscal reform. We must, however, note that the proposals afford the most effective strategy for creating the sustainable development that governments are striving to achieve.

The word *sustainability* has become fashionable at international congresses, but it is insufficiently defined to serve as a conceptual tool for designing workable policies (Harrison & Titova 1997). Nonetheless, the concept does persuade governments to think about the need for strategies that encompass the wider ecological consequences of their actions. The outcome is a willingness to countenance what are called eco-taxes. These are intended to be levied on finite natural resources such as energy to reduce consumption and limit the damage from the emission of carbon dioxide and other noxious by-products of production.

Advocates of this shift in the tax structure have accepted (since the UN's 1992 conference in Rio de Janeiro) that sustainable development is a two-track process. Enhancing the quality of people's lives is as important as preserving biosystems and conserving finite resources. But one fatal problem with eco-taxes is that their success would erode the tax base. This is how two of the leading exponents of eco-taxes put it:

The not so desireable side of the remarkable efficiency of an ecological tax reform is that tax revenues from this source...could fall away completely in the foreseeable future (Weizsacker & Jesinghaus 1992:55).

Eco-taxes, because they are framed within the terms of conventional tax philosophy, may reduce the rate of depletion of finite resources but they would also deplete the public exchequers of revenue. This is evidently an unsustainable arrangement. And if it were to be pursued, the logic of the philosophy would drive governments back to taxes that damage the welfare of people and their natural environments.

This dilemma dramatizes one of the virtues of the rent-revenue philosophy. If people were required to pay the rental value of the natural resources they used (as many, in fact, already do - to private owners) an adjustment in patterns of consumption would follow. The environmental goals would be achieved. But that success would feed through to the land market, which measures the attractions of the natural environment for living and working. People are willing to pay higher rents for such benefits. Consequently, instead of eroding revenue, **the rent approach expands the public's revenue so that everybody enjoys the benefits of cleaning up and conserving the natural environment.**

This critique of eco-taxes does not mean that we should not employ some of them as the fiscal route to moderating damaging behavior or reducing the use of byproducts that inflict costs on society and the environment. "Greenhouse" taxes that slow up and eliminate global warming are legitimate as alternatives to regulatory action. The important point, however, is that such taxes should not be viewed as revenue-raisers. They should be supplementary policies to support the general strategy of charging people the rental value of the resources that they use.

A similar dilemma confronts governments that levy taxes which affect people's health. Under the present fiscal regime, governments are locked into a dependency on revenue from tobacco, a killer product whose disappearance from the shops would cause financial hardship to nations. Governments cannot raise the tobacco tax to a level that "kills the golden goose". So the tax rate is held low enough for people to continue killing themselves with cancer. This is an untenable arrangement, from any point of view; one from which we can escape only by re-structuring public finance in favor of the benign, **renewable revenue**: the flow of income that people are willing to pay for the use of the resources of nature which sustain healthy lives.

Rights and responsibilities of governments The bureaucracies of some OECD countries have embarked on a reappraisal of public finance. There is a growing awareness of practical reasons for contemplating fundamental changes, such as the looming demographic crisis: the aging of populations will impose unmanageable strains on budgets early in the 21st century unless corrective action is taken.

There is also a growing awareness of the need to inject an ethical component into public finance. New Zealand led the way with its Fiscal Responsibility Act (1994). This influenced Britain's government into proposing a contract with Parliament to compel it to maintain "principles of responsible fiscal management". The intention was to avoid traumas inflicted by the boom/bust prone economy. **This attempt at fiscal prudence to nurture sustainable growth will fail.** The wishful ambition is grafted onto a tax regime that is the prime cause of instability in the economy. It encourages activities such as land speculation. The next recession will compel government to manipulate fiscal policy to try and minimize damage and rescue their economies from unemployment. Again, they will fail: for they will be trying to employ taxation as if it were a solution rather than the root-cause of the problem.

Governments have the primary duty to engage their citizens in a democratic debate. People need more facts upon which to base their choices. These facts must be provided by governments, but this entails a reappraisal of official ways of viewing the world. Governments have a democratic right to expect sufficient revenue to defray the costs of public obligations, but they also have the responsibility to employ the revenue-raising methods that most suit their citizens. This calls for a new era of radical reform from statesmen.

The Program of Reform

The changes that we offer for consideration entail no negative material consequences. They do, however, require a substantial shift in people's perceptions of how the world works. The reforms will not occur without a substantial democratic debate.

Actions from a state of mind

THE QUALITY of people's lives is routinely compromised by political decisions that rest on bad advice from economic and financial specialists. The errors are based on a false understanding of the important parameters of the market economy. An example will illustrate the enormity of the errors and the tragic scale of the costs that are imposed on people.

In the summer of 1997 the IMF issued a clean bill of health to the government of South Korea. The Directors of the all-powerful IMF "welcomed Korea's continued impressive macro-economic performance and praised the authorities for their enviable fiscal record" (cited in Williams de Broë 1997: 1). Before the end of the year, IMF officials were forced to stitch together a $56 bn package with which to rescue the Korean economy. There were strings to all that money: the traditional "austerity" measures imposed on debtor nations, the ultimate price of which is paid in unemployment and diminished standards of living. The IMF, from its plush offices in Washington DC, continuously monitors every economy in the world, so **it could have anticipated the crash of the giant Korean economy while it was in the making**. Why did it fail to forecast the crisis? Solely because of the fatal flaw in its basic theory of how markets work. This theory ignores trends in the land market. If, however, weight had been given to the visible trends, the IMF would have been able to monitor the build-up of pressures during the 1980s. Those pressures, we are time and again reminded by history, are defused through an implosion of the economy.

Table E presents a portrait of the Korean economy that will not be found in IMF reports. The looming crisis which it registers appeared in an unpublished Master's degree thesis. The statistics are not Top Secret: they are readily available from the Korean government's Economic Planning Board.

Table E
South Korea: economic indicators (1975 = 100)

	1975	1980	1983	1985	1988	Increase
Land price	100	328.1	440.5	533.5	839.0	X8.4
House price	100	355.3	328.7	397.0	466.5	X4.7
National income	100	142.1	178.6	204.2	287.9	X2.9
Wholesale price	100	225.4	284.4	289.0	293.9	X2.9

Source: Kang 1994: 13.

As the economy prospered, the price of the scarcest factor of production - land - escalated. The flow of income into the land accelerated the rate at which rent-claimants could extract the value added by others. Thus, once again, was triggered the process of dividing society. As the rate of increase of the price of land outpaced other categories
- land became increasingly unaffordable to users - the families and entrepreneurs who need it on which to live and work; but

- speculators moved in and, with the money loaned by banks, hoarded the valuable sites which people needed.

Banks were not concerned about this pincer effect (Harrison 1983; Foldvary 1997): their loans were secured against land as collateral! The IMF is one of the leading proponents of land as a necessary medium for protecting the financial sector from risks.

The outcome was inevitable: a crash in Korea that curtailed activity around the world, such as Samsung's cutback in its European investments.

Recommendation 1
Reappraise economic theory, to identify conceptual weaknesses. Scrutinize the intersection of theory and policy, to enhance the quality of political decision-making.

Reform the Land Market
LAND values are the Achilles heel of the economy. The negative macro-economic impact can be traced most immediately and clearly in the housing sector. It ought to be a highly visible process in the financial sector, but - on a worldwide basis - banks have become adept at concealing the accumulation of bad debts linked to land.

The OECD (1992: 15) chronicled the process by which some of the damage is inflicted on society by high land prices. They

- impede the acquisition of land needed for public purposes, especially infrastructure;
- encourage urban sprawl;
- cause the over-intensive use of land, with negative environmental effects;
- favor monostructures of high-rise central office buildings which crowd out residential and other land uses;
- induce negative distributional effects by increasing the price of housing; and
- reward speculation and hoarding and de-stabilize land markets.

Rising land values may be a rational - and affordable - response to scarcity. Effective market-based prices that signal the need to reallocate resources to the most efficient combination are an integral part of the working system. But how high do land prices have to rise before they begin to float on artificial scarcities, such as those induced by speculation? The OECD could not say "due to a lack of reliable data". **There is no shortage of such data for the labor market, against which economic ideology is biased**.

When land values skyrocket they become to the financial institutions what heroin is to a drug addict: the more you have, the more you need, until the implosion terminates the demand. Financial detectives can trace this process in the balance sheets of banks; but the human effects are most profoundly felt among the families who lose their homes and their savings as a result of the decimation in the value of their investments.

There is a qualitative difference between land and the rest of property in the workings of an economy geared to serving customers by adding value to the wealth of nations. The refusal to acknowledge this encourages the self-defeating actions that cyclically destabilize the economy. The solution is the fiscal-led market model. **Charging the full rental price for using land and natural resources removes the attractions of land as collateral and increases the real worth of labor and manmade capital.** Non-land assets can be used as collateral: these include personal talents and the business plans of entrepreneurs. For shareholders in banks, the major attractions of this reform of lending policies are

- elimination of the riskiest investments from the portfolio: the speculatively priced land whose value periodically collapses as the bubble bursts; and
- elimination of taxes on the interest from savings and dividends from shares. The real value of investments rises and the risks are reduced.

Central banks will need to play a leading role in re-educating their financial sectors. This would be more effective as a stabilization program than the proposal that emanated from the IMF after the collapse of the Asian economies in late 1997: the creation of a quick-response program to bail out financial systems that collapse when the land speculation bubble bursts.

The IMF crisis-management fund resigns the global economy to periodic breakdowns, which are becoming all too frequent. The bail-out of Mexico, followed by the $100 billion that had to be assembled to rescue the Asian economies, indicates a quickening of the tempo in financial instability. A stabilization program worth the name would target the propensity to speculate in capital gains from land. To eliminate the vulnerability of banks to this activity, a **once-for-all restructuring of the real estate sector is necessary to remove land as collateral**.

- If entrepreneurs want to borrow money, real investment that adds value to the economy should be their goal.
- If financiers want to lend money, profits from fixed capital formation and product innovation should be sufficient motivation.

The solution is not state regulation of either the land market or the financial system. Public finance is the route to the free market solution. The effect would be to eradicate the asset value of land, but improve the pricing mechanism based on rent charges.

This reform would cause some apprehension to bankers, but disruption would be restricted to a balance sheet effect. To control the process, however, careful planning is necessary, and funds may have to be earmarked out of the Public Rent Dividend to smooth the transitional period. The rewards: the clear waters of the speculation-free era that lie beyond the primitive economics of boom/bust cycles.

The costs of this reform could never approximate the current costs of bailing out banks - costs that fall on taxpayers. The regular taxpayer-funded bail-out of bankers is silently tolerated because the practical alternative is never canvassed. The bail-out costs are mounting. In the US, taxpayers were saddled with a bill of $500 billion to rescue savings and loans institutions as a result of land speculation and racketeering in the 1980s.

Recommendation 2
Financial institutions must develop a new risk analysis strategy, and prepare for the removal of land as collateral for debt-creating loans.

The People's Public Finance

THE SUSTAINABLE character of the new system was delineated by John Kenneth Galbraith in *The Affluent Society* (1987: 44) in these terms: "....if a tax were imposed equal to the annual use value of real property ex its improvements, so that it would now have no net earnings and hence no capital value of its own - progress would be orderly and its fruits would be equitably shared".

The synergistic rewards that flow from treating rent as public revenue cannot be challenged, but one issue does remain controversial: could the annual rental income of land and natural resources in all its forms finance the legitimate needs of modern society? Economists express the consensus view: "No!" The spurious basis of this conclusion (analyzed in Ch. 2) fails to take account of a number of key facts.

- A large part of government spending - that on national defense, law and order, administration of the democratic process - is currently funded out of society's net income. **It comes out of "wages" but is paid as a rent to the state.**
- A large part of government spending would not fall on the public purse in a society whose foundations were economic efficiency and social justice.
- A large amount of rental income is measurable in the economy today, which could be collected *in lieu* of taxes on people's wages and savings.

When all these considerations are taken into account, the Single Tax hypothesis that economists seek to discredit is found to be a fiscally viable philosophy for modern society.

But implementation of this policy does not exclude the retention of those taxes that are intended to penalize people who damage their health and impose costs on others. In the USA, the federal government incurs an annual financial commitment of $22 bn to treat smoking-related illnesses. Nor does the rent thesis exclude non-rent taxes that penalize people who damage the environment. In Britain, beneficiaries of the nuclear industry under-fund the decommissioning of plants by an amount that could rise to £70 bn, according to one estimate (MacKerron and Sadnicki 1997). Such costs ought to fall on those who cause the damage.

Recommendation 3
Harness the catalytic benefits that flow from treating land and natural resource rents as public revenue by first engaging the public in a democratic dialogue.

A New Style of Life
EMPHASIS has been placed on the prospects of the new public finance increasing productivity in the value-adding economy. This is not in conflict with people's environmental concerns, which may include the need to reduce levels of production and consumption if people freely choose this course.

Whatever now happens, in the 21st century choices will have to be made about the character of society. This prospect is forced on us by ecological imperatives. When government raises revenue direct from the economic rent of land and natural resources, people acquire a freedom to choose that is not now at their command. One prospect is a significant surplus of public sector revenue, which could be used to
- Reduce the public debt
- Improve the quality of social infrastructure
- Vary the living and working patterns of citizens.

This is the disbursement of the Social Wage on an equal basis. The re-patterning of the public's finances creates a new synergy that radically alters prospects at all levels. The free choice could be made to *reduce* the consumption of material products that deplete finite energy sources *without* lowering people's living standards. This is the model of sustainable development that provides everyone with effective choices that include the right to bias their lives in favor of greater spiritual content. An understanding of this dimension is already emerging, commissioned by organizations such as UNESCO (Young 1992) and the European Commission (Robertson 1997).

Recommendation 4
Governments should facilitate research that helps citizens to expand the effective choices at their disposal under the terms of the new society.

Neutralize the culture of dependency

THE POLICY option of rent as public revenue was long ago recommended by the UN (1968). The proposed revenue take was a modest one, but it would have established a principle. Today, the policy is not canvassed by institutions such as the World Bank which influence the former socialist societies, and which claim to combat poverty.

The former socialist countries want to learn about the "best practices" that would optimize the benefits that could flow from the market economy. But the advisers from the IMF/World Bank, and related institutions, continue to favor property rights and fiscal policies that give priority to the interests of banks. President Boris Yeltsin of Russia, for example, was persuaded to change his attitude towards land: he was continually informed by the IMF, on which he was dependent for loans, that land had to be privatized so that it could be used as collateral in the debt-creating process.

The bias in the ideology of global finance will prevent the eradication of poverty despite the objectives and possibilities articulated in the UN *Human Development Report* (1997). Existing policies favor the repetition of global crises such as the one that originated in Thailand in 1997.

Fiscal reform offers the only prospect of breaking the cycles of debt and dependency that repeat themselves through history. Temporary relief only can be expected from proposals to cancel the debts of Third World countries: their removal would signal the clearing of decks ready for a new round of fiscal imprudence and private indebtedness; leading to the first debt crisis of the third millennium.

Now that we have learnt the lessons of the bizarre strategies that engineered change in Eastern Europe, it is possible to design enlightened programs to facilitate investment in value-adding reforms. This challenge is not a financial or technological one. It is an issue of philosophy. An example will illuminate the deception that is being visited on the peoples of the former socialist countries.

Contrary to the claims, foreign capital is not a pre-requisite for investment in transitional or developing or "emerging" economies. **Investment in a closed economy would flow to sufficient levels if people had the benefit of the correct public finance: they would generate the resources they needed internally, and the investment would be self-financing.** People pay their way when liberated from taxation.

But this is not an argument in favor of protectionism. Under free trade, costs are reduced. This, in turn, yields maximum opportunities for people to work and save. And it also generates the maximum net income for spending through the public sector.

- This reality - people create their own opportunities, when freed to do so - was denied in the 19th century, for understandable reasons of class-psychology. Working people were said to be dependent for their wages on the capital of their employers.
- This reality - people create sufficient net income to pay for all the social services they want - was ignored in the 20th century, because the democratic call for a rational and fair public finance was defeated in the first decade of the century in Britain and Germany.

But under the global pressure of an over-warm environment and a perpetually over-heating economy, the reform of public finance is once again on the political agenda. The correct policy needs to be enshrined as a central principle for both private lives and social sectors in the 21st century.

Recommendation 5

Re-appraise foreign aid policies to developing countries, to link resources to the adoption of self-help public finance strategies.

Part 1

The Systemic Crisis

Fred Harrison

Chapter 1

The Social Surplus Income

1. Formation of Net Income

TIME HONORED arrangements appear as natural. For many centuries slavery was acceptable as a social institution because it had been consolidated into law and property rights. By looking back to origins we see that people were formerly free of that arrangement. People were correct to find that it offended their moral sensibilities. Similarly with taxation. By looking back into history we can establish empirically that exactions on people's wages and savings were not normal. Taking this as one analytical starting point - and linking it to the insights of theory - we can make sense of unemployment, poverty and social discontent. Otherwise, we are inclined to resign ourselves to these features of civilization as insoluble dilemmas.

Our starting point is the formation of net income, the surplus which has been used by all civilizations to create those cultural attributes which distinguished them from their tribal roots.

Net income results from the convergence of several factors.

In agricultural societies, fertility of the soil and productivity of people's labor predominate. The first civilization combined labor power with hydraulic engineering to channel a natural resource (water) into arid lands; the irrigation produced income in excess of what was needed for production and reproduction. That net income was pooled, through the temples, to pay for spiritual life, civil administration of law and defense of the realm, and development of intellectual pursuits (notably, writing). Net income originally came in the form of produce in kind: barley, cattle, etc. Then, with monetization of commerce, it became possible to measure with precision the productivity of one location compared with another: the rent of land and of natural resources such as copper.

From the earliest societies, customs and individual behavior were dovetailed to generate sufficient revenue to fund the investments of what we now call the public sector. This was one of the primary social equations of human evolution without which culture would not have evolved.

With industrial society, the same underlying realities apply. But by now, society was divided into a complex structure of antagonistic classes based on the ability to appropriate part of the net income. Social problems were largely the result of the privatization of net income, forcing government to invent new forms of revenue-raising which punished people who worked and saved.

A symbiotic relationship had existed between the governed and government in its various secular and sacred forms. The glue that held the earliest civilizations in place was the net income, the distribution of which is schematically illustrated in figure 1:I.

Figure 1:I

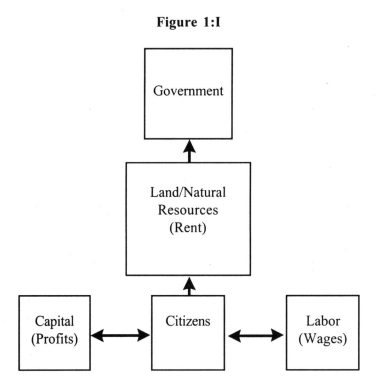

We can isolate the rent that is socialized by examining the status of the categories of public spending. We find that if an item is a socially necessary expenditure, it is financed out of net income. Spending on defense of the realm, the administration of justice and politics, are underwritten out of net income. People pay for these territory-based services out of their wages. This is revenue which, if it were appropriated into the private domain, would be called the rent of land.

This is not an esoteric part of philosophy. As we will see, it has a major bearing on the discussion over the feasibility of a fiscal policy which, by common consent, is the best one available to society - except that it (allegedly) cannot provide sufficient revenue to pay for public services. We can test this proposition about the status of payments for core public spending. What would happen if we were to renounce these commitments as public obligations? Anarchy would prevail. The first indication of this breakdown in order would be the elimination of the value of land. People would be reluctant to acquire financial commitments to land that they could not occupy with confidence. In other words, if the primary layer of land value is its natural fertility (for growing food), the next layer up is the value that people assign to land which they feel confident will be safe to occupy. They are willing to pay for that security attached to the land, which is why land in (say) the United States is more valuable than in (say) the Congo. (Migration patterns reflect this phenomenon.) People will pay for territorial security and the administration of civil order, and the amount they are willing to pay is measured by the value they assign to the occupation of land. That spending would come out of the net income generated by their economic activities. So, to put it another way, the powers that provide protection and enforce law and order exercise, *de facto*, eminent domain over their territory. Their charges to defray the costs of these security services are rental payments by the people who enjoy the benefits of those services. In feudal times, those charges were called rents.

That terminology is no longer used in the income accounts of modern nations, but that does not alter the economic reality: the payments to governments are out of the net income that people help to produce, and this was called (by classical economists) economic rent. They could not hope to live in a community and pocket that income themselves - there would be anarchy, constant fear of invasion from without, a collapse of the economy.... and the emergence, sooner or later of a Strong Man who would enforce peace. And he would exact a price for his services. We can call that price tribute, protection money, or rent. It is the revenue that exceeds what people need for production (of wealth) and reproduction (of their families): the economic rent of land and natural resources.

On the other hand, much of what is called social spending - on able-bodied people - is not net income: it is wages. Money spent to support widows and orphans would be from net income, a legitimate claim on the surplus value generated by a humane community. Money spent on educating and curing able-bodied people would be private income, which would remain in private hands (and be spent on those activities) through the private sector if these functions were renounced by the public sector. *The Welfare State came into existence only because a significant number of people were denied their right to work and earn their wages, so they needed help from the countervailing power of the state.*

Scientific treatment of the taxable capacity of the economy is necessary if serious policy errors are not to continue to be inflicted on citizens by their governments. Examples of hardship and international conflict stemming, in part, from the failure to correctly identify and measure the taxable portion of a nation's income include, from British history, Ireland at the end of the 19th century. The imperial government was extracting revenue and a debate occurred about the capacity of the people to supply income to Britain. The Irish population's perception of the burden was of a different order of magnitude from the cold statistics provided by the Foreign Office. Why? Because the people were paying both taxes and rents. The landlords were locked into a surreal struggle with the government over the net income. The tug-of-war was fought through intermediaries, the peasants who farmed the land as tenants, who paid the costs of that power struggle.

The issue was to have major significance for the distribution of income in the first half of the 20th century, when the countries of Europe had to decide how much they could extract from their dominions. This was not resolved by either objective economic calculation or the ethics of property rights. Naked power was the yardstick for measuring how much was extracted.

> The United Kingdom was first in the field, and taxed on the principles of residence, origins, control, and every other pretext it could invent, on the Donnybrook Fair principle, 'see a head, hit it' (Stamp 1922: 111).

This was calculated to foster dissatisfaction with the imperial powers and to nurture the liberation movements that became active after World War II.

Germany after the First World War: the issue that made taxable capacity

---

TAXES are defined as "compulsory, unrequited payments made to general government" (ONS 1996:70). Unrequited means not reciprocated or returned.

Resource rents payments to government are (1) not compulsory, as to size of payments: you choose where you live and work; and (2) they are requited, in that the payer selects the combination of services required, which determine the value of the location where he chooses to live.

a serious problem for the European powers was the amount of reparations the defeated country could be forced to pay. The miscalculations caused political strains that drove some people into the hands of the Nazis. That the size of the reparations mattered was known to some observers at the time such as John Maynard Keynes. In 1922, a leading statistician, Josiah Stamp, warned that Germany, defeated though she might be,

> [H]as her psychological limit too and only actual slavery and individual taskmasters can get production from her people if no *part* of the increased production can revert to the producers, and if they can never rise over subsistence levels for many years (Stamp 1922: 118).

Stamp knew that the method of raising revenue mattered. It affected the amount of production, and also the *character* of the productive process. As he said of Germany: "If the German becomes servile, and actually content with a bare existence, we may not get enough production for indemnities to be paid" (*ibid*:133).

The contemporary examples that ought to exercise us include the indebtedness of Third World countries. Some Western governments do wish to reduce the burden of payments, but this is no more a permanent solution than the Clean Slate proclamation of classical antiquity.

2. The dead zone
CONVENTIONAL taxation compels the State to adopt ruses to wheedle resources out of citizens. Some strategies are thought to be less painful than others. Death duties, for example "which come between the living and the dead" (Stamp 1922:129), are deemed to be better than taxing people from their current earnings.

The outcome of fiscal history is that citizens are locked in a continuous battle with government over the division of the nation's wealth. But the process of confrontation between Citizen v Government is complex. The individual citizen - and particularly employees who do not own land or who lack significant accumulations of man-made capital - is trapped in an unholy struggle between the government and those people who have now come to own rights to the net income of society.

This hidden conflict is at the heart of economic problems, and also the repeated failures of government to define the solutions capable of delivering a stable society with a sustainable economy. We anticipate the discussion by offering the outlines of a model of how this struggle proceeds. Figure 1:II provides a schematic illustration of the level at which the fight over society's disposable net income proceeds.

Figure 1:II
Net Income & the Dynamics of Rent Appropriation

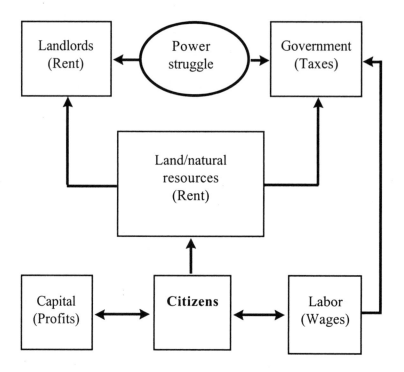

Two important points first need to be noted.

(1) The size of the surplus, or net, income, is not fixed. Under normal conditions we expect people to produce enough from their labors to yield sufficient additional revenue out of which to finance the public services that they need. But, the size of that pie is not fixed, as Dr. Tideman shows (Ch.6). Most importantly, it can vary according to the means by which finance is collected by government.

(2) The struggle between the people who believe they have a right to appropriate part of society's net income, and the government which needs that income to defray public costs, is not a simple one. It is a battle in which everyone is engaged, directly or indirectly, either as beneficiary or victim. Some examples will help to clarify the point.

● Government may restrict the share claimed by landowners by legal means, in favor of another group. One example is the control over rents charged to tenants in rented homes. In Britain, for example, two sharp increases in the share of employees' incomes (as a percent of gross national income), during or immediately after the two world wars, were both associated with limits imposed on the increases in residential rents (Feinstein 1968:118, 123-4).

- Government may claim part of the land owner's rent through the tax system, either from the annual rental income or when a piece of land is sold. This revenue is distributed equally, among all citizens, through public spending.

- It is the indirect struggle over rent that is most complex in its impact (Fig. 1:II). In this case, segments of the working population come into play. The first stage is the extraction of public value by private individuals, who thereby diminish the financial base at the disposal of government. This obliges government to impose taxes on people's wages. If they are weakly placed, as workers (unskilled, unable to move to new jobs or locations) they are literally trapped into having to bear the tax burden. But if they are unionized, or if they are occupationally mobile - such as scientists in the 1990s, who are part of the international Brain Drain - they can escape the tax burden by shifting it onto employers. Employers have to accept the tax-take as part of the costs of employing people. Some employers have no choice but to accept lower profits. Others, however, because of the conditions that rule in the markets they serve, are able to push the tax burden onto consumers through higher prices. Consumers, in turn, have less left out of which to pay rent to their landlords (if they are tenants) or out of which to buy land (if they wish to live in their homes as owner-occupiers). Ultimately, therefore, they transmit the tax-take onto landowners by their reduced ability to pay rent.

It is the indirect struggle over the division of society's net income that causes a large part of the misunderstood disruption to most of our important social and economic institutions.

Life would be simpler if governments adopted the rational approach, and levied revenue direct from the rent of land and natural resources. Unfortunately, they abandoned that approach - as a coherent fiscal policy - long ago. The result is the social warfare in which the rules are not specified and the spoils are not even correctly identified.

- Landowners push as hard as they can to hang on to as much of the rent as possible.

- Governments claw as coercively as their financial commitments necessitate to acquire the resources they need: directly, to a miniscule degree, from the rent of land, overwhelmingly, from the income people receive from their labor and their savings.

- Citizens, as employees, push their employers and fellow citizens (through the prices charged for the goods and services they produce) to retain the real value of what they produce.

The outcome is organized chaos. One of the consequences is a reduction in the size of the net income: the spoils out of which everyone wishes to extract his or her legitimate equal share. We all lose. This is why we need to inform ourselves that "The limit of taxable capacity may also fluctuate to some extent, according to the different ways in which taxation is raised" (Stamp 1922: 129). The amount of surplus income available to finance the public sector is reduced because government resorts to damaging methods to raise that revenue.

A democratic government that claims to champion the principles of social justice and economic efficiency would ask itself this question: What is the optimum policy to maximize total income for both the public and private sectors?

Government also ought to ask itself: Why, if people are willing to pay for public services, do they display such a strong resentment to *taxation*? People are willing to pay what they can afford as rent, after taking into account what they need to finance the costs of maintaining their families and their ability to continue to work. But they pay taxes with a grudging attitude, and many of them work strenuously to avoid those payments.

The size of the black economy indicates the scale of citizen revolt against government economic policy. In 1998, the estimated size of the black economy was 9% of the official economy in Japan and the US, 12% in Britain, 15% (Germany, France) climbing to 24% in Italy. Millions of people across the industrial world feel compelled to live in a twilight, lawless world, formally branded as economic deviants for no better reason than that they wish to retain the value of their labor.

People would be more willing payers if they perceived a direct correspondence between the payment and the services which they receive. That correspondence is absent, which is why they are resentful.

The struggle between citizen and government results in a dead zone: an area of life from which we are excluded. This zone is the stuff of both nightmare and fairytale. Under one set of rules it entails an enriched life for everyone to enjoy in which involuntary unemployment and poverty are banished. Under alternative conditions - the ones under which we now live - it is a zone that mocks people with riches beyond their grasp for no better reason than that their governments refuse to liberate them to produce the wealth that is within their talents and the nation's endowment of natural resources.

3. Exclusion as social process

THE EXCLUSION of people from work originates at the most vulnerable point in the system's structure. By addressing the issue rationally on the basis of social justice, policies can be developed to eradicate unemployment permanently.

Historically, criticism of the economic system was led by the left. In its most extreme form, this criticism was Marxist, whose perceptions were distorted by anger at the injustices that abounded in the 19th century. The emotional reaction caused theorists to develop complicated notions of exclusion that had little to do with the realities of economic life. Social processes were shrouded in conceptual confusions, which was all the excuse policy-makers needed to ignore the flaws in the foundations of the industrial system.

The outcome was the horrific 20th century. Indignities ranged from the physical traumas of the 1930s to the psychological anxiety experienced by blue- and white-collar workers in the 1980s who feared the arrival of redundancy notices. Throughout the century, a consensus developed that the problems of instability in capitalism were inherent in the system itself. In the 1920s, as the storm clouds gathered and the jazz-and-prohibition era moved inexorably towards the crash of '29, the Marxists encouraged that view: they were ideologically predisposed to proclaiming the onset of world revolution. This would be provoked by the "contradictions of capitalism", in which the growing pool of surplus workers would finally overthrow their chains and seek refuge in communism.

In response to the mass unemployment of the 1930s, John Maynard Keynes offered his famous diagnosis. He was a capitalist who made a fortune on the London stock exchange; but he, too, regarded the system as intrinsically unstable. There was no reason why the economy should return to full employment, he wrote, which was why it was necessary for government to intervene and prime the pump (through the manipulation of interest rates and fiscal policy).

After World War II and the (temporary) return to full employment - shattered economies had to be rebuilt - some of the most influential teachers like Paul Samuelson at the Massachusetts Institute of Technology also affirmed a socialist analysis. The economy was not self-regulating; therefore, it needed to be tuned from the Treasury with deficit financing. "Fine-tuning" achieved the height of popularity in the 1960s ⁓ only to disappoint by not having an answer to the monetary inflation in the 1970s.

That was the cue for the next school of thought to emerge.

Milton Friedman, in his work on monetary theory and regulation, rescued the reputation of capitalists. He said the problem was with central bankers, who zigged when they should have zagged, specifically in and after 1929. They exercised too much arbitrary power. That facilitated shift in influence in favor of officials in the Treasury. The bankers were the bad force that made the good forces (i.e., those influences that were from within the market system) go wrong. Right-wingers, who had been forced to retreat during the first half of the century, were able to relieve their frustration by elevating Friedman to guru status. Friedman said we could never count on fallible humans to do the right thing, so we should adopt rules to follow automatically, predictably. Then markets, guided by "rational expectations," would regulate everything in a correct manner. That view was falsified by the harsh events of the Reagan and Thatcher years.

The century ended on a wave of low inflation and rising unemployment. The search was once again on for a general explanation for economic instability, to explain why, in the 1990s, the industrial world experienced jobless growth.

The Marxist critique continued to account for unemployment as intrinsic to capitalism. Critics claim "that the nature of the capitalist mode of production is such that it precludes a smooth and peaceful transition from prolonged stagnation to long-term growth" (Friend & Metcalf 1981: 175).

Explanations associated with imperfections in the land market were not in favor. Why should they be? John Maynard Keynes had reassured the world that land was no longer relevant: as an economic issue it was relegated to a bygone agricultural age, replaced by problems associated with the system of money (Keynes 1936: 241-2).

For the new generation of politicians who were elected in the mid-1990s, globalization afforded an explanation. New technology (based on the computer) implied that people without work lacked the appropriate education and technical skills. Policy-makers narrowed their concerns to alleviating poverty and unemployment rather than confronting the causes. But joblessness and low incomes are part of a dysfunctional transmission mechanism which causes things like premature death and protracted

> The British government wants industry to modernize to compete in the global economy. But in 1997 it proposed to change corporation tax to penalize more than 50 research organizations by requiring them to pay tax for the first time. According to the Association of Independent Research and Technology Organizations, such a tax penalty would wipe £50 million a year off industrial research spending. At the same time the government sent out a Working Party to try and discover why Britain was not investing more in R & D!

suffering among individuals, and social disturbances in the community, which warrant correct analysis. To determine the fundamental causes of unemployment we have to retrace our steps. The explanations are to be found in history.

There were three primary ways to deny people their birthright and render them dependent laborers.

(1) Dispossession from land

Traditional rights of access to land were gradually transformed until most clansmen or members of tribes found themselves wandering the highways, landless. The objective of those who engineered this social transformation of property rights were seeking control over the rental income of land, which had previously been treated as public revenue. Britain exemplifies this process (Jupp 1997). So well known is the history of enclosures, in England, and the highland clearances, in Scotland, that the facts need no elaboration.

> In connection with enclosure new laws were introduced which blasted this freedom, these traditional rights - rights to pasture domestic animals and birds on the waste, to collect fuel, fruits, berries etc. from wastes and woods. The livelihood of many villagers depended on these rights: but now they were being stigmatized - and punished - as theft. This is the root cause of the widening gap between rich and poor in villages, and of vagabondage (Hill 1996: 234).

The landless were driven from their homes; most sought refuge in the towns, now - without independent means of economic activity - vulnerable to whatever was offered to them. Wage rates were at the barest subsistence level. Many of these people were forced to migrate to other lands in search of sustenance.

(2) Taxation

In land-rich continents such as Africa, the state had to be made to conspire with those who would extract the rent of natural resources. One mechanism for harnessing cheap labor was for the colonial authorities to impose a tax on the heads of tribesmen, which they had to pay in cash. As subsistence pastoralists they were not integrated into the cash economy. They were forced to leave their traditional lands and search for work that would pay wages. As our illustration we choose South Africa.

> At the turn of the century the supply of labor the problem that confronted the European investors who wanted to extract gold and diamonds. How could it be obtained at affordable rates? What would attract free-roaming people to work down the dirty, dangerous mines?

The state sought to attain these ends by various means, including (i) increased taxation (in money) of Africans, and (ii) a legal assault on the position of peasants and immobilized farm labor, restricting conditions of land tenure and the amount of land which could be occupied on state-owned land, seeking to "unlock" labor tied up on private land (Legassick and de Clercq 1984:146).

The state controlled taxation; it was persuaded to use this tool not to finance the needs of the community, but to coerce free people who would otherwise have no reason to abandon their economic activities on their traditional communally-owned land to migrate to the towns and mines to earn money. Taxation was overtly employed as a tool of exploitation: a link in the chain that locked people into a system in which their freedoms were written off in the interests of foreigners who wanted to plunder nature.

(3) Rigging the price of land

If prices are raised above what people can afford to pay, they are locked out of the land that they need on which to live and work.

Today, in the mature market economies, land becomes unaffordable on a cyclical basis. Land speculators drive prices above what working people can spare out of their earnings. But once upon a time, there was land to spare on continents like Australia. The solution was to persuade the state to impose artificially high prices for land. In that way, the landless settlers from Britain would be forced to accept wage-work. That scheme was documented by E.G. Wakefield (1788-1875). Marx reviewed the facts (*Capital*, Vol.1: Ch. 33), and noted:

> This [Wakefield's] "sufficient price for the land" is nothing but a euphemistic circumlocution for the ransom which the laborer pays to the capitalist for leave to retire from the wage-labour market to the land.

When land is free or affordable, people can choose to either work the land themselves; or, if wages were sufficiently attractive to them, they could choose to work for others. But that freedom meant landowners would not be able to extract the rent that they sought: somebody had to work for *them* on *their* land! That could be achieved only if they could monopolize access to land, which was possible only by controlling the police power of the state. Otherwise, as Marx noted, people would retire from wage-labor to the land!

These three processes were the variations on the grand theme of separating people from their traditional rights of access to the land that gave them life. Whatever else it was, it could not be described as intrinsic to the logic of that mode of value-creation called capitalism, and we have none other than Marx himself to confirm that assessment. He understood that paying money to buy land from owners out of capital was a systemic contradiction to capitalism.

And yet, analysts on the left continue to characterize unemployment and poverty in terms of *capital* rather than land. This seriously misrepresents historical reality. For example, one exhaustive study of mass migration and land occupation since the 15th century described emigration from Europe not as a response to dispossession of rights to land, but as due to "capitalization of the agricultural sector, industrialization" (Potts 1990: 200).

The labels we use matter. We need to characterize the origins of systemic unemployment and poverty, but that word cannot, logically, be derived from the concept of man-made wealth that we call capital. The indiscriminate use of words misdirects policy-makers towards solutions that cannot, by their nature, solve the problem. This is confirmed by a review of some strategies that were supposed to combat unemployment.

4. Policy Failures: European Union
MEMBER countries of the European Union spent £140 billion a year on supporting unemployed people in a strategy which EU officials acknowledge has not worked. About 18 million people in Europe were without jobs when the EU decided to hold a conference on unemployment in November 1997. The European Commission President, Jacques Santer, linked unemployment with taxation when he endorsed cuts in value added tax rates (VAT) in labor-intensive service industries, in the hope that new jobs would be created.

European governments were divided over policies for restoring full employment. German Chancellor Helmut Kohl championed the argument that there were "no patent cures". He insisted that employment policy was mainly a national and not a European challenge. Germany's concern was that other European governments might propose new policies to boost jobs that would involve member countries having to pay more to the EU. Policy-makers could not visualize a costless general solution such as the shift in the tax structure away from labor and capital and on to land. And yet, ironically, the European Commission had provided a well documented analysis leading to the conclusion that existing policies were under-using labor resources and over-exploiting natural resources. The common element which encouraged the abuse of both people and nature was the tax system. This allowed firms to avoid paying for many of the resources of nature which they used, while at the same time penalizing them for employing people (European Commission 1994: Ch.10).

The logic of this analysis required that Europe's leaders should systematically eliminate taxes of the destructive kind in favor of one in which the users of natural resources pay the market-determined rents as public revenue. Instead, however, Europe continued to admonish those countries that sought to hold down tax rates in order to reduce unemployment. Ireland became a celebrated case in 1997 when it was warned about holding its corporate tax rate at 10%. A number of countries claimed that this attracted investment out of their economies and into Ireland. German entrepreneurs were willing to admit that they had located in Ireland because of the low tax rate. The European Commission found itself arguing that this favorable tax regime was discriminatory against other countries and that the benefit would be treated as a subsidy to employers.

Globally, inflation was all but burnt out of the system. But unemployment remained at very high levels. The old explanations did not appear to work. To the credit of the Blair government in Britain, unemployment was restored to the political agenda when Chancellor Gordon Brown convened a summit meeting in London in February 1997 to try and motivate the leading industrial countries into taking action in the labor market.

The success of the initiative by Gordon Brown would depend largely on whether the right questions were asked. Research commissioned by Brussels had already begun to make it clear that there was a need to reverse the long-term trend towards higher taxes and charges on labor. This trend was part of the Rhineland Model, which combined the market economy with the public finance that enabled governments to regulate the labor market. But with the prolonged crisis of unemployment which was threatening to raise the budgetary obligations to insupportable levels, something had to be done. In France, the American Chamber of Commerce financed a study which showed that 92% of companies questioned claimed that the high level of social security contributions raised the level of labor costs to the point where these were the single biggest deterrent to foreign investment.

In Britain, there was no fundamental strategy for dealing with the problem as a structural weakness. The result was a retreat to a "tough love" philosophy, in which government ministers sought to place much of the onus on to the unemployed. Frank Field, the Minister responsible for reform of the welfare benefits system, did not mince his words when he wrote that welfare payments should no longer be viewed as a "simple entitlement" but as a contract. He blamed the welfare system "for the loss of key civic values of work, honesty and thrift" (Field 1997).

BRITAIN'S Minister responsible for welfare reform opposes the use of coercion to push unemployed single parents into work. Frank Field says: "I am convinced that lone parents are a vast untapped resource and that simply offering a helping hand should result in an immediate response. What is the point of applying sanctions when it is all too often a lack of child care which prevents large numbers of single parents from working?" (Field 1997). But Mr. Field will have his work cut out making sense of the tax system's contradictory pressures on lone parents.

- If a mother deposits her child in a nursery or crèche provided by her employer at the place of work, the company is not taxed for that free or subsidized provision of care.
- If the parent hands her child into the care of an independent nursery she cannot claim tax relief for paying for the service.

Gordon Brown recognized that his task included the need to adapt the tax system to encourage rather than penalize work. Although he acknowledged that tax reform in the United States had helped to reduce unemployment, it had failed to inject social cohesion. He was seeking a model that would deliver high and stable levels of growth with employment opportunity for all (Brown 1997). But his vision lacked that holy grail sought by all politicians, the Big Idea. In Mr. Brown's view there were "no quick fixes on jobs".

Meanwhile, however, the big winners in Britain were the beneficiaries of the lottery who did not even have to buy tickets. The Arts Council allocated £331 million for investment in capital projects during the first year of lottery grants and £340 million in the second year. The lottery was also used to finance multi-million pound projects to celebrate the millennium. The government emphasized that these investments created jobs. Some new jobs were created, but the real winners were the people who owned land close to the locations where this money was invested. The value of their land rose. Nobody was looking, least of all the tax man.

5. An experiment in detaxation: USA

GOVERNMENTS fail to pursue lasting solutions because they have not yet grasped that the tenure-and-tax model that was established to exploit natural resource rents created a corset of constraints on the industrial economy which they cannot override by addressing symptoms rather than causes. This corset imposed artificial ceilings on both the rate of growth of the value-adding economy and on the level of output.

An example is the attempt in the United States to bring people back into work by supplementing wages for families receiving the lowest incomes.

The US model echoed similar action in countries like Australia, where 300,000 working families received the "workforce additional family payment" in 1995, almost 20% of all working families. Canada and New Zealand also introduced tax credit schemes (Millar *et al* 1997: 3), indicating a trend in which the state, representing taxpayers, was assuming part of the role of the family breadwinner. This was an ironical trend in the market economies which were at the same time preaching to the former socialist countries the virtues of self reliance in the entrepreneurial economy.

In the United States the "earned income tax credit" (EITC) was received by 19 million people in 1994 at a cost to taxpayers of about $21 billion. What is the logic of the EITC? It was designed to help low earners, representing 15 million households. Its effect was, first, to offset the income tax liability, and second, provide an additional cash rebate that would help to offset the negative effects of consumption taxes. The average family received $1,151 in rebate checks. The scheme now benefits families earning up to $28,000, which is close to the median wage. In 1996 a family with two children could receive up to $3,500 in EITC cash, from a scheme which the tax authorities found had been abused through error and fraud to the tune of an annual $5 billion. The Congressional Joint Committee on Taxation estimates that households earning up to $39,000 will receive EITC cash by the year 2007.

The EITC program was not inspired by socialist thinking. In fact, it was fathered by a proposal from monetarist Milton Friedman, the Chicago School economist who floated the idea of a negative income tax (NIT). Friedman, because he placed the analytical burden of the market economy's problems on monetary policy, could not think through the damage inflicted on the labor market by taxation in general. To be fair, we must note that he did pronounce the following:

> In my opinion the least bad tax is the property tax on the unimproved value of land, the Henry George argument of many, many years ago (cited in Harrison 1983: 299).

In this, Friedman was restating a truth that most economists would not controvert. And yet, the insight was not used to improve policy-making in Washington. An example is offered by Martin Feldstein, Professor of Economics at Harvard University. He was appointed Chief Economic Advisor to President Reagan in 1982, and was therefore well-placed to shape fiscal policy, including the EITC type strategy. Professor Feldstein had noted the following:

> One of the reasons that economists have long been interested in the tax on pure rental income is that it is a tax without excess burden. Because the owners of land cannot alter the supply of land, the tax induces no distortions and therefore no welfare loss (Feldstein 1977: 357).

Despite such wisdom, the policy-makers continued to flout sound policies in favor of those that destroy jobs and undermine the willingness of people to finance their own family needs. In place of such a program, it appears that the advocates of free enterprise have been willing to endorse strategies that deepen people's dependency on the state - putting them at the mercy of the generosity of taxpayers. One consequence is a bill presented annually to taxpayers: $7.8 billion, the cost of operating the Internal Revenue Service.

After his re-election for a second term as President, Bill Clinton decided to add a new layer of action to encourage people into work. Evidence that his plan - reforming the welfare benefits paid to the unemployed - will not solve unemployment surfaced in a major study by the politicians in the front line in the cities across America. The US Conference of Mayors launched a 34-city survey and discovered that large numbers of citizens would sink into destitution when the law requiring people on welfare to take jobs came fully into effect in 1999. The survey revealed that the big cities were unable to provide the jobs needed to fulfill the legal obligation of welfare recipients to work. To achieve President Clinton's goals it was necessary to undertake fresh investment in mass transit systems, child care and health cover. People in the inner cities who were willing to work could not accept employment because they were not within the public transport network which they needed to travel to the jobs.

According to the Mayor of Philadelphia (Ed Rendell), chairman of the Mayors' welfare-to-work task force: "By the summer of 1999, for the first time since the great depression, there will be large numbers of Americans in American cities without any subsidies at all, without any cash payments. We cannot let that happen". The survey predicted a shortfall of jobs from a high of 75,000 in Detroit down to 1,200 in President Clinton's Little Rock, Arkansas.

6. Education, Education, Education: the UK
TONY BLAIR took his New Labour party into power in May 1997 on the promise to educate people back into work. Was this the solution for the global, computer-based market economy of the 21st century? The employability of people over their lifetimes will necessitate a continual process of re-skilling, to keep abreast of rapidly changing technologies in the workplace. This will be necessary to ensure that people maintain their

productivity levels consistent with both competition from people in other countries and the new technologies which would otherwise replace them. If the working environment were a benign one, this process of lifelong learning would be fulfilling for everybody rather than something to be feared. Unfortunately, the balance of existing forces in the economy do not favor full employment no matter how adept the workforce may become at acquainting itself with the latest developments in technology.

To understand the framework of power within which people's prospects in the workplace are sealed, we have to remind ourselves of the broad sweep of the history which brought us to the postwar confrontation between trade unions and the law. We have seen that defensive employee organizations were necessary as centers of countervailing power in the 19th century. This was always going to express itself as internecine warfare which would one day have to be resolved with the state - representing the population - acting as mediator in the confrontation between employer and employee. Successive Labour governments in the postwar years were unable to mediate, and it was not until the arrival of Margaret Thatcher on the world scene that a personality with sufficient power could stamp itself on the pushing and shoving that was the industrial relations of the 20th century. As Conservative Prime Minister, Mrs. Thatcher proceeded to dismantle laws which had cumulatively given power to employees acting as collective bargaining units. The legal protection over strikes and other disruptive industrial practices were outlawed, and by 1994 trade union membership had collapsed from 13.3 million (when Thatcher came to power in 1979) to 8.3 million. Wage councils which had set minimum levels for the weakest segments of the workforce were finally abolished in 1993. The Fair Wages Resolution, which provided a measure of support for public sector employees, was revoked. The overall effect was a reduction in the level of wages, particularly at the lower end, and a massive increase in unemployment.

A proportion of employees were formerly receiving higher wages than they would have under competitive market conditions. This was the effect of the exercise of a degree of monopoly power. But did the deregulation of the labor market create a balance of power leading to full employment and satisfaction all round? It did not. Mrs. Thatcher, as a result of her government's intervention, merely succeeded in transferring the financial burden from employers to taxpayers. By sabotaging the hard-won institutions of Britain's employees, Mrs. Thatcher increased the burden on the general population who had to carry the costs of the malfunctioning economy. One result was that households receiving family credit support

TAX-INDUCED WASTE OF LABOR

The European Commission estimates that the effective average tax rate on wage income in Europe rose from 28.7% (1970) to 42.1% (1995). Two Italian economists estimate that the increase in labor taxes since 1970 accounts for a 4% increase in European unemployment (Tabellini & Daveri 1997:4).

TAX-INDUCED WASTE OF CAPITAL

The IMF estimates that between 1970 and 1995 the ratio of capital to labor in Europe has more than doubled. This is the response of firms to the rising costs of employing people. In the USA, the ratio increased by only 25%. This permitted increased productivity. Writes Guido Tabellini, Professor of Economics at Bocconi University, Milan: "As capital is combined with less labor, it becomes less productive. Hence, labor taxes also harm investment and growth" (Tabellini 1997:8).

from other taxpayers rose from 285,000 in 1989 to 692,300 in 1996 under Conservative administration. The cost quadrupled from £566 million to £2 billion. This was just one measure of the deepening of people's dependency on the state.

The policy responses to poverty in the deregulated labor market were generally viewed as being limited to two possibilities.

The first was the regulation of wages to increase the lowest levels. The Conservative government did not favor this option, but was resoundingly defeated in the election of May 1997. The New Labour Party campaigned to introduce a minimum wage. But this was the use of coercive action by government as a substitute for coercive action by organized workers. Countries which had long employed minimum wage legislation, such as the USA, had not been able to abolish either poverty or unemployment.

The second option was to emulate the US approach to supplementing wages with benefits such as family credit. But this taxpayer-financed policy was also less than a comprehensive and permanent solution. Perhaps that was why Tony Blair sought election to Downing Street with the chant of Education, Education, Education.

Education is a fine thing, and nobody can have too much of it. But as a solution to unemployment as a social process of exclusion, in time it will be found that the Blair emphasis on education and the re-skilling of people for the computer age was not to be the answer. The root cause is to be found in the failures in the land market and related fiscal policies, but that is not how the problem is viewed by the statesmen and social scientists who shape public debate. An example illuminates the point. Home ownership imposes a constraint on the mobility of people who ought to move to new locations where jobs are available. This reduces the fluidity of the labor market and so contributes to unemployment. Exhaustive studies have linked home ownership to immobility (Hunter & Reid 1968: 50-51; a thesis most recently reviewed in Harrison 1997). But these studies persistently fail to recognize that it is the monopolistic character of the land market which underpins the frictions in the housing market and deters people from selling their homes and moving to jobs in other locations (OECD: 1992). No amount of re-education will override this constraint.

Government has a responsibility to understand how it aggravates that systemic crisis when it introduces new laws on taxes. When it cuts taxes, the net economic benefits accrue to the owners of land. When it increases taxes, a government is actually struggling through a complex indirect route to capture some of the net income which is held by private individuals. The failure of government to build this dynamic relationship between taxation and the community's net income into its policy formulating process has been the major cause of instability in the modern economy and society.

Chapter 2

Flat-earth Economics

1. A "virulently negative force"

ALAN GREENSPAN looked into the abyss and feared what he saw. Next to the President of the United States, he is probably the single most influential person in the world of economics. One wrong word, and billions of dollars can be wiped off the value of assets that are traded on the world's stock markets. As Chairman of the US Federal Reserve, he oversees the welfare of the largest economy in the world, which is locked through the banking system into more volatile economies around the globe. So Alan Greenspan has to keep a wary eye on what is happening beyond the shores of America, and what he saw in the Fall of 1997 left him with a growing sense of anxiety.

He voiced his fears in the guarded language of someone who could cause turmoil. Before an audience of America's finest economists, Greenspan delivered a speech in which he cast doubts on the value of some of the prime statistics on which governments base their policies. It was enough to send gold bullion prices tumbling on the bourses: Alan Greenspan had raised the specter of a return of deflation to the United States. Deflation: ingrained into the collective psyche of the American people are the images of dustbowls and the soup kitchens of the 1930s so vividly portrayed by William Faulkner in *The Grapes of Wrath*.

Alan Greenspan was careful not to predict the return of that tragedy. He felt his way forward carefully, sending out a coded message wrapped in a critique of the statistics.

Inflation, he said, was not what it seemed. That was why he warned that "The challenge for policy-makers is to make our best judgments about the limitations of existing statistics" (Wessel 1998:9). But he could not conceal the problem that really troubled him: the effects of a rapid decline in the price of stocks and real estate. This could be "a virulently negative force in the economy," he told the American Economic Association in Chicago on January 3, 1998. *It had been the collapse of asset prices over the previous six months that had caused the crisis in Asia.*

51

The risk of the world being infected by the Asian disease had injected a similarly somber feeling of anxiety among economists who advised the leading financial houses in the City of London and on Wall Street. Quietly, they began to warn clients that the world could be heading for a deflationery slump. The elements for a repeat of the catastrophe of the 1930s appeared to be present. Inflation had been tamed by the brutalism of the Reagan and Thatcher era. This was followed in the 1990s by the success of the Asian "Tigers", whose competitive spirit had forced down the prices of consumer goods on the world markets. Then came the crash in 1997. It began in Thailand and spread like wildfire through Malaysia, Indonesia and northwards as far as South Korea. One effect was a savage reduction in the value of their currencies. This threatened further downward pressure on prices as the Asian exporters, most of whom were saddled with multi-billion dollar debts which they could not finance, sought to trade their way out of trouble. Underpinning the fears was the risks to the world financial system: bad debts in Asia exposed some of the leading European and US banks to major losses.

From his office in Washington, DC, the Chairman of the Federal Reserve had to anticipate the trends. His economists found that their statistics were not reliably monitoring what was happening in the real world. For example, in the services sector the price rises were lower and output much higher than was being chronicled by the official figures. But it was not a general decline in prices that worried Greenspan. He knew that cheaper products and services were good for consumers and for the economy if they were the result of increased productivity. Computer manufacturers led the way: they cut their prices while achieving healthy profits. This meant they were commercially viable enterprises.

It was in the realms of stock prices and real estate that the market economy was vulnerable. Banks advanced billions of dollars to firms and governments around the world. Their collateral? Stocks and shares, and real estate. Firms and even governments might default on the repayments for the loans - as happened in Latin America in the 1980s, and Mexico in 1994 - but so long as the value of the collateral held firm, they would get their money back. Cut away the collateral, however, and the banks themselves could be bankrupted. This was what Alan Greenspan had in mind when he cautiously called for deeper reflection on the risks associated with the decline in asset values.

He associated stocks and shares with real estate, but there is a difference between the two. This was dramatically illustrated by the collapse in the value of shares on the world's stock exchanges in 1987. Zeros were wiped off the ledgers, but the "crisis" was no more than that: a book keeping transaction. People did not lose their jobs. Firms were not priced out of business.

Real estate is another matter. No, not real estate - land. In the US, 70% of loans are now linked to the value of land. What would happen if the US were confronted with a crash of land values on the scale it experienced in 1925? The effect would be similar to the trauma of Japan in the 1990s. The collapse of the Japanese economy was associated with the bursting of the land price bubble in 1990. It was the same story in Thailand. In fact, if we look at any substantial economic recession in the past 200 years we see catastrophe looming first in the land market. Given such a historical reality, one would think that rational governments would give priority to monitoring trends - in prices and the volume of transactions - in the land market. With the exception of Japan and Hong Kong, however, no government presiding over a market economy troubles itself to compile a barometer of land prices that would be of value to the economists who are supposed to routinely monitor the health of the economy.

This was Alan Greenspan's problem. Even his own agency's statistics on the value of land in the United States are a disgrace. They are of no value to policy-makers, who therefore expose their citizens to the dangers that stem from operating in a void: bombarded by background noise, but devoid of the shafts of intelligence that would improve the quality of their judgments.

Greenspan feared the consequences of a crash in land prices. But if a government does not equip itself with sensitively monitored price data showing an upward trend, it cannot press the Red Alert button when those prices falter, stall....and they cannot take evasive action as the prices start to fall, then plummet....

The official numbers on real estate values do not add up. They conceal the full story because some of the numbers are missing from the books. That being so, as we shall now see, it is not surprising that policy-makers have repeatedly failed to implement corrective policies to neutralise "a virulently negative force in the economy".

In Chapter 3 we shall explore some of the consequences of the failure to focus attention on the land market. One of them is that agencies like the IMF are able to penalise working people in countries like South Korea to protect the financial interests of banks in New York, London and Paris - the banks that had profligately sponsored the boom in land prices. Before analysing this fissure in the foundations of the industrial economy, however, we need to investigate why the statistics are so poor that the Chairman of the US Federal Reserve is forced to make judgments without the benefit of the sound statistical information that could be gathered for everyone's benefit.

- Why do governments spend fortunes compiling data on the price of cabbages when they are reluctant to offer comprehensive information on the flow of rent in the land market?
- Why do legislators who take meticulous care to assess the impact of their laws on their constituencies remain silent on the effects on land prices?
- Why do statisticians analyze trends with theories that are mute on the macro-economic impact of land speculation on people's jobs?

Awkward questions, few answers. That is why the most powerful unelected individual in the market economies of the world is obliged to grope his way into the future without the benefit of the information that he needs. To develop meaningful answers we have to detour into an exploration of the state of economic theory as a social science. The excursion is unavoidable, for without it we could not begin to assemble the clues that point in the direction of workable solutions to contemporary problems. Without an appreciation of the pitiful state of economic theory, we cannot begin to realize why science and technology - and the arts of governance - cannot provide the antidotes we need for the "virulently negative force in the economy".

2. Disarray in economic theory

ECONOMISTS are puzzled. Economies that appear to be buoyant are suffering unemployment rates that have stabilized at high plateaux. Why are sufficient jobs not being created in the richest nations of Europe and North America? Why has there been a slowing down of economies, despite the global deregulation program that was inspired by Ronald Reagan and Margaret Thatcher?

Economists are puzzled. That is why they have resorted to observation rather than explanation. Globalization is the fashionable word: domestic economies have to adjust to a global market (as if international trade over the past century was not a global process). But some prominent economists are also frankly disenchanted with their discipline. Books with titles like *The Death of Economics* are appearing, the confessions of economists who no longer believe in the textbook theories that have been taught to generations of students.

If the problem of unemployment is to be solved, we need to understand why economists cannot prescribe with confidence a solution based on uncontroversial theoretical principles. It is important for policy-makers to understand those reasons, if they are serious in their pursuit of full employment. Discovering the answers is not an easy challenge. It is an enterprise strewn with treachery and traps, in which we cannot even rely on the language used by governments.

- Decoding of language is a prerequisite to this enterprise. For the words used by government do not correspond with the realities of economics.

- Understanding how the financial sector has - as if by magic - apparently transformed the character of large flows of income is also an analytically necessary prerequisite.

- We have to come to terms with the unsavory realisation that governments, through their tax codes, have systematically discriminated against millions of citizens who believe that they are treated equally before the law.

- Fiscal favoritism transforms entrepreneurs into get-rich-quick merchants whose objective is not to add value to the economy, but to extract value created by others: that reality makes sense of statistics that would otherwise appear to be nonsensical.

- The retreat of governments from their responsibility to collect the value which they create - by investing public resources, acting as agents for citizens-in-community - also features in this story, and must be appreciated if we are to penetrate the logic of current policies.

The impression with which we are left is of governments operating as card-sharps, tricking people out of money that belongs to them - and shuffling the proceeds into the pockets of bystanders who are not players in the value-creating process.

Social scientists are supposed to expose such behavior - by insisting on treating the concepts of economics with scientific integrity - but they have made our task more difficulty by failing to meet their professional obligations. This is a serious charge, but economists assist us to substantiate it. We begin our analysis by reporting the views of a professor of economics who established an international reputation as a popularizer of economics: Robert Heilbroner.

As Norman Thomas Professor of Economics at the New School for Social Research, New York, Robert Heilbroner was to achieve world fame with his first venture into publishing: a survey of the great thinkers who constitute the history of the science of political economy. He called the book *The Worldly Philosophers*, and - because they had done such a good job on him - he dedicated the volume to his teachers. The first edition was published in 1953, and it has remained in print ever since.

Robert Heilbroner's views on the state of economic theory, and the social environment within which these are expressed, amounts to a frank confession about the ideological allegiances of the practitioners and the unscientific status of economics as it is taught today.

The opportunity to review the world of economics was offered by the publication of studies on global unemployment in the 1990s. In noting the persistent malfunctioning of the US economy, Heilbroner offered a pithy summary of the psychology of policy-makers and the markets:

> These malfunctions begin with levels of unemployment that would have been judged unacceptable only a dozen or so years ago but are now regarded as "normal"; worse, given the near paranoid reaction of financial markets to the slightest hints of rising prices, they are considered desirable. Between 6% unemployment and 3% inflation, there is little doubt that the great preponderance of public, as well as political, opinion regards the former as the lesser evil. More distressing, one suspects that the majority of economists would concur (Heilbroner 1996: 173).

The pessimism that resigns scientists to mass unemployment is, indeed, distressing; but how did it come about? Why are economists not able to prescribe scientific solutions? Heilbroner's frank explanation, if valid, disqualifies economics as a scientific discipline; in which case, it would be wrong of policy-makers to rely on exponents of that discipline for solutions.

Drawing on a lifetime experience as teacher, Robert Heilbroner claims that "differences in sociopolitical premises powerfully affect the content of economic theory" (*ibid.*: 177). In other words, subjective preferences rather than principles imbue the subject. This "in turn leads to sharp differences in both the interpretation of events and the choice of responses to them". In such circumstances, the economic interpretations are worth little: for it means that those groups that happen to manage the sociopolitical process at any given time can buy the testimony of economists. This is how Heilbroner put it:

> [V]ariances in sociopolitical constraints make it exceedingly difficult to declare with certainty whether the success or failure of a given policy is the consequence of its theoretical validity or its institutional setting (*ibid.*: 178).

Economics, then, is not grounded in the rules of other sciences. It is the plaything of ideologues. The repeated failures of successive schools of thought serve not to raise fundamental questions about the approach to economics; rather, to foster yet more schools. The dismay over the failure of Keynesian economics to anticipate inflation, notes Heilbroner, was the signal to unleash a raft of new schools of thought, among them: rational expectations, monetarism, new classical and a new Keynesian economics. Economists, it appears (if Heilbroner is correct), are unable to disentangle their discipline as a scientific subject from their private views as citizens. It is not surprising, therefore, that the professor should conclude that "economics becomes an unreliable - worse, an untrustworthy - discipline" (*ibid.*: 179).

But that does not prevent Heilbroner from offering his economic assessment of the cause of global unemployment: new technology, which is now able to perform the functions previously undertaken by human labor. The problem with this explanation is that the history of industrial society is made up of successive waves of advances in science and technology. All of these have rendered employees redundant. And yet, often as a result of the onset of war, full employment was restored. But there is no logical reason why rational people in a cooperative system should not adjust their working routines and rules to become the masters, not the victims, of technological innovation. The fact that so many people *are* victims reveals something important about the social rules under which we live; about how the beneficial attributes of technological innovation are not shared to everyone's advantage. Those rules ought to be the subject of careful study by social scientists, including economists. But it seems that we cannot turn to economists for help, for they now lack confidence. According to Heilbroner, "the confidence reposed in economics seems to me at a low ebb [because] we lack the confidence once bestowed by Keynesian doctrine, and before that by Marshallian, and still earlier by Millian, Ricardian, and Smithian views" (*ibid.*: 179).

The reason why Marshall, Mill, Ricardo and Smith felt comfortable with their discipline is that they sought to offer an objective description of the way in which the economy worked. They presented a comprehensive account of all the categories of economic activity; they defined their terms, and they attempted to test their theories against the observable evidence. They did not seek to conceal ideological prejudice or ignorance with obscure mathematical formulae. In terms of Heilbroner's list, economics as a social science came unstuck somewhere between Marshall and Keynes. By the time Keynes wrote *The General Theory of Employment Interest and Money* (1936), economics had been fatally impoverished. Many of its practitioners had lobotomized their subject. Of the three factors of production, they still acknowledged labor. They also acknowledged capital. Land was made to disappear in response to what Heilbroner characterizes as "the sociopolitical belief systems from which economic policy ultimately springs".

There is a world of difference between policy and theory. In a democratic community, the policy-makers are free to choose whatever policies they wish to pursue, even when these offend the hypotheses of science. In a scientific community, however, practitioners are supposed to champion the fundamental laws that govern the operations of that which they purport to study; leaving their private belief systems outside the laboratory.

The sidelining of economics as a scientific discipline has been documented by a professor of economics at the University of California (Mason Gaffney), who explained the primary purpose of the stratagem. Economics from Smith through Mill and Marshall had accurately identified the optimum conditions for public finance. To achieve the best economic results, they found through scientific reasoning - which was further endorsed by moral reasoning - it was necessary to treat the rent of land and natural resources as public revenue. Otherwise, they warned, society would be left with second- and third-best systems of taxation which would exact a heavy price. These great thinkers were willing to advocate that policy to governments. The vested interests in society would one day have to find a way of submerging that knowledge and policy out of the public's consciousness (Gaffney 1994b). The need to do so became politically urgent at the beginning of the 20th century, with the full extension of the right to vote to all adults, and it was successfully executed. We know that the operation was successful, because Heilbroner was to note the fate of the income that flowed to the resources of nature:

> The problem of rent has become almost an academic side issue in the modern Western world (Heilbroner 1983: 77).

Robert Heilbroner was to become both a victim of this intellectual process and, as we shall see, an unwitting mouthpiece for those who had successfully neutralized economics as a socially-relevant problem-solving tool for policy-makers.

3. The Single Tax Hypothesis
THE PATHFINDERS of economics developed and advocated the scientifically correct and ethically appropriate theory of public finance, beginning with the French Physiocrats (Tideman 1994). The major advances are attributable to European theorists, and largely to scholars from the British Isles. In these Old World societies, there was little risk of the discoveries disturbing the power base of those who controlled society (the

landlords), for they were strategically located within the network that regulated the law-making process.

Social conditions in America were more fluid. Here, anything was possible for the democratic process to accomplish. And it was here that Henry George (1839 - 1897) took the theory of public finance and most forcefully built it into a philosophy of social reform. He was able to show that poverty and unemployment could be alleviated only by detaxing people's wages and savings and eradicating land speculation; and he was consistent in offering the solution that would wipe out the propensity to deal in land for no purpose other than to extract other people's incomes without adding value to the deal.

It was necessary, said Henry George, to leave property rights intact: there should be no disturbance of possessory rights. But the rental income of land in all its forms would have to be swapped for those taxes that were imposed on labor and capital. This proposal became known as the Single Tax.

George eloquently explained how most of the grievous social crises could be traced back to distortions caused by unjust systems of land tenure and taxation. His exposition, in *Progress and Poverty* (1879), became the focus of political controversy at the turn into the 20th century which spread around the world. George can be credited with originating the first global reform movement.

George was not a scientist. He was a journalist. But when he wrote his book, he complied with the norms of science. He did not allow his personal preferences or social prejudices to intrude in his theorizing. Disagreements over ideological preferences were legitimate; but there was no room for disputes over the methodology of economics as a social science.

The rent of land, noted Henry George, was a publicly-created value that was the sole legitimate and sufficient source of funds out of which to defray the costs of the community's public activities. The democratic popularity of this proposition was put to the test when Britain's Liberal government sought to turn this recommendation into practical politics in 1910. The country landowners formed defensive organizations. The government was left in no doubt, however, as to the theoretical validity - and, as it happened, moral legitimacy - of its position. The fiscal reform was endorsed by Alfred Marshall (1842-1924), who at the time was the leading Cambridge economist. He recorded that the rent of land and natural resources *was* a publicly created value which, if devoted to defraying public services, would enhance the quality of people's lives. In a letter to *The Times* (Nov.16, 1909), he wrote:

[I]n so far as the Budget proposes to check the appropriation of what is really public property by private persons, and in so far as it proposes to bring under taxation some real income, which has escaped taxation merely because it does not appear above the surface in a money form, I regard it as sound finance. In so far as its proceeds are to be applied to social problems where a little money may do much towards raising the level of life of the people and increasing their happiness, it seems to me a Social Welfare Budget.

Henry George had argued that the shift of taxes off wages and savings and on to the rent of land would lead to full employment and stable growth. Many employers concurred and became active advocates of tax reform. One of them, Arizona entrepreneur John C. Lincoln, argued that "the ground rent provided by the Creator for the expenses of the government will be found to be ample for such purposes. Our land laws prevent the community from collecting this natural source of revenue, and they compel the government to collect from its citizens taxes on wealth to which the government has no natural or moral right". What if this view was empirically wrong? What if the rent of land and natural resources was not sufficient to defray all legitimate government expenses? People like Lincoln had no doubt that such a hypothetical possibility did not compromise the ethical considerations. He was to write:

Those who do not believe that ground rent would pay all of the reasonable expense of economic government would have to admit that all ground rent should be collected, and only then should the government have any right to collect any part of the wealth of its citizens (Lincoln 1957: 40).

Employers who advocated tax reform understood that they had to make out their case scientifically, whatever the additional moral or theological arguments they wanted to deploy in support of the correct distribution of property rights and income. One of them was a generous British philanthropist. Joseph Rowntree bequeathed a large part of his fortune to alleviating poverty. He willed that his money in trust should, *inter alia*, be used to investigate the potential for removing poverty by reforming the tax system. In his Trust Memorandum dated 1904, Rowntree noted that "Every social writer knows the supreme importance of questions connected with the holding and taxation of land, but for one person who attempts to master this question there are probably thousands who devote their time and strength to relieving poverty and its accompanying evils". Rowntree wanted his money used to redress the balance, for "the taxation of land values, or the appropriation of the unearned increment - all need a treatment far more

Box 2:1
GDP: Grossly deceiving prices

Governments manipulate peoples' lives by responding to changes in statistics. One of these is Gross Domestic Product, which is defined as "measuring total economic activity". It "equals the sum of all incomes (whether individual or corporate, etc) earned [sic] in the UK from the production of goods and services" (ONS 1996: 66).

People assume that economic activity involves the addition of value to the economy to increase the total disposable goods and services. This is not true with the land market. When rents are capitalized into selling prices, trading in them does not add any value through the production of goods and services.

The payment of land rent is a straight transfer of value generated by a producer to someone who, as landowner, is the recipient of income which has not been earned by the provision of goods or services of an equivalent value. Thus, when the index of GDP rises this may reveal an increase in the value of goods and services; or it may be monitoring the increase in the price of land, in which case there has been no improvement in the quantity or value of goods and services in circulation.

thorough than they have yet received". Ninety years later, the gap in public understanding has not been corrected; an omission, ironically, which Rowntree's trustees have not sought to rectify, even though they direct millions of pounds annually into research aimed at clarifying the causes of poverty.

We can only wonder why the empirical attributes of the Single Tax have not been investigated despite the wishes of philanthropic employers like Rowntree and Lincoln. For 150 years, economists had routinely acknowledged that the tax system was capable of thwarting people's employment and wealth-creating prospects; and that the solution was to redistribute the burden of public finance off labor and onto land. And yet, today, as a result of the negligence of the economics profession over the past 80 years, government statistical services even fail to provide a vaguely accurate estimate of rental income. But that has not prevented academic economists from pronouncing verdicts on the economics of Henry George. In doing so, they expose themselves to the fatal criticism of compromising their subject through ideological prejudice.

The starting point for evaluating rent as a base for public finance is the size of the revenue. This is an empirical question that ought to be beyond controversy. Unfortunately, economists remain ready to opinionate without displaying the care and attention that we expect of scientists. Robert Heilbroner, for example, pronounced on this fundamental question in these terms:

Rents are not frozen in archaic feudal patterns, but constantly pass from hand to hand as land is bought and sold, appraised and reappraised. Suffice it to point out that rental income in the United States has shrunk from 6% of the national income in 1929 to less than 2% today (Heilbroner 1983: 145).

The measurable return to land (received or imputed) in the real estate sector alone was more like 20% in 1996 - if we include capital gains. That computation is but the beginning of a calculation of income which will exceed 30% of national income. That is a far cry from the trivial numbers that are now cited in textbooks.

4. Economists defy the ground rules

ECONOMISTS publicly assert that the rent of land and nature's resources is insufficient to defray the financial obligations of the modern state.

A healthy skepticism of that claim is necessary, for by their theoretical, manipulation economists have played a part in submerging rent as a category in its own right. In doing so, they have helped to obliterate from people's minds the one reform above all others that would restore full employment, abolish poverty and create the conditions for sustainable development.

The truth about rental income is concealed beneath layers of analytical confusion and statistical misrepresentation. The neo-classical economists, the school that emerged at the turn into the 20th century, redefined economics to eliminate the unique characteristics of land and natural resources. These were conflated into the concept of capital, as if there was no distinction between man-made equipment which we use to manufacture wealth and the land on which we rely for our lives.

Excavating the truth entails a forensic examination of the books. Taking the US national income accounts as a case study, we can haul up buckets of information from the black holes to reconstruct a more accurate portrait of the economy than the one offered by economists and government statisticians. That this investigation is necessary today implies a great deal about the way in which policy-making has been seriously disadvantaged by the exponents of economics.

If an astro-physicist announced that the laws of gravity were now no longer relevant - an anachronism of a bygone age - is it likely that he would be employed by the US government to advise NASA on the power systems for boosting rockets into outer space? It is highly unlikely. And should the mistake be made, the inquest into the first crash would identify the culprit, whose services would be dispensed with before he could be instrumental in causing further wrecks.

Yet social scientists with eccentric views on the laws of economics are engaged by governments to advise on how to power the economy. *The economies keep crashing, but the economists go from strength to strength in stature and salary.*

The booms and busts that afflict the economy appear to confirm that economics as a discipline is at a pre-scientific stage, and therefore ought not to be held responsible for the persistent failures of the economy. This view is encouraged by the wide variety of schools of thought that pass for economics as a social science...if you have a point of view you can create your own school advocating how your ideas might be experimentally tested in the workplace. That leaves the awkward problem of having to explain to people, not least those who lose their jobs, why the economy keeps grinding to a halt under the influence of the competing prescriptions. The solution has been to claim that the business cycle is a law of nature over which mere mortals can exercise no corrective influence. This is an explanation particularly welcome to the Ministers of Finance who are periodically mortified by the loss of steam in the economies over which they have presided (Harrison 1997: 4-5).

Economists routinely abuse the norms that are applied in the natural sciences. That explains why subjective views preoccupy the scholarly journals in the place of scientific discourse. Nowhere is this better exemplified than in the realms of public finance.

Governments determine the social framework within which people work, save and pursue their private goals. The rules of the game are set in the public sphere. The public sector provides the cultural and material infrastructures that facilitate the interplay between people. That public sphere of life has to be powered. The "fuel" that drives the public sector is that share of resources that defrays the costs of funding the services that cannot be provided by individuals. In a sustainable social system we would expect that public sector finance would be underpinned by laws that ensured a smooth operation to compliment people's private activities. To test such hypotheses, however, we need hard data.

If, as is explained in Ch.6, taxes on wages and savings curb the output of the nation's income, can we shift to rent as the alternative way of funding the public sector? Would economic rent generate sufficient revenue to meet the costs of legitimate social services? According to some of the most distinguished economists, such a proposition is hopeless.

Mervyn King is deputy governor of the Bank of England. With his co-author John Kay he felt bold enough to declare, without offering any evidence in relation to the British economy: "...it is apparent that the total of economic rents, of all kinds, is not now a sufficiently large proportion of national income for this to be a practicable means of obtaining the resources needed to finance a modern state" (Kay & King 1990: 179).

In the United States, Nobel prize winner Robert Solow was confident enough to pronounce (a throwaway remark between parentheses, such was his confidence in his knowledge): "Whatever was the case in 1879, however, it is no longer true that the proceeds of such a tax would be enough to cover all the legitimate expenditures of government" (Solow 1997: 8).

These and other authors (*see Box 2:II overleaf*) were echoing the views of earlier economists who felt confident enough to issue pronouncements without troubling their readers with evidence. One of these was economic historian Joseph Schumpeter (1883-1950), who declared that George's fiscal remedy for the ailments of society "involves an unwarranted optimism concerning the yield of such a tax" (1954: 865).

And yet, working from first principles and direct observation, we can conclude that the classical economists were correct to share the view that, with the passage of time, the proportion of rent in the national income, far from decreasing, would *increase.* Land is finite. The only addition to earth is 25 tonnes a day of meteor dust. But there is an infinitely expanding demand on the resource base, that thin crusty exterior around Planet Earth. This demand comes from the increase in the number of people who are born every day, and the desire for higher living standards that are made possible by the infinite possibilities in the advances of knowledge. People are multiplying their demands on nature at a faster rate than their demands on the capital and consumer goods which can be manufactured. It follows that the economic rent of land and natural resources can command an increasing share of total income. And yet, economists have sought to reverse this logical conclusion. They have stood reality on its head. For them, people or man-made capital must be growing scarcer relative to land and natural resources; hence the diminishing share of land-rent in the income of the nation. This self-deception is possible in part because the statistics that would reveal the truth have been doctored to disguise the reality.

5. Excavating truth from statistics

HOW MUCH rent is there in the economy? This question had long nagged a distinguished professor of economics at Columbia University in New York. Dr Lowell Harriss favored the Georgist proposal to extract more revenue direct from the rent of land. He was to become Executive Director of the American Academy of Political Science, and also a director of a New York think tank, the Robert Schalkenbach Foundation.

It was at the Foundation that Dr Harriss and his colleagues decided to finance an expedition into the darkest recesses of the nation's accounts. Who was earning what? Specifically, how much rent was tucked away from prying eyes? How was it concealed? The Foundation commissioned Dr Michael Hudson, a Wall Street economist who had specialized in the flow of funds and international finance, to begin excavating the truth from the statistics. Hudson, as it happened, was pre-disposed to digging: he had cultivated an interest in tracing the evolution of debt and credit in the economies of ancient civilizations in the Near East (Hudson and Levine 1996). It became clear that, as the first step to establishing the scale of net income, it would be necessary to decode the concepts that shaped the nation's books. These accounts were as impenetrable as the hieroglyphics chiseled into stone and clay tablets buried in the Near East tombs that scholars have to decipher to unearth the principles that regulated the economy of classical antiquity.

The quest was on, and the results were astonishing. The remainder of this chapter draws heavily on the reports submitted by Hudson (1977) to the Schalkenbach Foundation. The challenge was to unearth the answer to the question: What part of income would flow to land and all natural resources as rent if the US were a tax-free society? It was not a simple matter of looking up the relevant line in the accounts compiled by federal government agencies. The starting point was an intimate acquaintance with the financial superstructure of the modern state. And the point of departure is the recognition that credit and debt rests primarily on the land.

Disguising rent as "interest" Most savings from the end of World War II through to the bursting of the global real estate bubble in 1990 were recycled by the banking system and by the insurance industry into mortgage lending. About 70% of US business loans took the form of real estate credit. This means that most of the economy's flow of interest payments are paid out of the real estate sector's rental revenue. *We call it interest, but part of it - that portion linked to land - is actually rent.*

What the statisticians - and textbook economists - represent as "rent" appears in Table 8.10 of the national income and product accounts (NIPA) as "rental income of persons." This is an imputed figure relating solely to homeowners. These owner-occupants are treated as running a business by buying their homes and, in effect, paying rent to themselves. Their "rental income" is supposed to reflect the hypothetical rent they would

Box 2:II

US National Income : Statistical Illusions

ECONOMISTS offer students data on the changing distribution of income without explaining the impact of taxation. The percentages for the US monitor the official version of what happened to "rental income".

Income Approach to GNP : % (USA)

	1929	1933	1960	1980	1987
Wages & Salaries	58.9	73.1	71.0	75.5	72.8
Proprietors' Income	17.5	14.6	11.2	5.5	9.0
Corporate Profits	12.0	-3.0	12.0	8.6	8.4
Rental Income	6.2	5.1	3.8	1.5	0.5
Interest	5.4	10.2	2.0	8.9	9.3

SOURCE: Byrus & Stone 1989: 637

Their presentations offer a distorted impression of shares in the nation's income. For example, Byrus & Stone (1989: 637): "Throughout this century, wages and salaries have increased as a percentage of National Income, growing from less than half in 1900 to roughly three-fourths now". The economists fail to explain how this effect was largely the result of distortions caused by tax policy, not the relative improvement of employees' economic condition - as a breakdown of these incomes net of tax would reveal.

To their credit, the two economists note that "The declining share of rental income is misleading because rapid depreciation schedules (tax breaks) cause rental income to be severely understated in recent years". Even so, that did not inhibit them from claiming that "A single tax on land sounds appealing, but it suffers from several flaws....potential revenue would probably not cover today's total government spending...." (*ibid*: 639)

In fact, land rent and capital gains from the real estate category alone in the USA, although statistically conjured almost out of sight, are up to at least 20% of national income under the present tax regime; and counting....

Advocates of the rent-as-public-revenue policy do not expect the rental income that can be measured under *today's* fiscal regime to "cover today's total government spending". (*See Ch.5*).

have earned if they had acted as their own landlords and paid a net rent to themselves after deducting state and local property taxes, interest and amortization on their mortgages, and even charging off depreciation (capital consumption allowances) for the wear and tear of their homes. The resulting figure - $115.8 bn in 1996 - was 1.85% of national income.

A search elsewhere in the national income accounts for the term "rent" turns up nothing. Revenue earned by the mining, oil and gas industries on their natural resources, and the revenue generated by forestry, fisheries and the radio spectrum is called "profit," *but that part which is attributable to the resources of nature is actually rent.* The estimates contained in this chapter do not include an assessment of the rental value of these natural resources.

Nor does the full official term, "rental income of persons," include the returns to commercial real estate investment, or corporately owned real estate, or even farms. It also does not include mortgage interest, which is paid by real estate buyers out of their rental revenue, whether it takes the form of money proceeds (from renters) or "in kind" benefits (for owner-occupants). The statistic does not even include real estate taxes, despite the fact that the land portion of these taxes represents part of the pretax rental revenue.

The NIPA figure for "rent" also excludes capital consumption allowances (CCAs) that the tax laws permit owners of buildings to deduct from gross earnings. Business analysts add these depreciation allowances to profits to derive "cash flow," and use that as the basic measure of current returns to real estate. Adding the rise in real estate prices (called "capital gains") to this cash flow produces a final comprehensive measure: total returns.

Economists who wish to classify economic activity, and those who are interested in reforming public finance, must first factor these items into account when calculating the taxable capacity of the nation's land and natural resources. The categories are listed in Table 2:I.

We can now proceed to disentangle the official figures to arrive at an impression of the rental value of US real estate.

In 1996, estimated net rental revenue of homeowners as reported by the Commerce Department was $115.8 bn (NIPA Table 8.10). But home-owners nearly double this figure to $225 bn in their disclosures to the Bureau of Labor Statistics (BLS). Noncorporate real estate (the category to which most commercial real estate partnerships belong) generated $145 bn in cash flow (real estate profits of $44 bn, plus $101.5 bn for capital consumption allowances). The corporate real estate sector registered a

Table 2:I
Tax-deductible expenses in US real estate (1996)

	$ bns
Local real estate taxes	?
Mortgage interest	?
Capital consumption allowances for buildings	
- non-corporate real estate	?
- corporate real estate	?
Profits or losses	
- for non-corporate real estate	?
- corporately owned real estate	?
Federal taxes on net reported income	?

modest net book-keeping loss of $2.8 bn but kept $8.4 bn of real estate cash flow (CCAs) in the most recent year available (1994).

These revenues represent what was left after paying local and state property taxes of $202.3 bn, and the substantially larger flow of interest charges of $356.6 bn. The sum of all these various components of rental revenue amount to much more than the 2% or so claimed by some textbook writers. They add up to nearly a trillion dollars: $935 bn in 1996. According to Dr. Hudson:

> About 60% of this, or $561 bn, is plausibly assignable to land. Land-price gains add another trillion dollars or so in each of the boom years, pushing land's total returns to $1.5 trillion.

In Hudson's judgment, based on the most exhaustive analysis of the federal government's national income records, "land-rent of real estate alone represents a quarter of national income, even without taking into account the returns assignable to land and natural resources from other land-based industries."

This sum is almost equal to the US tax-take. How was a value of this magnitude made to disappear in the national accounts?

Real estate represents by far the economy's largest tangible asset. In its *Balance Sheets for the U.S. Economy: 1945-94*, the Federal Reserve Board (FRB) estimated real estate's value at $13.4 trillion, about two-thirds of the economy's $20 trillion in overall assets in 1994. Of this sum, land values were very conservatively estimated at $4.4 trillion. Hudson's adjustments to the official figures, after discovering the bizarre way in which the FRB biases its values in favor of buildings, yielded a land value closer to $9 trillion.

It would seem that real estate's corporate and personal income tax payments ought to be substantial. Yet the NIPA statistics show the real estate sector's reported earnings to be so small as to give the impression that it operates virtually on a charitable basis. *Most commercial real estate records net losses (for tax purposes) year after year.*

Do real estate investors use "Hollywood book-keeping" of the sort found in movie studios that manage to turn out $100 million blockbusters without declaring any profit for their investors? Dr Hudson worked out that the appropriate model was the oil industry, which showed little taxable income decade after decade as a result of the depletion allowance. The real estate, mining and oil industries, as well as finance and insurance, have long been the major beneficiaries of a similar fiscal largesse. In the case of real estate, the capital consumption allowance and the right to count interest as a pre-tax business expense are the two major factors freeing real estate investors from income taxation.

Many real estate investors do operate on the margin of solvency. They do so out of choice, however, in the pursuit of "making a killing" out of capital gains. They mortgage their properties to the hilt by using other peoples' money rather than their own. To the extent that the low net earnings of real estate in the national income statistics make sense, then, it is by showing the degree to which real estate investors have been willing to turn over most of rental income to mortgage creditors as "interest". The strategy is to ride the wave of increasing land values and to "cash out" by selling their property for more than they paid.

The tax laws tempt real estate holders to use as little of their own money as possible - that is, to borrow as much as they can - by allowing them to deduct interest charges as an operating expense. Homeowners also enjoy this privilege. The effect has been to buoy up prices, by enabling buyers to carry a larger mortgage after taking into account the tax savings.

Creditors provide an expanding pyramid of mortgage credit to bid up real estate prices, the macro-economic consequences of which are silently ignored in the textbooks.

In addition to not owing income taxes on the two-sevenths of rental cash flow that is paid out as interest, landlords are allowed to set aside a tax-free portion of their gross rental earnings to reimburse themselves for the wear and tear of buildings, over and above their out-of-pocket maintenance and repair expenditures. The result is that real estate owners deduct most of their gross rental income, and hence are not taxed on it. *Thus is "rent" made to disappear.*

The same technique operates in the FIRE sector (Finance, Insurance and Real Estate), which pays a uniquely small portion of income tax in comparison to the magnitude of its assets and cash flow.

Although the Internal Revenue Service (IRS) collects and reports realized capital gains (and losses) as part of its income statistics, no conceptual basis has been developed to incorporate these capital gains into the NIPA format. There again, the exercise would not be particularly enlightening: the tax code permits so many exclusions and deductions that the bulk of capital gains are not declared or taxed. Thus, the major objective of real estate investors - capital gains - appear nowhere in the national income accounts.

Does all this matter? Dr Hudson thinks so. He points out that, only when the earnings of each sector are known and compared to the magnitude of investment, can the fairness and symmetry of the tax system be evaluated. Such an assessment requires that each industry's cash flow and total returns be known and compared to its tax burden. When it comes to real estate, the statistics camouflage the reality.

Reflecting the symbiosis that has developed between the real estate sector and the financial and insurance sectors since World War II, most rental income now ends up neither in the hands of developers nor those of the tax authorities. Rather, it takes the form of interest paid to banks, S&Ls, insurance companies, real estate investment trusts (REITs) and money market funds.

Curiously, however, despite the fact that many properties were changing hands at rising prices, there was little net income to show for all this activity. At least, little income was reflected in the NIPA statistics. This statistical illusion is explained largely by the fact that with each sale at rising prices, the mortgage debt tends to grow, along with depreciation allowances. Unlike consumers who borrow money to buy cars, ppliances, or for other non-business purposes, real estate owners are able to pay off their creditors out of pre-tax income.

Mortgage interest payments in the mid-1990s were running at $326 bn annually, absorbing almost half of the gross rental revenue. This mortgage interest now absorbs an amount equal to 7% of national income. A mortgage debt of $4.3 trillion represents some 46% of the economy's $9.3 trillion private nonfinancial debt, and a third of the total $12.8 trillion U.S. debt. Home mortgage interest also exceeds the reported rental value of owner-occupied homes and individually owned real estate. By 1991, interest payments rose to $343.2 bn, over two and a half times the total of reported net rental cash flow of persons ($42.7 bn), the $1.2 bn loss for real estate corporations, and $88.6 bn cash flow for partnerships.

In 1996 the real estate sector generated some $346 bn in interest payments. This was 75% higher than the $202 bn paid out for state and local property taxes.

Compared to interest charges and taxes, the figures reported for rental cash flow are relatively small, and net taxable income smaller yet: $24 bn rental income (and $86 bn cash flow) reported by homeowners, $130 bn earned by partnerships, and a $4 bn net loss (but $3 bn net cash flow) reported by real estate corporations.

Added to real estate's other deductions during 1989-93, depreciation allowances exceeded gross rent by so much as to create (for the benefit of the tax authorities) a net book-keeping loss for the economy's corporate and noncorporate real estate sectors. Overdepreciation thus turns out to be a legalised scam.

6. The revenue capacity of land

ADDED TOGETHER, the various forms of gross rental revenue of land in the real estate sector represent about 14% of National Income.

In clawing towards an estimate of the rent that must be apportioned to land, Dr Hudson insists that we have to include the revenue that is disguised in its various forms. No matter how you slice it up, the values listed in Table 2:II are attributable to the services provided by the use and occupation of land. For analytical clarity, this revenue should be called *rent*.

Table 2:II
Fiscal cost of the real estate sector's fiscal privileges: $ (bn)

Deduction	1996	Tax yield (at 33% rate)
Mortgage interest		
- business	97	32
- homeowners	260	87
Over-depreciation	200	67
Capital gains tax benefit	300	100
Total:	$857	286

About $857 bn is additional rental income that would have to be declared if the loopholes were removed.

But we must not forget capital gains. In Dr Hudson's view, "It is the community's economic development that adds value to real estate. An argument therefore may be made that the capital gains rightly should belong to the community rather than to developers and mortgage lenders. It is preferable for the economy to invest its savings in some way other than to bid up real estate prices and thereby inflate a real estate bubble". In the absence of a fiscal policy based on rent as an annual stream of income, there is a logic in targetting capital gains. This issue was analysed by a doyen among economic commentators in Britain (Samuel Brittan of *The Financial Times*), who observed:

> The moral is not that we should give up redistribution but concentrate the tax burden on the less mobile elements. The least mobile factor of production is, of course, land. The case for land taxation has been made by many generations of political economists...
> [T]he best bet might be to concentrate on taxing long-lived capital structures which embody a large element of land in their price - that is, not plant and machinery, but commercial buildings and domestic residences (Brittan 1997).

To tax capital gains in real estate (which the FRB estimates at some $550 bn in 1994) at the same rate as normal earned income is taxed would have yielded $183 bn, assuming a 33% tax rate (including state and local taxes). The reported federal deficit for that year was $195 bn.

7. Where Did All the Land Go?

IN REACHING conclusions about US land values, however, caution is the key word. For example, Dr Hudson examined the Federal Reserve Board's methodology on a sector by sector basis. By 1993 the FRB estimated that the land held by all nonfinancial corporations had a *negative* value of $4 bn. This nonsensical number was the result of the way the FRB imputed land values: it subtracted the estimated replacement cost of buildings from overall real estate market prices. This "land residual" method leaves little room for land value, for it makes the replacement value of structures absorb most of the rising market value of corporate real estate. Replacement values are typically made to rise even when market prices are declining.

Yet real estate represents an economy's largest category of wealth. The FRB estimates that at yearend 1996, U.S. households and non-profit institutions held $11.4 trillion in tangible assets. Nearly 80% ($8.2 trillion) of gross household wealth took the form of real estate while non-profits held $0.8 trillion. Real estate also accounted for nearly half ($3.4 trillion) of the $6.9 trillion in tangible assets owned by non-financial corporate business.

In view of this dominant economic importance of real estate, it is ironic that the statistics are so pathetic. The methodology by which land values are assessed undervalues them by as much as $4 to $5 trillion - a sum as large as the Fed's estimate of total economy-wide land value. Land appears only as a residual, not as having a site value in and of itself.

In drawing up balance sheets for the economy, the Fed's statisticians divide real estate into land and structures. The Fed's methodology meant that the Balance Sheet breakdowns of land and structures no longer represented current market prices. Subtracting buildings at their replacement cost from the property's current market value left land with only a scant (if any) residual value.

This creates danger for the innocents who want to invest their savings. Assuming that the estimated values for buildings were realistic, the inference was that corporate balance sheets were in stronger condition than many people realized. Those who thought this, however, did not understand how the Fed had derived its figures. Every overestimate of building value reflected a corresponding underestimate of land value (to the tune of $1.5 bn, in Dr Hudson's view).

Faced with the statistical disappearance of land values, the FRB terminated the publication of land estimates. *It was embarrassing to report that all the corporate land in America had a negative value in 1993 of $4 bn.*

A recalculation of the Fed's figures provides the estimates that appear in Table 2:III. This doubles the estimated land value, from $4.4 trillion in 1994 to nearly $9 trillion.

Table 2:III
U.S. Land Values: $ trillion

Corporate	2.0
Non-profit sector	0.5
Residential	4.0
Non-corporate	1.3
Farmland }	
Corporate }	1.0
	8.8

SOURCE: Hudson (1997), derived from Federal Reserve Board estimates published in the National Income Accounts. The first three categories are from data for 1996; the second group is derived from 1994 data.

8. Political influences encourage underestimation

IN DR. HUDSON'S view, further research will to lead to an upward revaluation of land relative to structures by $1.5 trillion for corporate real estate, another $2 trillion for owner-occupied residential real estate, $0.6 trillion for non-profit real estate, and $1 trillion more for noncorporate real estate partnerships.

Why is such research not being done to enhance the information that is vital to the competitive spirit of the entrepreneurial economy? Our survey of official statistical malpractice - all of it lawful, sanctioned by the democratic process; much of it the outcome of horse-trading behind closed doors - provides little comfort for Federal Reserve chairman Alan Greenspan. For the deficiencies in the data on the prime asset - land - cannot be deemed an accident. Attempts *have* been made to improve the data; notably by the late Henry Reuss when he was chairman of the House Committee on Banking, Finance and Urban Affairs. He recommended the compilation of an index on land prices (Harrison 1983: 303, n.3). A Working Party of leading economists and statisticians in Washington was established to explore the ways in which the data could be compiled, but the project was killed when Ronald Reagan was elected president.

Meanwhile, the need to chronicle price trends mounts with every successive wave of chaos in the markets. The banking crises are now recurring with greater frequency, from the US and UK property *debacle* in the 1980s, the collapse of many of Scandinavia's banks in the early 1990s and the excruciatingly drawn-out financial fiasco in Japan that lingered through most of the decade. Price indices for commodities - from copper and gold to oil - were tracked on the bourses, but the land on which we live, work and play was assiduously ignored.

The FIRE sector has a self-interest in not tracking land gains more closely. Government agencies have acquiesced in this industry bias, even though state and local fiscal authorities would benefit by creating a tax system that encouraged capital investment rather than speculation. Private consultants do track land values for their clients, but the aim is to buy stocks in corporations with undervalued land rather than to improve policy-making for everyone's benefit.

But what of the dilatoriness of economists? They display a surprising inertia towards the incompleteness of information on land. Many of them would reject such a charge; including, no doubt, Nobel prize winning economist Paul Samuelson of Massachusetts Institute of Technology. He wants economics to be judged as the "realistic science" (1967: 792), a standard against which he would agree to be judged. His stricture appeared in the 7th edition of his *Economics*, a textbook which *The Economist* of London has characterised as influencing several generations of university students.

Yet realism is what economics cannot deliver, if it will not call a spade a spade. For example, in the 12th edition of his book (1985: 114-115, co-authored with William Nordhaus), Prof. Samuelson deals with rent as requiring "only one explanation". That explanation defined rent in the national income accounts as the income of persons (which, for 1983, is shown as 2% of Net National Product). No realistic attempt is made to enlighten students about the flow of rental income to persons who own the choicest of locations in the commercial and industrial sectors, or to decode categories like "Net interest" or "Depreciation".

Such a charge could not be leveled against Columbia's Professor of Economics. Dr Harriss, unlike many of his peers, knew that the tax base that Henry George had in mind was *not* what the national income accounts classified as "rental income of persons". He had written that "much that would belong in the base consists of the fruits of parcels of land that are not subject to lease." This included, he noted,

> the land owned and used by a corporation, as for factory, office space, or commercial occupancy, with the net yield appearing, presumably, as profit or in payment of interest on debt. The economic rent of much agricultural land appears as 'farm income.' *Probably most of the land value in the country does not yield a rental appearing as such in the national accounts* (1979: 369, n.13. Emphasis added).

Without that realistic appraisal of what lies behind the official labels, it is not possible to achieve a working appreciation of the order-of-magnitudes in the distribution of income between land, labor and capital.

Without the hard information it is difficult to "prove" that the economy is biased by taxation in favor of the pursuit of capital gains (the ethos of the casino) rather than the production and construction economy (the ethos of the value-adding entrepreneur). The blind spots in the law-making process, nurtured by the paucity of relevant information, are

● driving the global economy towards the first major depression of the new millennium, and

● encouraging economists to disparage the one fiscal policy that remains unassailable in theory and morality.

Yet the rent of land and natural resources, in all its forms (overt and disguised by the tax system and a subjective economics: *see Appendix 1 for a comprehensive list*), is sufficient to introduce the Single Tax philosophy in the United States today. All that this requires is the democratic will.

Chapter 3

Globalisation:
the Looming Chaos

1. Of bankers and scapegoats

THE LAND MARKET is one of the most sensitive barometers of the state of health of the economy. It literally alerts government to the net income which can be spent on behalf of the community. Under the current rules of the economic game, land prices provide the earliest warning signals of trouble ahead.

But this barometer also sits in judgment on the record of government. Like a seismograph it registers the ripple effect of laws passed, and policies pursued, by government. If a law improves the condition of society - up goes the value of land in general. If a tax or policy reduces the quality of people's lives - down goes the value of the land that they occupy. This second aspect of the land price barometer will be discussed in section 4 below. Here we need to clarify the process by which politicians and economists sit in judgment on what happens in the real world. Our case study is the collapse of economic progress in the Asian countries which resulted in a IMF-sponsored rescue operation costing more than $100 million in 1998.

By the 1990s, countries like Thailand, Malaysia and South Korea enjoyed growth that was more than double the rates achieved by the advanced economies. In Korea, government and employees built an economy that rose to 11th position in the league of industrial nations. It achieved an average annual growth rate of 8% over the previous two decades before imploding The people worked hard, and saved hard (with a personal savings rate of 20% of disposable income). Manufacturers like Samsung became brand names in the shopping malls around the world. And yet, when the financial crisis struck Asia in 1997, South Korea was found to be saddled with short-term foreign loans that exceeded $200 bn. How could it have happened, and what corrective measures ought to have been taken?

The consensus view of the the IMF and financial analysts was that the blame lay with the government and its cozy relationship with the conglomerates, known as *chaebol*. The general explanation canvassed in the world's press was that Korea had suffered because her commercial and financial systems were not sufficiently deregulated. The medicine that she was forced to swallow in return for $57 bn. arranged by the IMF entailed bankruptcies and the opening up of the Korean economy to foreign investors. The country was forced in to recession through a tightening of fiscal and monetary policy. The security enjoyed by employees was eliminated as part of a restructuring of the manufacturing sector. Despite the government's agreement to comply with the IMF's austerity program, the credit worthiness of Korea was reduced to "junk bond" status. How could a country with massive reserves and a huge surplus on its trading account with the rest of the world be humiliated in this fashion?

South Korea is the classic case of a country overtaken by its own success. It produced value-for-money goods which the world's consumers wanted but that was no protection against the malevolent influence of the land market. As the profits flowed in, so the value of land rose even faster. The *chaebol* invested in fixed capital equipment to increase the sale of their products abroad; but they also recognised that the highest returns could be got from the land at home. Real estate became the black hole into which vast sums were poured. The North American and European banks were happy to oblige. They were willing to lend at low rates of interest to such a prosperous country. In the summer of 1997 the IMF supplied a glowing report on the South Korean economy and the government's policies: its economists in Washington viewed the flourishing Asian economies through a theoretical prism which deflected attention away from over-valued real estate. Even when Thailand gave the game away in June 1997, the Western analysts were unwilling to acknowledge that the problem was with a systemic flaw. Instead, they censured the Asian governments for their lax controls over the financial sector. A little prudence in time, it was implied, would have prevented the disaster.

But Korea would not have fallen so far without the help of the international banks. They were delighted to pour money into South Korea. They, too, ignored the risks associated with tying money to land that had become the object of speculative activity. But when thecollapse came, the foreign banks were not going to suffer. The IMF framed its rescue operation to inflict the pain on Korean workers and ensure that the foreign loans were repaid.

To their credit the financial press did see through the injustice of the IMF's policies. The anomaly behind the IMF philosophy could be overlooked if the crisis had involved a banana republic. But South Korea was the 11th largest economy in the world. The Western banks were put under the spotlight. They "retain and secrete information that markets need, not least information about the banks themselves, their sources of profits, lending policies, asset quality and location, and hedging activities," wrote Martin Mayer in *The Wall Street Journal* (January 2, 1998). "The IMF has got it all wrong. Foreign lenders are the beneficiaries of this bail-out. US, European and Japanese banks are being rescued for the losses they would face if Korea defaulted. The blame also lies with them. Banks financed real estate speculation..." wrote Brian Reading in *The Financial Times* (December 20, 1997).

On the other side of the world, in a court in Germany, the financial and moral probity of banks was subject to a withering analysis by a judge. Heinrich Gehrke sent Jurgen Schneider to jail for six years following the collapse of his property empire with debts of DM. 5bn (£1.69 bn). Schneider had forged documents to deceive Germany's largest banks into advancing larger loans than his development projects warranted. But when the time came for assessing culpability, the judge said Schneider was not alone in responsibility. Judge Gehrke pronounced:

> Schneider was neither a professional fraudster nor a Robin Hood of the property world. The banks knocked down his doors with almost unbelievable recklessness. They didn't check asset valuations, and if there were shortcomings in his loan applications they simply accepted them. The case is a sort of picture of Germany's society, and of the German banks especially, where the rule holds that appearances take prominence over reality. If someone wants a small bank loan they're strictly controlled, but if someone wants millions and pretends to own billions, then the bankers will carry the money to them (Staunton 1997).

The judge singled out Deutsche Bank for behaving with "almost incredible negligence". It was an observation that could legitimately be directed at all the banks in Europe, the United States and Japan which had poured billions into the land market in South Korea without weighing the risks. But why should they worry about the defaults on their loans when they could rely on the IMF to bail them out?

The people of Korea had fallen victim to the crushing logic of the economic philosophy that nourishes the land-and-tax laws. The tragedy was spelt out as it confronted the dirt farmers of Oklahoma in the Great Depression.

A man can hold land if he can just eat and pay taxes; he can do that. Yes, he can do that until his crops fail one day and he has to borrow money from the bank. But - you see, a bank or a company can't do that, because those creatures don't breathe air, don't eat side-meat. They breathe profits; they eat the interest on money. If they don't get it, they die the way you die without air, without side-meat. It is a sad thing but it is so. It is just so (Steinbeck 1939: 35).

The government takes its taxes and the landowner extracts the rent: the age-old tussle for the net income generated by the producers of wealth. Add in the compound interest required by the banks, and somebody has to be bankrupted. That somebody is not the banks. They can always reclaim their collateral - land - without spilling tears. So what is to be done? Financial speculator George Soros, known as the man who broke the Bank of England for his successful dealings on the money exchanges, proposed the creation of an insurance system to remove the prospect of financial disasters that could wreck the global economy (Soros 1997). But insuring the banks against imprudent loans will not stop land speculation. In fact, it would enable banks to take more risks. They would write their own insurance policy, the cost of which would have to be financed by their customers.

Soros argued that the private sector was notoriously inefficient in the international allocation of credit. It did not have the information with which to form a balanced judgment. "Its goals are to maximise profit and minimise risk. This makes it move in a herd-like fashion in both directions," he wrote, even as he personally intervened to offer help to the government in Seoul.

In fact, the fundamental problem is not one of information. The problem is one of theory, which shapes the way we view the world. We see the effects of a distorted theory: it injects blindspots into our outlook and exposes working people, such as the population of Korea, to the speculators whose downfall is usually guaranteed by greed and bad timing.

The information in the form of a land price index, *if its significance was understood*, would provide government - and the banks - with the barometer they need. This would improve their analysis of risks associated with loans. Such a barometer does not exist, however, which is why people have to pay a heavy price for the errors of policy. If governments are to be rebase their policies on a rational footing, they must first re-learn the economics of land and natural resources.

2. Law of Economic Absorption

AS THE governments of the industrialized nations prepared to enter the third millennium, in the sphere of economic policy two issues were of more substantial concern than the immediate fate of the Asian economies. Both of them concerned the Globalization of the economy.

The long-term problem related to the ominous portents for public revenue. Tax-dodging multi-national corporations could now be even more effective at switching their profits around the world. And tax-dodging consumers could use the internet to order goods and bypass the tax collectors. This was a new spatial layer over the long-running fiscal crisis.

The short-term problem concerned jobs. Governments warned their citizens that, if they wished to remain in employment, it would be necessary to hold down the level of wages. People had to remain competitive, to survive in the new world in which they would compete with low-cost countries. Labor markets would have to become "flexible". By this means could the rich nations remain, if not exactly fully employed, at least no more under-employed than they already were (*see Box 2, page xiii*).

Overlaying this cajoling of workforces was renewal of the debate about free trade and protectionism. This controversy surfaced in its most acute form in Washington, where President Clinton unsuccessfully sought legislative endorsement to deepen his open-borders policy. He wanted to accelerate the free flow of goods between nations. Congress, which resented the flow of American capital into Mexico where wages were lower and environmental impact laws more lax, resisted. Republican politicians favored the protection of the US economy against competition from Third World countries. But once again, the debate on international trade was devoid of the depth of understanding that would guide policy-makers to an informed decision.

Who gains, and who loses, from protectionism? This was not a question posed on Capitol Hill, beyond the clichés that focused attention on jobs. Which cats got the cream? It was a question posed by Vilfredo Pareto (1843-1923), an Italian who came to economics after 20 years as an engineer. He had been well-exposed to the workings of the world, in both its social and "natural" forms. He became professor of economics at the University of Lausanne. His name survives in the literature in the concept of *Pareto Optimum*. This defines the conditions required for the optimum use of resources, and of how to get there: if it is possible to be made better off without making another person worse off by changing the use of resources, Pareto-optimality has not been achieved. The most efficient use of resources is attained when no person can move to an alternative position except by displacing another person into an inferior (less preferred) position.

Pareto's main contribution to economics was published in 1906 as *Manuale di Economia Politica*. In this, he committed himself to discovering rules of behavior which, tested against his training in engineering, he wished to characterize as laws. He wrote:

> Human actions display certain uniformities and it is thanks to this property alone that they can be made the subject of a scientific study. These uniformities also have another name. They are called laws (Pareto 1971: 3).

It was, he said, his intention to follow the practice of John Stuart Mill, and study economics not as a do-gooder reformer, but rather as someone searching for "the uniformities that phenomena present, that is to say their laws, without having any direct practical usefulness in mind, without concerning himself in any way with giving recipes or precepts, without seeking the happiness, the benefit, or the well-being of humanity or of any part of it. In this case, the purpose is exclusively scientific; one wants *to know, to understand*, no more" (Pareto 1971: 2; Pareto's emphasis).

On international trade, Pareto wanted to know who would gain and who would lose in the distribution of income, if obstacles were placed in the way of people's freedom to exchange goods across national borders. His quest for laws drove him to define ultimate - and regular - consequences. This was his conclusion:

> Obviously protection changes the distribution among certain individuals. The combinations which can occur are infinite; we can say roughly and in a very general way that agricultural protection especially favors landowners for whom it increases *rents*. Industrial protection favors the owners of industrial sites in a permanent way, and entrepreneurs in a temporary way. The latter, at first, get some temporary *rents* which the competition of other entrepreneurs reduces and nullifies more or less rapidly (Pareto 1971: 375. Pareto's emphases).

In the corridors of power where politicians champion the cause of protectionism, we hear much about the need to preserve people's jobs; we are lectured at length about the need to retain the capital invested in the factories of home-grown entrepreneurs, whose profits would be threatened by competition from abroad. But never, never do we hear a word about the general and actual outcome: the enrichment of the people who, though they contribute nothing to the value-creating process, claim increased rents (and therefore a larger share of the nation's income) as a result of protectionism.

If a government were to pronounce: "We must favor protectionism because we want to raise the rents that people pay," what would be the democratic (and, perhaps, in some cases, less-than-democratic) response? It would be a negative attitude towards restrictions on international trade.

Pareto did acknowledge that others might also benefit from protectionism:

> It favors skilled workers, who get wages higher than those they would have been able to get if the protected industries had not been established, but it is a detriment to the workers who work in the unprotected industries or in agriculture. Finally, a part of the bourgeoisie belonging to the liberal professions also benefit; industry, more than agriculture, has need for engineers, lawyers, notaries, etc. (Pareto 1971: 375-376).

As a spin-off for the general enrichment of the land-owning class, some people in the supporting trades and professions gain an advantage. But this is not a Pareto-optimum situation. In the protected economy, people are made better off at the expense of others. To move closer to the ideal, people must be free to trade their goods and services wherever they can get the best return on their labor and savings, *but by doing so without exploiting others.*

The laws of economics, then, prescribe free trade. But who are the ultimate beneficiaries of open-border trade? The case is usually put in terms of the increased prosperity of workers, and new opportunities for the investment of capital. That is true, but is only part of the story.

What happens when the effective labor market is extended to include the work forces of two or more countries? Competition is intensified, which affects wages: these are adjusted to common levels throughout the new commercial territory. The wages of some people may rise, but those of others may be moderated in a downwards direction. The same is true in the capital market. The new opportunities for selling goods results in a reallocation of fixed capital so that the returns to some investors will rise, but that of others will decline to a common level. Overall, we see the emergence of an economy at a higher level of efficiency and productivity. Costs are cut. It is at this point that the story ends, so far as economists and policy-makers are concerned.

But there is another consequence, one that escapes the notice of the statisticians who compile the data on national income. It is a general effect of the kind that Pareto calls a law. As a result of the cost-cutting competition - the leveling out of wages and dividends - the benefits surface as an increase in the net income: the surplus after defraying the costs of production. Revenue flowing into the land market is increased.

Now, once again, what would happen if a government were to pronounce: "We favor free trade because we want to raise the rents that people pay"? People would not favor free trade on those grounds. And yet, whether through free trade or protectionism, there is no way to avoid an increase in the rent of land and natural resources. The share of net revenue in the economy will increase either way. That is a law which can be distorted by governments, but only by imposing costs on the economy (through lower efficiency), such that the majority lose.

Thus, we see in operation what we might call the Law of Economic Absorption. As people become more efficient in their economic activity; as science and technology advances, giving rise to new ways of satisfying human needs by using fewer human and material resources, so the net benefits are soaked up by the sponge that is the land market.

Good or bad?

The answer depends on who appropriates the net income. If it is *privatized*, citizens are confronted with all the crises that characterized the 19th century: poverty and class divisions, social conflicts and human degradation. But if the net income is *socialized* - which would eliminate the need to socialize people's private incomes - everybody shares equally in the Social Wage. As governments spend the increasing pool of rental income, on the basis of decisions agreed by democratic process, everyone is additionally enriched by his or her equal access to the facilities provided in the public sector.

This ideal outcome is not generally elaborated in the economic literature. The result has been an economic dialog severely distorted by the prejudices of economists who shy away from the consistent advocacy of the uniformities, or laws, which can be discovered through the application of economic reasoning.

Among those who failed their students was none other than Pareto himself. In his view, "where there is a landed aristocracy, as in Germany, agricultural protection strengthens that aristocracy, and helps it avoid being destroyed by other aristocracies. It is for this reason that agricultural protection is perhaps indispensable for the preservation of the present social organization in Germany" (Pareto 1971: 376). Pareto was a wealthy heir who had married into the Russian aristocracy. His wife was a Countess. It comes as no surprise to learn that, *pace* his desire to seek optimality through the laws of economics, when it came to political prescriptions he was staunchly on the side of those who wished to reserve the net income of society in the hands of aristocratic landowners (Gaffney 1994b: Ch.7).

This species of schizophrenic behavior (which is discussed in Ch.4: *see pages 112-117*) is the primary source of conceptual confusion which then feeds its malevolent influence into people's lives. But the damage inflicted on the public's perceptions is not restricted to a flow of contradictory statements from the Right. Economists on the Left are equally responsible, as we note with their attacks on Adam Smith and on the "the invisible hand". Their attacks are dishonest. Smith's vision of a future economy included the clear advice to governments: treat the rent of land as a peculiarly suitable source of public revenue (1776: Bk.5, Ch. 2, Pt. 2, Art.1). To do so would not result in a rise in the rental charges paid by the users of land; nor would it discourage industry. Thus, if governments had adopted Smith's advice, the Law of Economic Absorption would have been at the command of the common good. Instead, by ignoring that advice, it became necessary to impose taxes on labor and capital, with all the grievous costs that this policy entailed.

And so, as the world moved into the third millennium, the 19th century controversy over free trade was fought all over again. The conventional wisdom is fatalistic. It says that globalization entails unavoidable sacrifices that have to be made by working people to meet the challenge of competition from the "emerging" economies.

But there is no ambiguity over who benefits from the gains - the lower costs of production - that flow from the "more flexible labor market". The answer was neatly summarized by William Vickrey, who was awarded the Nobel prize for economics in 1996. A few days after the announcement he was to have made a speech based on two unpublished papers (Vickrey 1995); a speech that he was not to deliver, for he died just three days after being awarded the accolade. Dr Vickrey was to have declared: "In starting from an inefficient situation, if labor and capital are fully mobile in the long run so that returns to labor and capital are determined by nation-wide or region-wide conditions, any gains from an improvement in efficiency would redound to the owners of the fixed factor, land." And: "Given high mobility of capital and labor, which tends in the long run to equalize returns to these factors over the region, landlords ultimately reap most if not all of the benefit from an increase in the efficiency...."

Applying this well-attested analysis to the global scale, we see that the owners of land gain the benefits in a country where people are forced to be more flexible ("mobile"). Not a word of this appears in the think-tank reports or the financial press; which is why the process of economic exploitation - seen in its most concentrated form in land speculation - goes unmonitored.

3. The propensity for Land Speculation

AS THE sponge effect absorbs more of the productive gains from the economy into the rent of land and natural resources, prudent investors (under the present rules) should direct more of their savings into the land market rather than into fixed equipment with which to manufacture new goods and provide additional services to the public. The reason is clear enough: over the course of the business cycle, the rate of return from land increases faster than it does from other forms of investment (taking capital gains into account).

If rent is available for private appropriation, it acts like a candle drawing a moth into its flame. There is an inevitable thrust of investment activity away from job-creating enterprises and into speculative activity in the land market. There is a clearly defined pattern of cyclical behavior to this activity, which has an inevitable consequence: a boom followed by a collapse in the economy.

Table 3:I
Net Household Savings as percentage of Disposable Household Income (national definitions): 1991

Treatment of interest deductions

Most generous		Least generous	
Finland	5.5	Australia	7.4
Netherlands	1.3	Belgium	17.0
Norway	2.6	Canada	10.3
Spain	6.7	France	12.8
Sweden	3.4	Germany	12.8
US	4.9	Italy	18.6
		Japan	14.9
		UK	9.2
Average	4.1	Average	12.9

Sources: OECD, cited in Tanzi 1995: 95.

When the market collapses into one of its periodical bouts of disruption, analysts level accusations against none other than "the market". In truth, the primary flaw is not with the economic agents, who act in what they perceive to be their best private interests with the information at their disposal, and within the permitted rules of the game. The blame must ultimately attach to governments that decline to reform their tax regimes. Taxation distorts the natural inclinations of people to produce and exchange goods and services on a value-for-value basis. Perverse tax policies encourage people to pursue unearned income from land speculation, and they act rationally when they to take advantage of the opportunities.

But there is a price to be paid as a result of this rational private action. The price is a collective one, in which we all lose The ground rules as they apply in the land market are not designed to generate the optimum result. Someone's private gain is everyone else's social loss.

The manner in which the rules are rigged to favor disruptive land speculation can be most clearly traced in the sector that supplies housing. First, note that it is a general rule that people are less likely to save and invest where taxation enables them to avoid paying the full cost of an activity. Thus, as we see in Table 3:I, those countries which offer generous treatment in the deduction of interest from taxable income are liable to save a smaller proportion of disposable household income than those countries where governments are less generous in the treatment of interest in their tax codes. The data was analyzed by the IMF's Vito Tanzi, who observed:

> If the difference in saving rates is attributable to the tax factor, given the deep integration of the world capital market and the facility with which capital moves, the conclusion must be that this feature of the tax system must be promoting major flows of capital across countries. These capital flows do not reflect real differentials in the productivity of investment but simply the influence of tax systems. *They must thus be associated with large misallocation of resources on a world basis.* At the margin, the last dollar invested in housing and in other expenditures is unlikely to have generated the same benefit across countries (Tanzi 1995: 96. Emphasis added).

Tanzi does not draw attention to the fact that the net benefits of these distortions end up as higher rental income. This outcome renders land unaffordable to people on the lowest incomes. This then necessitates the provision of housing through the public sector (government has the overriding clout to tax and redistribute, in the forlorn attempt to equalize the economic game).

The fact that the United States is generous in its treatment of interest is significant. In the past 20 years the US has absorbed a large slice of the world's capital available for investment. One potential has been the raising of the world real rate of interest (Tanzi: *ibid*). Tanzi notes that this has encouraged over-investment in housing and in buildings in general. "For sure, the average American consumes far more housing space than the average Japanese or European. Tax factors are likely to play some role in bringing about this result," he notes. This is a mild representation of the facts. The favorable tax treatment of investment in real estate has had a crippling effect in skewing the US economy in favor of land speculation: a damage inflicted on its citizens which has reverberated around the world to transmit similar negative impacts on the innocents abroad.

Tanzi notes that the differences in the treatment of interest deductions among countries has so far "not been the subject of frictions. There has been no call for harmonizing or at least reducing the disparity in that treatment" (*ibid*). That there has been no heated dialog over what has been a massive waste flowing from the misallocation of capital across territorial borders should not surprise us. This debate will not occur until people have developed an understanding about the impact of favorable tax treatment in swelling the sponge that is the land market. To understand the negative economic and social consequences implies the need to develop corresponding corrective policies.

Globalization promises greater efficiencies in the production of wealth in the 21st century. But before we celebrate that prospect, the lessons of that double-edged sword that is the Japanese economy need to be taken into account.

4. Japan & the policy errors
A POLITICALLY embarrassing role of the land price barometer is its capacity to track the performance of government. Good policies liberate the economy, enabling it to flourish. Bad policies crush the productive capacity of people, which reduces the income that is at the disposal of government to spend on social programs. This function is dramatically illustrated by Japan, whose government does take the trouble to chronicle the trend of land prices. Figure 3:I illustrates the two bubbles of the early 1970s and the late 1980s.

In 1990 the government in Tokyo thought that it had shaken loose from the grip of land speculation. A note of relief was struck by the President of the Ministry of Construction's Research Institute. He wrote:

> The economic bubble that has driven many corporations and citizens to extraordinary and speculative economic activities has finally burst and the country's economy is returning to normal, based firmly on real demand. The land price hike during those heady days was the major obstacle hampering housing and social overhead capital improvement, depriving the people of a feeling of affluency. Most Japanese did not benefit from the

bubble. They feel their lives are hardly affluent but yet burdened with long working hours, lengthy commuting times, high living costs, low housing standards, a poor living environment and delays in accumulation of social overhead capital (Shishido 1992).

In 1985, the year before the onset of the land boom around the world, the OECD sought to compare the value of the land in Japan with asset values in other countries. The value of Japanese land was reported to be 317% of GDP. This contrasted with the United States where land value was said to be equivalent to 74% of GDP, and in Canada it was 70%. According to the OECD "the value of land in Japan was *one-and-a-half times* greater than the value of land in all of the United States, and it was thus 'worth' more than the land of the United States, Canada and France put together" (OECD 1988: 75). Such a comparison was dangerous: the analysts were trying to assess the health of the G7 countries with data that seriously misled them. The statistic for the US land values relied on data supplied by the US Federal Reserve. This information, as we saw in Ch. 2, is worthless. And yet, the information is vital to understand the motives behind the fateful decisions taken by families and corporations both at home and abroad. The Paris-based Secretariat of the OECD did understand this and was able to analyse the prospects for Japan, because sound information was available.

Graph 3:I
Japan's residential land prices: % change

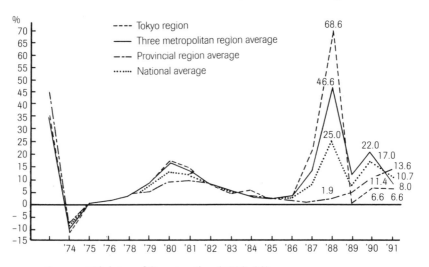

Source: Ministry of Construction (1992: 98).

- **The debt trap**. As residential land prices escalated - the price of an average apartment in Tokyo reached seven times the annual income of an average wage-earner household (OECD 1989: 14) - families felt wealthy. They could borrow more on the strength of the collateral value of their land. So long as interest rates were not raised to dampen down an overheated economy, all was well. But there always comes a point where people can no longer afford to play the game of Monopoly. Prices collapse, and the earliest signals are the downturns in the land market. Families find themselves marooned with debts which they cannot finance. And that is when the banks find themselves holding "non-performing" loans.

- **The investment trap**. Japanese banks, whose books were swollen by the inflated value of land which they held as collateral, borrowed from foreign banks to re-invest in the lucrative property deals abroad; Hawaii was one of the meccas for this hot money. In the 1980s, external assets held by Japanese banks grew at more than double the rate of domestic lending, which "gave rise to concern about the 'overpresence' of Japanese banks abroad"(OECD 1991: 87). When the foreign land markets collapsed - as they all did - the Japanese banks were left with real estate that was worth less than the loans. Strings of hotels in California were sold off at knock-down prices as the banks tried to stave off insolvency.

Japan, the second largest economy in the world, developed a productive capacity in the postwar years that was a world beater. But the nation that could take on all-comers in the commercial arena could not defeat the sponge effect on its own land. The character of the speculative activity in Japan differed significantly from that in the UK for institutional and cultural reasons. In Japan, people and corporations tend to hold on to their sites whereas in the UK there is a greater willingness to trade these assets in the market. So in Japan, small-time speculators sought capital gains once removed: they traded in the shares of those corporations that were land-rich. The outcome was the impoverishment in the quality of family life in Japan.

But in the 1980s the families that already owned paddy fields within the metropolitan areas were happy to overlook their cramped lifestyles as they saw the value of their land soar into the stratosphere. The "bubble" was deflated by 1990. It was a case of "the bigger you are, the harder you fall". By the mid 1990s, most of the OECD economies were managing to pull themselves out of the depression. The major exception was Japan, where in 1997 land prices across the nation continued to drop for the sixth consecutive year (Harrison 1997: 29-32).

A distinctive feature of the Japanese problem was the government's reluctance to confront the problem of the debts held by the banks. The banks were shy about acknowledging that they had accumulated huge losses as a result of loans to land speculators. In January 1998 the Japanese government admitted that the level of potential risky loans held by banks was ¥76,710bn (£361bn).

The 1997 financial crisis triggered in Thailand afforded economic analysts and government policy advisors the opportunity to identify the primary source of instability. The analysis was barely clear to the readers of the press, and there was certainly no discussion about appropriate solutions. Professor Feldstein of Harvard University had no doubt why the banks were in a state of palsy. He wrote in 1997: "Japanese banks were weak long before the recent currency crisis began, primarily because of the 65% collapse in the price of the Japanese urban land" (Feldstein 1997a: 8). The analysis did not match the quality of the data. *The Wall Street Journal's* editorial of November 26, 1997, referred to "The unwise real estate and financial market frenzies". Unwise? Nobody questioned the wisdom of speculation as *the* intrinsically weak spot in the foundations of the market economy.

It will all happen again unless Japan takes remedial action. The correct solution is to be found in history. Japan could relearn the lesson taught by the Meiji emperor who defended his feudal state against American trade aggression in the 1870s. He decided that the most effective weapon was to fight fire with fire. If American wanted to sell manufactured goods, his country would go into that business as well. But that meant industrialising a rural economy. The transformation had to be completed fast. From where would he get the money? How would the farmers learn to work in factories? Would his people tolerate a division of society along the class-and-money lines of European societies?

The emperor chose as his key instrument of public policy a modified version of the traditional system of public finance. He and his civil servants decided that the rent of land ought to be used to finance the public infrastructure and the educational system that was needed to equip a modern workforce. For two decades, as the agricultural society transformed itself in double-quick time, the rent of land provided over 70% of the government's revenue (Table 3:II).

That policy was abandoned by the landowning politicians who insisted on parliamentary democracy in 1890, but the seeds for a cooperative system of wealth-production were sown. The rest is history.

If the politicians in Tokyo cast their minds back to that earlier era -

Table 3:II Japan in transition (1870 - 1930)
Composition of Central Government Tax Take: %

	Land Tax	Excise Taxes	Income Tax	Business Taxes	Customs Duties	Misc.
1870	73.9	-	-	-	7.1	18.9
1880	72.9	10.0	-	-	4.5	12.6
1890	51.7	21.8	1.4	0.4	5.7	19.1
1900	24.6	28.6	3.4	3.8	8.9	30.6
1910	15.9	18.7	6.6	6.8	8.3	43.6
1920	6.2	31.6	16.0	9.8	5.8	30.5
1930	4.8	37.4	14.2	7.9	7.4	28.4

Source: G. Ranis (1958-59: 446).

which faced a crisis comparable to the one that confronted Japan in the 1990s - and if they decided to reinstate the rational public finance, the demographic problems of the 21st century will be overcome. Japan Inc. would also overcome the USA to become No.1 in the world markets, but there is nothing to stop the USA from neutralising that prospect. Washington could level the playing field by adopting the same enlightened public finance for the people of America.

5. The coming crash in the 21st century

THERE IS NO law of nature that ordains that the global economy must be subjected to another round of "paroxysms" in the 21st century, but this outcome is inevitable unless the appropriate reform to public finance is undertaken. None of the alternative interventionist measures (or the appeals to deregulation which served as their alternatives for policy in the 1980s) will serve the purpose.

Globalization brings new opportunities for prosperity, but the tax system remains an unavoidable part of the perennial problem. It is instructive to note the analysis of the IMF's tax specialist, Vito Tanzi. He recalls that the heightened flow of capital around the world has stimulated "a phenomenal growth in the world capital market...bringing about a considerable reduction in the dispersion in long-term real interest rates across countries" (1995: 1). This ought to be a cause of celebration. The territorial and legal obstructions that impeded people's access to capital have been almost totally removed. This ought to mean that the humblest entrepreneur in the farthest flung corner of the world has access to capital at affordable rates, to enable him to create new forms of self employment. Unfortunately, as Tanzi notes, "the more deeply integrated the world economies become, the greater the distorting effect of non-harmonized taxation" (1995: 74). But the IMF limits its concern to an appeal for a level playing field, without any consideration of the economic impact of the sponge effect of the land market.

> If the playing field for investment were leveled, both within countries and across countries, and if there were no obstacles to the movement of capital so that it was free to flow everywhere, an efficient allocation of capital would result and a world rate of return to investment would come to be established. Each investment in the whole world would be pushed to the point at which its rate of return would equate the world rate of return. As a consequence, both the gross-of-tax and the net-of-tax rates of return would be the same in all countries and in all sectors, and the difference between these two rates of return would reflect the average, effective tax rate on capital income (Tanzi 1995: 72).

Such a dynamic redistribution of capital levels the rate of return downwards, yielding an increase in productive efficiency and an increasing net income. This, it would seem, is something for which we should be grateful. But we know, now, that - under the present tax regime - it is something to fear. For despite more than 1,000 tax treaties among countries seeking security in the harmonization of their tax codes, nothing whatsoever is even being contemplated to control the absorption capacity of the sponge. And this, we also now know, leads inevitably to the speculative boom/bust. At the end of the first decade of the new millennium we can expect the world economy to be decimated by the first of the depressions of the 21st century.

It need not be so, but the prospects are not good. The best chance for change came - and went - in 1997. IMF economists scattered throughout Asia, proffering tens of billions of dollars to shore up the collapsing economies of the "emerging markets". They could have prescribed rational reforms. Instead, it was the conventional medicine that was dished out. The IMF's money came with strings attached: nations that were once proud of their economic record, such as South Korea, were forced to swallow "austerity" measures. These entailed the compression of their quaking economies into the institutional framework favored in Washington, DC. The IMF was willing to advocate structural reforms; but these were limited to fit the conventional wisdom.

The 21st century depressions will be of a different magnitude and character from those experienced in the past. It is not just the scale of the looming crisis that is novel. There is also, for the first time in five millennia of spatial displacement across the globe, an end to horizontal territorial expansion. The world is entering a new phase of spatial expansion on a vertical scale. In the short-term, emphasis will continue to be placed on exploitation of the untapped natural resources of the "emerging markets" which are being privatized at give-away rents. But also shifting into gear is the quest for the rents of outer space, and the rents of natural minerals below the surface of the ocean beds. And there are also the rents from our genes....

These will not require labor-intensive methods of extraction. This brings a new risk with the next phase of rent-appropriation. Previously, the land grabbers did need people to lay railway tracks or cut down the trees. Now, robots and computers will undertake much of the dangerous work on the seabed; and few astronauts will be needed to keep the telecommunication satellites and experimental platforms orbiting in space.

The principles that shape the formation of net income remain the same, from variations in fertility/resource endowment to the impact of distance/ transport costs on differences in the rent of sites. The centers of gravity of the new operations are rapidly shifting, but the underlying process of exploitation - of nature and of people - remain the same. And unless we democratize the processes, untold hardship will be inflicted on the peoples of the new millennium.

Chapter 4

Public finance fit for people

1. The crisis of governance

THE FISCAL crisis reflects the more general problem of the insecure relationship between people and government. A new foundation is necessary, but the bridge to a new relationship needs to be built on a deeper appreciation of the dynamics of power. A review of history and political philosophy is warranted, as a preliminary to offering a sketch of how public finance could alter significantly the distribution of power between people and their elected representatives.

Liberal political philosophy was developed in the 17th and 18th centuries. The majority of people were attempting to reclaim power from the feudal aristocracy that had wrenched power from the community and its leaders. Philosophers were disposed to view one of the primary challenges of politics as the restraining of government, on the assumption (valid to observers) that government was hostile towards the governed. This hostility was the result of abnormal arrangements inherited from the past, which separated people from government and the disposition of power. In terms of our present interest, this meant the separation of people from control over the net income which they have produced. As a result, government was forced to resort to taxation, which therefore did, indeed, generate conflict between itself and the people.

In America, that the Founding Fathers should evince suspicion of authority exercised from London is not surprising. Thomas Jefferson put it graphically:

> It is better to keep the wolf out of the fold, than to trust to drawing his teeth and claws after he should have entered (Jefferson 1905: 165).

The wolves were, in fact, already inside the fences being thrown up in the New World - if the settlers knew what to look for. Most settlers directed their suspicions at the old monarchies and aristocracies from which they had fled. Their concerns, however, were not identical to the fears of the

94

influential investors in the land speculating companies that had begun to create the new fiefdoms. These two groups shared a common hostility towards government, but their concerns were nourished from two different sources:

- The land speculators did not want government in the mother country to arrogate to itself the functions of public service, which would have to be financed out of the rent of the colonies (one way or another).

- The victims of land appropriation from Europe associated government with the controlling landlord class, and they were psychologically disposed to suspicion of authority.

That was the history, sustained by conflict, but we now need to question the wisdom of preserving this hostility. We need to challenge some of the primary psychology-based assumptions on which our system of "checks and balances" is based. Is it true that all men are power-hungry and are disposed to abuse power? What are the limits of "good government" as J. S. Mill called it?

There is a sphere of life which is necessarily social, co-operative, community, which requires collective action. Human beings, it is trite but necessary to observe, are the product of social evolution through the processes of biology and culture. It comes as a shock to have to admit that governments have acquired lives in conflict with the interests of citizens. Keynes recognized the incongruence when he referred to the temptation of governments to "debauch the currency" and thereby "overturning the existing society" through inflation (Keynes 1920: 236). A government that does this is operating within a society in which the natural order has already been overturned. Primarily, this means that the legitimate revenue of the state has been diverted, so governments find occasion to covertly tax people by debauching the currency, which is an indirect tax and a symptom of an existing misorder of society.

The separation of people from their natural source of public revenue results in an absence of principles that demarcate public from private activities. To restore a natural basis to government and its finance, which would establish the correct relationship with citizens, we have to re-integrate the correct philosophy of public finance into our lives. Revenue comes with the performance of service, and public activity is (or ought to be) a value-creating activity which pays for itself.

This is not to say that every activity in the public sector has to directly display commercial characteristics. But to put it in this way is to play with words. Seemingly non-commercial activities (such as defense of the realm, maintenance of good public health, etc.) do create a value which is reflected in a tangible value: the rent of land.

We can no longer afford to postpone a fundamental revision of the rules of public finance as one avenue to the new society. Existing rules are not set in cement.

> Some of the rules we live by are grounded neither in physical reality nor in the social evolutionary process but are, instead, the product of design and intent. From this recognition it follows that some rules of social order must be subject to modification and change, to 'reform' (Brennan & Buchanan 1980: 206)

Our principle political problem stems from the fact that the rules of income distribution were designed by, and in the self-interest of, a minority which had no concern for the commonwealth. They were not interested in fair play on "level playing fields" (giving value-for-value, for example). They were solely interested in appropriating the value that belonged to others. So we now need to determine the rules for good judgment in formulating a public finance that serves everybody's equal interest. In our search for the source of legitimacy in the construction of a new system for distributing income, we can appeal to

● The empirical record. We know that there are net gains from shifting taxes off people and on to land. See, for example, Ch. 8 for a review of the benefits that accrue to those states in the US which rely most heavily on the property tax against those that heavily tax people's incomes and consumption.

● The consistency of the conclusions of the great philosophers, from the founders of economics as a science in France in the 18th century through Adam Smith, John Stuart Mill, Alfred Marshall to William Vickrey.

Two tax economists, Brennan & Buchanan, claim that "it is perhaps not surprising that modern economists. ...become uneasy when issues about choices among constraints are raised. How can individual choice behavior outside the standard paradigm be modeled?" (*ibid*).

We should not be too concerned about the feelings of modern economists. Their predecessors had no difficulty in modeling an optimum public finance system by testing hypotheses both conceptually and empirically. The need to engage in such an exercise now is suggested by the following observation:

> Neglect of rules ensures drift into constitutional anarchy, a state of affairs

that many modern diagnoses suggest has already been attained. In such setting, confusion abounds, and the tentacles natural to a Hobbesian jungle take root, grab, and hold (Brennan & Buchanan 1980: 207).

We cannot rely for leadership from modern economists. For a start, they still talk about "fencing government in" (Brennan & Buchanan 1980:155). This is a negative spin on what ought to be seen as a fruitful partnership between the public and its government. The new rules ought to be presented as emancipating government from the daily routine of crisis management (which is now the basis of modern democratic politics). We need government to be a partner in the liberating process of enabling people to achieve their private and social goals, by providing the necessary supportive services (which includes the removal of obstacles to people's liberties).

The starting point for challenging the legitimacy of public finance - and therefore implicitly challenging the power base of governing institutions - is the general discontent with taxation. This discontent is legitimate, given the fact that "quite arbitrary discrimination in the distribution of the benefits of public spending among persons and groups seems to be characteristic of modern fiscal systems" (Brennan & Buchanan 1980: 161). This is the asymmetry of taxation: arbitrary exactions from private income with the reciprocal of arbitrary distribution of public benefits. We need a set of rules that offers symmetry in public finance: payment proportionate to benefits that are received.

There is only one way to achieve this symmetry. Benefits from all levels of public spending are summed into the rent of each and every location (Ch. 1:1 above). The intrinsic value attributable to nature is not publicly provided but nor is it privately created separate from the co-operation of people in community.

The new rules must replace the asymmetry between what people can afford or are willing to pay, and what government wishes to receive. When rent is treated as public revenue, the symmetry emerges between what people want to pay and what government needs to receive to provide the services demanded by citizens.

Tax reform is now a popular slogan for politicians. But if their proposals are not linked to a review of the basic rules governing public finance, their actions are reduced to shadow boxing. Alterations in tax rates give the impression of change when all that would be accomplished would be the cruel deception of those people (the majority) who are disadvantaged by taxation.

2. Ethical principles of public finance

THE GLOBALISATION of the economy invites us to reassess the workings of the market system, and that is another reason why the time has come to review the principles of public finance. Like a good mechanic who cannot figure out why the car keeps breaking down, the sensible strategy is to take the engine apart and put it together again, guided by the best available knowledge. If any parts need replacing, that would be the stage at which to do it - rather than, as has been the case throughout the 20th century, bolting *ad hoc* policies onto the system (policies shaped by the fashionable school of thought that managed to prevail at the time) in the hope that these would stabilize a very unstable economy.

People are entitled to a social framework which integrates systems of work and wealth production, balancing private needs with social obligations; and synthesizing the rights of citizens with the rights of the community and the environment. The catalyst for this balancing act has to be a public finance based on the principles of economic efficiency and social justice. If we construct an honest public finance we restore the partnership between private and public sectors; and between people and the biosphere.

There is reason to believe that governments are interested in developing an ethically-based public finance. Decisions in Australia and New Zealand may be the forerunners. Unfortunately, fine words may mislead: an example is the Fiscal Responsibility Act passed by the government of New Zealand in 1994. This was intended to enshrine "principles of responsible fiscal management". The Blair government in Britain was so attracted to this concept that Chancellor Brown declared his intention to adopt a Code for Fiscal Stability. His quest for stable growth and a flexible economy stressed the need for "Openness and Predictability".

The New Zealand law was not based on principles that could pass the tests of efficiency or ethics. One critic was to write:

> In reality, the Fiscal Responsibility Act was designed to embed the current fiscal strategy of budget surpluses, repayment of debt, privatisation and low taxation in law (Kelsey 1995: 232).

These goals, on the surface, may seem appropriate. But they are embedded in a system that had been allowed to deteriorate into a state of permanent instability.

The New Zealand law was not the reasoned product of a review of public finance and the responsibilities of government towards the electorate. Rather, it was the attempt by one political faction to permanently entrench its ideology, which happened to be the fashionable one at the time. Its philosophy echoed the Thatcherite attitude that government should be treated as if it were a business in the private sector, subject to the prevailing rules of the market economy. The outcome cannot be what was claimed by those who devised the Act. For there was no associated attempt to remove the basis for cyclical instability - speculation in capital gains from land.

The Treasury in New Zealand claimed that the Act would shift policy-making from short-term tactics to long-term strategies, leading to inter-generational equity and the efficient allocation of resources. Fiscal stability, it declared, would deliver a sustainable rate of growth that would benefit everybody.

These claims were repeated by Britain's chancellor in his pre-Budget Report to Parliament in November 1997. The British Treasury's document opened with the following statement:

> A key role for government is to provide a stable economic environment in which people and businesses can plan for the future, and growth and employment can prosper. Openness and Predictability about policy is an indispensable ingredient in this. This is one of the reasons why the Chancellor proposed... that the IMF, in conjunction with the World Bank and the OECD, draw up a Code of Good Practice for openness and transparency in fiscal and monetary policy (Treasury 1997b:1).

The intention was honorable but the action is not consistent with the aspiration. Openness of policy-making by governments today will not provide a stable economic environment for reasons that we have now explained. It is not possible to eliminate the damaging boom/bust cycles on the back of a stable implementation of conventional fiscal philosophy.

Mr. Brown is to be complemented for stressing the need for honesty and transparency in the management of public finances. But the standard he sets - "public finances in the best long-term interests of Britain" (*Ibid*.: 2) - imposes an onerous burden on the Blair government. One of his principles for managing taxation would be

> stability in the policy-making process and in the way fiscal policy impacts on the economy (*Ibid*.: 4).

If this principle were to be enshrined in law, it would be open to the citizens of Britain to take their government to court to seek redress for the damage that remains to be inflicted on them. In 1997, the UK economy was pronounced by the World Bank to be in a reasonably sound state (viewed from the perspective of conventional economic wisdom). That happy state of affairs would not last beyond the beginning of the new millennium. We can expect fiscal discipline to be abandoned in the face of cyclical booms and busts. A Fiscal Stability Act of the New Zealand kind makes no provision for neutralizing those forces that encourage speculation in land, which is the primary cause of instability. The ideals used to promote the Act were fine; the means were missing. Indeed, if anything, there is a risk that the Blair government would be so "prudent" that it could sow the seeds of an austerity program that could cause further misery in the millennium. For the new zeal for openness caused the Treasury's economists and policy-makers to develop a commitment to prudence, a prudence that was not consistent with economic analysis. In a review of the previous economic cycle, the Treasury acknowledged that it had consistently erred on the wrong side in its predictions about the growth of the economy (Graph 4: I).

Graph 4:I
The UK Treasury's formerly unpublished illustrative projections: real GDP (1988 - 1995)

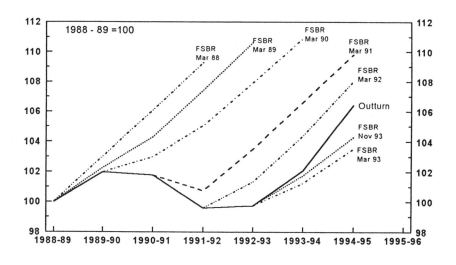

Source: Treasury 1997c: 3

The astonishing range of errors in the 1980s drives home the one key lesson that was not acknowledged in its discussion paper (Treasury 1997c):

that its basic theoretical framework is irrelevant to the task of predicting turning points in the economy. Not until production was well on the downswing in the 1990s did it revise its predictions in a downward direction - and then it continued to show optimism about a premature upturn. And once in the trough, the Treasury went to the other extreme, and displayed pessimism about the recovery.

So, when the New Labour party came to power in May 1997, lessons had to be learnt. But New Labour was no better equipped to analyze the underlying causes of economic instability. In 1997 the Treasury concluded that, after the protracted loss of output of goods and services during the 1980s and 1990s, the economy was back to the cyclical position which it occupied in 1986 (Graph 4:II).

Graph 4:II
GDP (actual and trend, log scale): Britain, 1980-2001

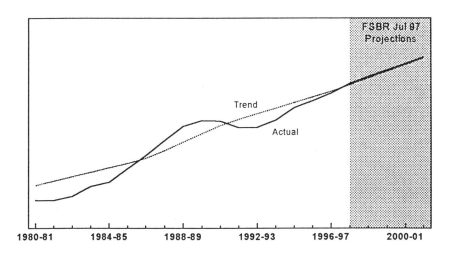

Source: Treasury 1997c: 7

The alarm bells started ringing. Gordon Brown was not going to preside over cyclical turbulence of the kind which he had promised would be banished from the UK economy! Fiscal prudence was necessary to prevent a re-run of the Lawson-style boom of 1988. The result was an approach to fiscal policy that locked the economy into the historical trend.

The real lesson was not being discussed in the Treasury's corner of Whitehall, overlooking the Houses of Parliament. What Britain needed was not a tightening of fiscal policy. Rather, it needed a *transformation* of the fiscal system. Without that change, the appropriate policies that were supposed to modernize Britain could not be adopted. The prospect of raising the economy to a higher plane of stable growth was no longer an option.

That did not stop the government from harboring expectations of new strategies that would efficiently integrate the operations of the private and public sectors, but the policy-makers did not have at their disposal the theoretical tools that elaborate the preconditions for such a qualitative change. The outcome, therefore, was most likely to be a continuation of the downward slide in the welfare of the British people. The Professor of Social Policy at the London School of Economics predicted that the Blair legacy, at the end of the first five years of New Labour - if policies were not changed - would be up to two million more people in poverty (Piachaud 1998).

3. Geopolitical struggle: the fiscal territory
AMONG THE new realities that surfaced with the global economy was the transformation of the struggle for power between sovereign nation-states. For five millennia the principle field of dispute was over the direct control of territory. A nation was not sovereign if it could not defend its physical space against all comers. With the nuclear age and the inter-dependence that was the global economy, a subtle shift in the rules of engagement are taking place. Governments are now seeking to influence the activities in other countries not by military means, seeking supremacy over land; but through reshaping the tax regimes to try and gain advantage over the trading prospects. We are now witnessing the direct interference by one government with the right of another government to determine its fiscal regime. The disputants play out the conflicts within the realms of diplomacy and the law courts, rather than with the aid of lethal weapons, but the outcome can be as fatal for the future independence of formerly sovereign nations.

A low tax regime offers producers an advantage - through lower product prices - in the markets. This highlights a general principle that ought to encourage governments to adopt a strategy for full employment based on the progressive reduction of taxes. Instead, they have preferred to force other governments to share the misery inflicted by adopting tax rates that equalize the damage across international borders. Such strategies are clothed in fine words like *harmonization* and *fairness*; in fact, these are attempts to make everybody suffer equally. Far from expanding people's choices within a stable system, they narrow life-chances by concentrating power (hegemony) and impoverishing cultural diversity (homogenization). Social scientists have not yet explored the attendant risks on populations, but history does warn us that the intensification of social tensions leads to the scapegoating of minorities (in domestic politics) and diplomatic conflicts (in international politics).

The sum of such problems may converge on issues of differences which, on the basis of past performance, had led to grievous consequences. The contribution of fiscal policy to such crises has not been studied, but for the sake of global harmony in the 21st century the implications ought to be analyzed by the peace-making statesmen while there is time and opportunity for reform. Otherwise, compromises under the pressure of crises will have to be adopted. These have never delivered principled agreements based on justice, but rather deals based on *real politik*. To illustrate the sorts of issues that need to be reanalyzed from a new perspective, three examples of tensions are sketched below. They highlight the scope for potential conflicts that can flow from the failure to agree upon property rights that are consistent with every person's desire for peace and prosperity.

European dis-Union. The economic integration of Europe after World War Two was a rational attempt to institutionalize harmony into one of the world's bloodiest war theatres. The further attempt at political integration - consolidated by monetary union, which would inevitably entail fiscal integration - was a logical progression. Ultimate success for the venture, however, would depend on whether the fundamental causes of historical conflicts were removed. They were not. This may mean, according to some informed analysts, that the initial success of the enterprise could become the cause of the next war in Europe. Such a prospect has been aired in Germany and analysed as a serious possibility by Harvard's Martin Feldstein (1997b). If conflict were to occur, it would undoubtedly be attributed - yet again - to notions of ethnic and cultural incompatibilities; whereas the actual cause would be the failure of governments to develop economic policies capable of overriding the built-in propensity to instability, poverty and unemployment.

Paradoxically, therefore, if the experiment in political harmony is defeated this will be the result of a sincere search for harmonization! How that is possible in principle ought to be understood, if the aspiration - permanent peace and prosperity - is to be fulfilled.

The proposal that tax policy should be harmonized between countries illuminates the problem. In 1997, objections were raised that some countries (such as Ireland) were taking unfair advantage of high-tax countries (such as Germany) to attract capital across borders. With the advent of the high-speed train connecting Paris and London through the Channel Tunnel, the Kent county of England attracted French companies which chose to relocate operations primarily for fiscal reasons.

It is understandable that perplexed governments would want to eliminate competition. By standardizing second- and third-best practices, however, they deny access to the evidence that might persuade them to change course. In the United States, for example, people can challenge their state and local governments with the news that, by downgrading the property tax (which is in any event the crude way of capturing part of the rent of land) they prevent an increase in *per capita* incomes. On average, people would be more prosperous if tax regimes were restructured away from taxes on incomes and consumption (*see Ch. 8*). *By standardizing bad policies, governments make everyone share the pain rather than the gain.*

But political tensions arising from tax-driven cross-border economic disadvantage are likely to be overshadowed by a more serious prospect. What happens to harmony if Euro-policy is dominated by German self-interest? That is not a remote prospect, as Europe was to find in 1992. Although other countries made mistakes, it was Germany's concern with her own interests that disrupted the European Monetary System (Grahl 1997: Ch.2).

Few observers doubt that Germany will set the pace over policy in a politically integrated Europe. How will European Monetary Union (EMU), complete with a central bank dominated by the German ethos, threaten the goodwill that all member countries direct towards the European Union? The added prosperity may be the cause of the Union's undoing. Through equalization, there will be a downward pressure on interest rates. This ought to be a cause for celebration: it implies that entrepreneurs will be able to borrow at cheaper rates to create new businesses that could reduce unemployment. But the lower interest rates will also provoke a more intensified round of land speculation. Is this a credible prospect?

The monetary effect of Germany's notorious fear of inflation was displayed in the run up to the Crash of '92. In the late 1980s, money was cheaper in Germany; but as the business cycle peaked the brake was applied more harshly in that country, whose real interest rate was below those in Italy, France and Britain. A European central bank would pursue policies that favored German financial principles. This will emphasise the need for greater efficiency, which in principle also ought to be good. But the leveling of returns to capital has, as an Iron Law, the reciprocal increase in net income. Under the present tax regime the incentive to speculate in land is increased, with all the disruptive consequences that this entails.

Britain will be the first and the biggest victim, because it will attract the larger share of the increased pool of footloose capital. Speculators will act rationally in seeking to exploit the culture that most overtly encourages the extraction of rent against investment in the value-adding processes. As these crises unfold, monitored by the rise in unemployment, national governments will come under pressure from their citizens to take remedial action. That is when people will start to question the value of the European Union. For they will discover that national parliaments no longer enjoyed the freedom to use monetary and fiscal policy to stabilize their economies. And, furthermore, action that was taken by the supranational agencies within Europe were clearly shaped by German preferences. That was made plain by Sir Nigel Wicks, the chairman of Europe's monetary committee, who - in response to a question on unemployment from a member of the European Parliament - replied: "I would not regard monetary policy as an instrument for solving unemployment. It is an instrument for dealing with inflation" (Walker 1998).

But we do not have to rely on the inauguration of EMU to anticipate this outcome. Europe's economic fate is sealed. The business cycle is progressing logically - under the present tax regime - towards the next land-led boom and bust early in the 21st century. The depth of the first depression in the new millennium will be in 2010. This is not a prospect to be relished, for the addition of new members from Eastern Europe will necessitate income redistribution policies that will impose breaking-point strains on national budgets. Whether the Union avoids disintegration before then will depend, in part, on whether the policy-makers learn the lessons of economic history.

Europe v USA   Commercial conflict between between the United States and Europe is a serious business. Trade between them reached £250 billion in 1996. US companies employed three million Europeans and 8% of American factory workers were employed by European companies. That they would profit from re-evaluating the basis of co-existence is evident from the degree of inter-dependence which has now ensured that each shares the fate of the other.

In November 1997 the European Union declared hostilities against the USA, claiming that its producers were disadvantaged by the improper subsidies provided to US exporters. The EU claimed that this was unfair under the rules of international trade. The subsidy was actually a tax rate which eased the burden on American manufacturers who exported their goods. The EU estimated that this reduced tax rate was equivalent to a subsidy worth over $2.3 billion (Coleman 1997).

The vehicle for the tax advantage was the foreign sales corporation (FSC), which is typically a subsidiary of a US company. Under US laws, FSCs are granted tax exemptions on exports. The EU complained that this allowed FSCs to exempt 65% of their foreign trade income from taxation. Corporations further reduced their tax liabilities by becoming incorporated in foreign tax havens.

For the corporations, the lower tax obligation enables them to price their goods at an advantage over their competitors. In 1992, FSCs disclosed profits of $9.6 billion and avoided tax bills totaling $2.3 billion which they would have paid if they were treated as normal US companies.

Under the World Trade Organization rules it is illegal for a country to treat a product differently when exported than when it is sold in the home country. The European Union, faced with a tax regime for its member states which is on the average more onerous than the US tax regime, had no option but to seek to change the US tax code despite the wishes of the US government. Such action was necessary, according to EU Trade Commissioner Sir Leon Brittan, because the US tax law gave American companies "an unfair advantage over their European competitors".

There was no suggestion from the European Union that it would equalize the competitiveness of European manufacturers by similarly reducing the tax burden on the manufacturers of the 15 member states.

Japan v USA The United States spent most of the 1990s persistently trying to persuade Japan to reshape its tax regime and regulatory codes to accommodate the exports of American manufacturers. This was, ironically, a re-run of the confrontation over a century previously, in which American gunboats threatened Japan if she did not open her markets. Washington had no doubt about its right to influence fiscal policy in another country. The sovereign rights of the nation-state were not uppermost in the mind of the US Deputy Treasury Secretary, Larry Summers, when he repeated Washington's demand for tax cuts in 1997:

> The pace of fiscal consolidation is something that is going to have to be looked at very carefully... in light of economic conditions [in Japan] (Tett and Hutton 1997:1).

But the level of Japanese tax rates in the 1990s had little bearing on the scale of the conflict between the two nations that will surface early in the 21st century. Japan will *need* to become more aggressive in its exporting policies to cope with the budgetary problems of an aging population. Table 4:I suggests that the amount Japan will have to spend out of GDP is two to three times greater than the two English-language G7 nations. This will lead to heightened tensions as the USA, in particular, finds her dominant position in world markets threatened by Japan, with the Chinese challenge looming closer on the horizon.

Table 4:I
Projected Pension Expenditure
G7: per cent of GDP

	1995	2020	2050
Canada	5.2	6.9	8.7
France	10.6	11.6	14.4
Germany	11.1	12.3	17.5
Italy	13.3	15.3	20.3
Japan	6.4	14.3	14.4
UK	4.5	5.1	4.1
USA	4.1	5.2	7.0

Source: Randall S. Jones (1997: 34)

The data indicates the potential for serious social and political tensions as a result of the rise of claims by pensioners and from the decline in the size of the working population. Rapid aging "creates additional pressure for public spending and calls into question the sustainability of the social-security system" (Jones 1997: 34). Additional self-financing methods for funding pensions are required; which, to be effective, must entail a cut in those taxes that damage the productivity of the factors of production. Unless the remedy is sought in this area, the prospect of geo-political tensions will increase as Japan seeks to deepen her share of world markets at the expense of other countries.

Japan, with less than half the US population, is not far short of the same share of world output as the USA (Table 4:II). The currency devaluations that followed the Asian crisis of 1997 will make Pacific rim exports even cheaper in the world markets. If this persists over the early years into the

21st century, the economic strains in Europe and North America will unleash some potentially ugly social reactions.

Table 4:II
Share of World Output & Population

	Output %:1995	Population Millions:1996
Europe	31.5	325.0
USA	21.4	266.5
Japan	18.4	125.6
All Others	28.8	

Source: World Bank.

How the relationship between Japan and the USA shapes up will depend largely on how Tokyo develops a vision of the future for its people. Despite the enormous capacity for material prosperity, the quality of life for households is well below what families could expect and would enjoy if it were not for the level of land prices. The signs are not good. In fact, in the late 1990s, Tokyo adopted policies which may deepen both her internal economic problems and her trading relationship with the US.

The government in Washington had been pressing Tokyo to expand domestic consumption so that Japanese families could consume more of the products from American producers. This issue had become a running sore in the relationship between the two countries. So what did the Japanese government do? It raised the consumption tax from 3% to 5% in April 1997. The predictable outcome was a drop in retail sales. The increase in this tax came at a time when the economy was stalled, as it was to admit for the first time in November 1997. The Japanese economy needed people to spend more, not cut back their consumption. The increase in the consumption tax rate was something akin to a kamikaze pilot's death wish. It was the economy that "died", and the families of Japan that paid the price.

How the 21st century will shape up will be determined, to an important degree, on how Japan resolves the crushing problem of the 1980s land boom. In 1998 the ruling Liberal Democratic Party's experts advised the government that it ought to revive the land market by suspending the land tax. This had been introduced *after* the prices had soared beyond affordable levels. Too late: *it could not prevent the speculation which created the "bubble" in prices.* In the aftermath, Japan's corporate land speculators lobbied for the abolition of the tax, which fell on holdings that exceeded 1,000 square meters. A special LDP panel received a report from a private think tank which argued that the abolition of the land tax would result in a revenue loss of Y152 billion, but that this would increase GDP by about Y240 billion three years later. Wrong: the reverse would happen, the shift in emphasis onto earned incomes and consumption serving to reduce output in the economy.

What happened to the Japanese economy was of concern to the authorities in Washington, DC, for the US economy was vulnerable to the capacity of Japanese banks to sell their U.S. securities. Japanese investors, including the ailing banks, owned $291 billion of U.S. Treasury bills in July 1997. To realise the cash they needed to stave off bankruptcy, Japanese banks could sell its assets in the US. And that would affect US taxpayers. There was a mutual interest in reshaping political economy, but this would not happen without a revision of the philosophy of governance.

4. False philosophical dichotomies
FISCAL REFORM cannot be separated from a vision of an evolving society. The reform advocated in this volume would qualitatively transform society from the one that now impairs the lives of millions of people. And yet, although political philosophers continue to engage in discussions about the kind of society to which we ought to aspire, they do not offer a vision of a correspondingly appropriate public finance. Without that fiscal reform the better society could not, in fact, come into existence.

Much of the contemporary dialog is based on a false dichotomy. This emerges in the controversy between the *libertarian* philosophy, as articulated, say, by Murray Rothbard (1962), and the *communitarian* philosophy, which is most prominently associated with Amitai Etzioni.

In the case of libertarians, the overriding concern is to diminish the scale of government (Harriss 1979). We shall not review the problem implicit in appeals for the removal of government and a reduction in the scale of social functions in people's lives, which favors the atomization of society. The important point is that libertarians, with a very few exceptions (Foldvary 1994), wish to preserve existing property rights; very definitely so with respect to the rent of land. Ultimately, therefore, short of hermetically sealing themselves away from society, they cannot achieve their goals. For the problems that inexorably flow from their preferred set of property rights guarantees the social and personal dislocations that necessitated the Welfare State in its variant forms.

Communitarians do bring something important to contemporary discussions. They remind us that citizens are social creatures. Most importantly, they have reminded us that responsibilities have been decoupled from rights. The strident claims people make to *rights* have resulted in the fragmentation of society; and the restoration of social cohesion will arise when we restore the responsibilities that are the reciprocal of rights. Unfortunately, the communitarians have not yet developed a sophisticated theory of property rights - one that would necessarily be linked to public finance - to articulate a practical strategy for rebuilding social cohesion. Interestingly, this weakness is identified in Etzioni's example of how people can be divided by apparently competing claims to rights.

> The moment, however, that I claim a right to the same piece of land or property or public space as you, we start to view one another like the Catholics and Protestants in Northern Ireland or the Palestinians and Israelis in the Middle East (Etzioni 1995: 7).

This particular example of conflict is an illuminating one. It dramatically integrates the problem of claims to land at both the collective and individual levels.

- Why do many Protestants and Israelis die in defense of "their" land, even though they do not own an inch of the soil? We need a philosophy that resolves competing claims at that level.
- Individuals claim to enjoy equal rights to life, but they are divided between those who own land - the means of life - and those who are excluded from land, who have to pay rent to the gatekeepers. This is a palpably odd situation, when viewed in terms of the fine phrases embedded in the declarations about human rights. Since there is a finite amount of land, how do we protect the legitimate claims of every person, including those who are excluded from land?

A social philosophy is needed which is capable of resolving these dilemmas to the satisfaction of every society, and every individual within each society. It would be invidious of the present author to proffer a formula for the character of such a society; but we do claim that the equal sharing of the net income of the community, through public sector spending, is the only mechanism for achieving a permanent and fair solution to competing claims to land and natural resources. This public finance policy is consistent with both cultural and economic diversity. It is the universal solution to the problem of property rights and public finance.

A new debate about the legitimate divisions of property rights, linked to public finance, needs to be brought into the public dialog; otherwise, these issues - the redivision of property, the continued intrusion of abusive taxation into people's lives - will continue by default. We shall illustrate the point with two examples. One is taken from the sphere of government: the obligation of democratically-elected leaders to preserve, or retrieve, people's individual *and collective* rights. The other concerns the discussions among economists on the principles of taxation.

- Governments continue to intrude on people's property rights without securing their agreement. A pertinent example from the current anxiety about the environment illustrates the point.

Prior to the 1960s, "individual citizens in the United States were, for the most part, unconstrained in their access to and their usage of the air and waterways.....(T)he government simply enacted laws that embodied direct prohibitions on specific types of activity....Individuals were simply prevented from being allowed to do things that had previously been available to them. In a real sense, government used the taking power; it took valued rights from persons, and without questions of due process being raised, and without compensation" (Brennan and Buchanan 1980: 165).

The US government achieved this diminution of people's rights by enacting prohibitions on certain kinds of activities. It may be that it was in the public's collective interest to alter individual behavioral rights; but in that case, there ought to have been a public debate about the fate of each person's former rights, in which he or she had a vested interest. One question relates to the alternative to regulatory constraints. The authors who cite this example were seeking to define the principles for limiting the rights of the state - Leviathan. The alternative to which they referred is interesting. They state:

> In a reconstructed scenario different from the one actually followed, the government could have, in recognition of the pollution-environmental problems, declared "clean air" and "clean water" to be "public goods." It could have then levied taxes for the financing of such "goods," which in this case would have involved the purchase of individuals' agreements to reduce polluting activities (*ibid.*).

Here we have the conventional - and convoluted - solution based on (a) taxing people, and (b) paying people compensation for the loss of the right to pollute.

Such policy strategies are now at the heart of the current problem of how to resolve satisfactorily the international political crisis following the failure of nations at Kyoto, Japan, in December 1997 to deliver a convincing agreement to eliminate "greenhouse" gases.

In the case to which Brennan and Buchanan refer, there was a third course of action. Rather than taxing people and then paying them, why not introduce a general rental charge for the use of the clean environment? Those who need to use more of that environment (i.e., dumping waste into the atmosphere) would be required to pay a higher rental charge. The revenue would be shared equally among all citizens through public spending. This policy is entirely consistent with the principles of paying for benefits received. That solution was the correct one for the US, at that time, but it was not one that tax economists would trouble to enter into the public dialog. It is to this problem that we now turn.

● Economists, while they are fully acquainted with the optimum fiscal policy, never allow their knowledge to intrude in problem-solving public discussions.

There are a very few honorable exceptions to this rule. One of them was the late William Vickrey (Box 5:III, page 144). He saw rent revenue as a catalyst for solving some of the major social and economic problems, including urban sprawl and inner city decay. He wrote: "Use of land rents, or, at least, of a major fraction of them, for public purposes is.....not merely an ethical imperative, derived from categorization of these rents as an unearned income derived from private appropriation of publicly created values, but is, even more importantly, a fundamental requirement for economic efficiency" (Vickrey 1995).

But to reach such crystal-clear conclusions it is necessary to subject the concepts of public finance to scrutiny. As things stand, "virtually any policy can be supported by a selective reading of the existing public finance literature" (McLure and Zodrow 1994: 203). On that basis, the views of one expert are as good (or as disposable) as another's. If this is the frame of mind of the social scientist, it is not surprising that politicians (those who are sincere in their quest for solutions) should be confused.

Thus, the Nobel prize winning economist who is noted for his work on "public choice" offered a study titled "The Political Efficiency of General Taxation" in which he took, as his premises, "individual liberty, private ownership of property, and a market economy" (Buchanan 1993: 401). He made no attempt to define these premises or reconcile them. They do need reconciling. At the core of the tensions in both political philosophy, and in our communities today, is the conflict between the private ownership of land (more correctly: the private ownership of the rental income from land) and individual liberty. Private appropriation of rent constrains the liberties of those who do not share in that net income (and distorts the market economy); and, to rub salt into the wounds, people consequently become the victims of the corresponding tax system, which abuses their rights to the property that they create with their labor.

Analysis of the fiscal crisis, then, takes us back to the fundamental question of power, and of the individual's relationship with everyone else and the institutions of the state. By posing challenging questions about the character of taxation, and about the power to tax, we are aware that cherished beliefs have to be challenged. Brennan and Buchanan (1980:2), concede that "asking these logically prior questions suggests that much of the traditional economic analysis of taxation is either irrelevant or profoundly misleading". This is a completely unsatisfactory state of affairs. Statesmen - and a democratic citizenry - need coherent statements from the social science specialists, and they are not receiving that service. The shakedown in thinking - the separation of shibboleth from science - would very quickly arise from the public's demand for a new debate.

That debate needs to focus on the character of the society to which we aspire. The sterility of current dogma will not take us far, and yet the capitulation of socialism does seem to warrant a radical reappraisal of the fundamental tenets of the western model (if only to revalidate existing values and institutions). But the new debate needs fresh guidelines, to arouse the prospect of worthwhile creative thinking. These guidelines must be practical and must hold out the prospect of enabling us to synthesize the libertarian's values with the communitarian's perspectives into a consistent framework. Otherwise, discussions about holistic visions will remain relegated to the ethereal sphere of spiritualism.

One of the starting points for that new debate is the resolution of rights to land and natural resources, as distinct from the rights to property in those things to which value has been added by people's labors. We have also now seen that the resolution of property rights requires a parallel adoption of the correct principles for public finance, principles that have to be consistent with the rights of personal and social property.

5. Of Denial and Deception
THE POSTWAR consensus broke down in the 1970s, and that provided statesmen with a historic opportunity to redesign democratic society. The

opportunity was grasped in the 1980s by politicians who lacked vision based on coherent principles. The champions of the political Right - notable Ronald Reagan and Margaret Thatcher - came to the fore, determined to push back the boundaries of government, reduce taxes and diminish such collective power as was exercised by employees. Absent from their manifestos was the promise to restructure public finance to one that was fit for the needs of people. Instead the scale of extraction of people's incomes by taxation was *increased*, and many more people were made dependent on the state for their economic survival.

Was that opportunity lost through ignorance? It was not. In the US, one of the influential economic philosophers was Milton Friedman; we have seen (page 46) that he was well acquainted with, and acknowledged, the principles of the virtuous revenue-raising strategy. But Friedman did not integrate this understanding into his over-arching proposals for systemic reform; and a prospectively influential voice in favor of freedom was lost.

From her stronghold in Downing Street, Margaret Thatcher - the Iron Lady - strode the world stage, exercising considerable influence over the policies of other governments; especially over the privatization of public property. One of the luminous influences on her intellect was an Austrian economic philosopher who had made his mark with a trenchant attack on Soviet socialism. *The Road to Serfdom* was compared to John Stuart Mill's *On Liberty* when it was published in 1944. Friedrich von Hayek attracted the attention of the Right. He consolidated his influence with *The Constitution of Liberty* (1960). One of the Conservative politicians who had imbibed the philosophy of Hayek was Keith Joseph, who was to achieve the rank of Cabinet minister; but more fatefully, for the course of history, he was to become the mentor of Margaret Thatcher.

In her memoirs, Mrs (now Lady) Thatcher chronicled the influence of Hayek:

> I cannot claim that I fully grasped the implications of Hayek's little masterpiece at this time. It was only in the mid-1970s, when Hayek's works were right at the top of the reading list given me by Keith Joseph, that I really came to grips with the ideas he put forward. Only then did I consider his arguments from the point of view of the kind of state Conservatives find congenial - a limited government under a rule of law - rather than from the point of view of the kind of state we must avoid - a socialist state where bureaucrats rule by discretion. At this stage it was (to my mind) unaswerable criticism of socialism in *The Road to Serfdom* which had an impact....He alerted us to the profound, indeed revolutionary, implications of state planning for Western civilization as it had grown up over the centuries.

Nor did Hayek mince his words about the monopolistic tendencies of the planned society which professional groups and trade unions would inevitably seek to exploit. Each demand for security, whether of employment, income or social position, implied the exclusion from such benefits of those outside the particular privileged group - and would generate demands for countervailing privileges from the excluded groups. Eventually, in such a situation everyone will lose (Thatcher 1995: 50-51).

It was from the reading of *The Constitution of Liberty* and Hayek's 3-volume *Law, Legislation and Liberty* that Mrs Thatcher formed her political philosophy around the concept of "the rule of law" (*ibid.*: 85).

Here, clearly, was the opportunity for a philosopher, preaching from his professorial seat in the University of Chicago, to influence destiny through a reformer, a tough lady who was determined to take the battle for change to the cutting edge of politics. It was a fateful alliance that was to mishandle an opportunity.

If the modern state was to be tamed of its socialist proclivities, there was little prospect of reshaping government - and some of the key institutions of society, such as trade unions - without a corresponding change in the character of public finance. Unfortunately, Friedrich von Hayek, the champion of free market economics and property rights who placed the liberty of the individual at the heart of his *problematique*, failed to recognize the flaw in his philosophy.

In *The Constitution of Liberty* he restated the inviolability of his key rule: everyone should be equal before the law. The reasonableness of that principle is seductive. It disarms the reader. We do not question the framework of inherited values within which Hayek wishes to apply the rule; certainly not insofar as it affects property rights.

Everyone should be equal before the law. But *whose* law? Now we have a problem. The foundations of the laws of western democratic societies, and especially those with respect to property rights and the associated tenets of taxation, were laid in the feudal era by an aristocracy that had no interest in guaranteeing the equality of every citizen before the law (Hill 1996). That aristocracy was exclusively interested in advancing its class interest. This meant the transformation of rent as a social value - with a social obligation - into a private income from which social obligations had been decoupled.

For Hayek, there was no substantive problem about the character of the existing legal system or the values that it embodied. In an interview with one of the present authors (Harrison), he explicitly affirmed his endorsement of the current distribution of rights to the land market, which is intrinsically monopolistic. The fact that people could, in principle, buy land under the law, meant to Hayek that there was no problem for his principle of equality. This is how he put it in *The Road to Serfdom:*

> [T]o call private property as such, which all can acquire under the same rules, a privilege, because only some succeed in acquiring it, is depriving the word privilege of its meaning (1962: 60).

In one bold sentence he arrogantly dismisses without mention the process under which people's natural rights were eroded to the point where they could no longer hope to accumulate property, no matter how hard they worked. The aristocracy replaced the rule of natural law with their private rule; disguising their orderly anarchy with a veneer that they called "the rule of law". That rule was the one with which Hayek wished people to comply; a rule that had at its heart the exercise of monopoly power that was an abuse of people's rights.

What did Hayek have to say about public finance? He was the giant slayer who exposed the wicked behavior of Soviet bureaucrats and western trade unions in defense of civil liberties; what about the state's arbitrary appropriation of people's earned incomes? He did, in fact, offer his views on the policy advocated in this volume: the treatment of rent as the primary source of public revenue. He wrote:

> If the factual assumptions on which it is based were correct, i.e., if it were possible to distinguish clearly between the value of "the permanent and indestructible powers of the soil," on the one hand, and, on the other, the value due to the two different kinds of improvement - that due to communal efforts and that due to the efforts of the individual owner - *the argument for its adoption would be very strong* (Hayek 1960: 352-353, emphasis added).

We can now only fantasize about what would have happened if Margaret Thatcher had been persuaded to follow through the implications of the "very strong" argument in favor of this reform of taxation. Her doing so would have been consistent with her commitment to market economics. For the land market is acknowledged to be monopolistic in structure, thereby prejudicing the equal interests of people outside it. For the free marketeer, the choice is between these options when challenged by monopoly power:

- destroy it by adding new competition to the market;
- neutralizing it by regulation; and
- sharing the benefits equally, between all citizens.

The first option is not practical (we cannot manufacture more land). The second option had failed lamentably between 1947 and 1979, the monopolists having defeated a string of laws promulgated by successive Labour governments. That left the third option only for Mrs. Thatcher to contemplate. She was not to do so, however, because her guru had perceived a fatal weakness: one based purely on implementation.

While constrained to endorse the wisdom of the policy, Hayek retreated from it because, in his opinion, there was a professional problem associated with valuing land. Thus, he was driven to conclude that, "Though we might often wish that things were as simple as the single-tax program assumes, we will find in it no solution to any of the problems with which we are concerned" (*ibid.*).

But the difficulties he perceived were baseless, a product in part of his caricature of what is intended. Nobody has suggested that the value that Ricardo said stemmed from the "indestructible powers of the soil" should be separated from the value attributed to land by communal investment and activity. There is a composite value which is accurately measured *by the markets* every day, delivering the pricing signals that are monitored by an army of valuers in both the private and public sectors. Land dealers, of course, would be astonished to be told that it was not possible for them to accurately measure the value of land which they bought and sold on a routine basis.

Hayek's pragmatic objection is spurious. It disappears under a welter of evidence of the kind to be seen in Denmark (Banks 1989: Ch.11); evidence that is routinely collected for fiscal purposes in countries as widely dispersed as New Zealand and South Africa; evidence that is used to monitor the state of health of the Hong Kong economy (as the *Wall Street Journal* noted in its report of land auctions on December 12, 1997). Which leaves us with Hayek's concession that the arguments in favor of the adoption of the policy are "very strong".

Hayek retreated from the logic of his insight. He did not wish to propound a simplification of public finance. The basis on which he did so was that his spurious distinctions could not "be drawn with any degree of certainty".

So what was bequeathed to us from the pen of the writer of constitutions of liberty? Having rejected - on the grounds of an absence of precision - the policy that he would otherwise have very strongly recommended, he abandoned his students to the conventional system of taxation. That system is arbitrary, not principled; grotesquely imprecise in its impact and philosophical formulation; and amenable to the manipulation of governments that claim to champion the liberty of the individual.

Thus was the historic opportunity of the 1980s lost to the world. But it was a close call. Other champions of individual liberty, spanning the tradition from Adam Smith, John Stuart Mill through to Alfred Marshall, not only saw the wisdom of the need to limit private claims to the rental income of land; they were willing to advocate rent as central to good governance. But Premier Thatcher, as she sallied forth to slay the socialists, operated within a safe philosophical *cordon sanitaire*. Perhaps she will one day see the irony of the comparison that she made when, analyzing the socialist propensities that she witnessed in Scotland, she wrote with exasperation:

> There was no Tartan Thatcherite revolution. That might seem strange. For Scotland in the eighteenth century was the home of the very same Scottish Enlightenment which produced Adam Smith, the greatest exponent of free enterprise economics till Hayek and Friedman (1993: 618).

Scotland was, indeed, the home of the Enlightenment. Smith - and another of his professorial contemporaries, William Ogilvie (Ogilvie 1997) - had delineated a new economics that identified rent-as-public-revenue at the heart of free markets and free individuals. It was the policy that Friedman and Hayek acknowledged as correct; and yet, from which they flinched when it came to counseling the statesmen of the world.

Friedman and Hayek have become part of a tradition in western political philosophy that nurtured both scientific objectivity (they acknowledged the truth about the optimum conditions for public finance), and denial and deception. This is behavior of a schizophrenic kind. The denial was of everyday realities, about the practicability of the optimum system for funding the expenses of the nation. The deception was of the people, who yearn for stability in society and fairness in the dealings of powerful governments.

6. The Business of Freedom

A WINDOW on history was opened in the 1980s, but was closed without letting in the breeze of fiscal freedom.

But the pace of change is quickening. We now appear to live in an era that is a continuous process of history-in-the-making, meaning tectonic shifts in social systems. In the 1990s, two new windows were opened. The first one was in Eastern Europe, with the collapse of Soviet socialism. Western governments, supported by the financial inducements offered by the IMF, prevailed heavily on the Yeltsin government in Russia to adopt a carbon copy of the Anglo-Saxon model of markets. At the time of writing (January 1998) the conflict in Moscow over the two key legal codes - the Land Code and the Tax Code - had not been resolved; the future was still one of possibilities.

The second window opened in the Pacific rim countries. The collapse of the "Asian model" enabled the IMF, armed with over $100 billion in rescue packages, to tour the capitals to sell (again) its favored model of markets, property rights and taxation. The possibilities of an enlightened solution remain open. For despite the region's needs for the funds from the West (and Japan), they retained a sense of cultural independence that suggested the possibility of adopting new social and economic forms in preparation for the challenges of the 21st century.

Could it be that the lessons of Hong Kong, among others, will be learnt? When it comes to freedom, it seems that pro-market Westerners are impressed by the former British colony. It was top of the rankings of free countries for 1998, according to the *Wall Street Journal* and the Heritage Foundation, a Washington DC-based right-wing think-tank. Nobody could accuse either of these institutions of being soft on socialism. Their annual investigation into the performance of countries around the world is motivated by the belief that "government coercion and control over the entrepreneurial process are deadly forces" (Johnson *et. al.* 1997). The Index of Economic Freedom assigns scores in 10 areas, including taxation, property rights and the black market. L. Gordon Crovitz, vice president of Dow Jones, publishers of the *Wall Street Journal*, concluded: "In terms of strong institutions, Hong Kong is a role model for Asia and beyond" (Crovitz 1997).

The land of Hong Kong is in the public domain, leased to users via auctions; and the government relies heavily on that revenue to finance public infrastructure. Perhaps this fact was not the cornerstone of Hong Kong's freedom? Well, if that sceptical view prevails, at the very least we can conclude that this arrangement, while being eminently practical (for more than a century), is also not at variance with economic freedom. We have the editorial word of the *Wall Street Journal* for that! And the IMF acknowledges that Hong Kong has a growth rate of productivity at the top of the world league, ahead of the G7 giants (*see Box 1, page ix*). How many coincidences does it require to suggest a common cause?

Singapore was ranked second in the Index of Economic Freedom. And that state holds most of the land on the island in the public domain. And yet, that economy prospers. The empirical evidence in favor of a new kind of land-and-public finance nexus begins to emerge.

New Zealand was placed in fourth place (behind oil-rent rich Bahrain). In the 19th century, Henry George contributed his influence to the finance philosophy in New Zealand, which was to rely heavily on the rent of land as public revenue. To this day, a majority of municipalities levy a direct tax on the rent of land.

In joint seventh place in the freedom league was Taiwan. That country built its market economy to compete with the mainland communists: it did so by undertaking fundamental reforms to land tenure and taxation - again, drawing a significant proportion of public revenue direct from the rent of land (Cheng 1961; Harriss 1977). The Taiwan leaders operationalised a philosophy attributed to Sun Yat-sen, China's first republican president, who in turn attributed his land-and-public finance policies to John Stuart Mill and Henry George.

Four nations in the Top Seven which, without any ambiguity, could - to a more or less degree - point to a distinctive public finance that acknowledged the overt significance of the rent of land. Could that be a coincidence? Hong Kong, Singapore and Taiwan are in the business of making money; despite the criticisms that can be leveled at some of the variances from the pure Anglo-Saxon model of democratic institutions, these nations are acknowledged as leaders in the freedom stakes. They achieved their success by giving citizens a real stake in society. Their social models are of varying degrees of perfection. Even so, they have claims to freedom which many unemployed people in western countries would envy. Which of the world's statesmen will learn the lessons, and refine an even freer model for *their* citizens? This issue is not one restricted to rates of growth, productivity and employment. It is, in fact, a matter of life and death for large numbers of people in the richest nations of the world (Miller 1998).

Privatized rent is the last great injustice inherited from the earliest civilizations. The anti-social prejudices that protected it through four millennia ought not to be tolerated by any society with a claim to being democratic and governed by principles of justice. But because private rent has been nurtured deep into our collective experiences, reform will not occur without a full democratic debate. And that cannot take place without an honest reappraisal of rent. The facts *were* known to previous societies. In France, the center of European culture in the 18th century, the Physiocrats identified the *produit net* as sufficient to finance the social needs of the Agricultural Age. Then, Adam Smith anticipated the factory system that would shift global influence to the British Isles in the 19th century; and he prescribed urban land rents as the suitable public finance for the Industrial Age. In America, Henry George analysed the rents of nature as sufficient for the coming Combustion Age of the 20th century. And today, at the dawn of orbital traffic jams, we affirm the sufficiency of rent for the Space Age. By reforming public finance, we herald an age fit for a new millennium.

Part 2

The Public Rent Dividend

Chapter 5

The People's Stake:
Resource-rents and the UK budget

Ronald Banks

1. Detaxation: the first People's Budget

ONE AND A HALF MILLION people could be rescued from the income tax trap almost immediately, and within two years, with income tax halved, Britain would become one of the most productive economies in the world. Britain could completely abolish income tax within three years of the first reform Budget, and taxes on people's consumption within five years. This program of modernization would lay the foundations for permanently full employment and social justice in a way that cannot be achieved by any other means. The end result would be a real stakeholder society, the first one in modern times.

Britain could abolish corporation tax, the two local government taxes (council tax and the uniform business rates) and halve income tax in its first budget after completion of a full valuation of land which would take two years, including appeals. The income tax reduction would be skewed towards the lower end of the earnings scale by increasing the tax threshold by £1,000 and introducing a basic rate of income tax at 10p in the pound, with the higher rate reduced to 35p. Other taxes could also go, *in full*, including capital gains tax, inheritance tax, stamp duties and the employers national insurance contributions. The figures are given in Tables 5:IV and 5:V (pages 132 and 133).

This revenue would be replaced by collecting the value that the public creates on a communal basis: the annual rent of land and natural resources. **This method of raising public revenue allows each and every citizen an equal share in *all* the land and natural resources of the United Kingdom, including the most valuable sites.**

For this study, a figure of 17.5% of national income has been taken as the rental value of land and natural resources under the present tax regime. For 1996, national income was £675 billion, using the United Nations definition, which gives a land rent of £118 billion. The rationale for using this figure stems from a number of studies. A summary is given in Box 1. The original conservative estimates, which were published in *Costing the Earth* (Banks1989), are shown in Table 5:I. They offer a statistical portrait of land rents in Britain.

Table 5:I
Estimated rental value of land,
Britain: 1985-1990 (£ billion)

	(1) Land Rent	(2) National Income	(3) Land Rent as % of National Income
1985	58.2	260.3	22.4
1986	55.2	76.5	20.0
1987	66.2	303.3	21.8
1988	85.7	36.7	25.5
1989	104.6	363.6	28.8
1990	118.8	387.3	30.7

Source: Banks (1989: 40)

The late 1980s were a period of ever increasing land values, which terminated in the property boom and the recession of 1992. The pre-boom year of 1985 could justifiably be taken to represent a "normal" percentage of rent to national income, i.e. about 22%. Similar considerations encourage us to select 1995 data as representative of average long term trends. A study by Treasury economists shows that the UK economy in 1996 was in a similar position, in relation to trend, to 1986. (Treasury 1997c Introduction). This view is also supported by an examination of UK residential land values between 1979 and 1996 (Savill's Research, London). The figures suggest that we would be justified in adopting a land value/national income ratio higher than the 1985 figure in Table 5: I. However, we will continue to err on the side of caution by working, initially, on an even lower figure.

The case for taking the figure of 17.5% of national income as the rent of Britain is supported by figures from the Danish economy. Denmark's tax authorities employ a sophisticated and accurate method of assessment

Box 5:I
Land values in the United Kingdom

IN *The Chaos Makers*, Prof. Frederic Jones uses official figures relating to property sales to estimate UK land value. He admits that his estimates are conservative. Even so, his estimate of land rent is sufficient for a complete abolition of Income tax!

Denmark values property and land annually for tax purposes. Experience has shown that their computerized valuations are remarkably accurate. The cost of valuations and collection is only 1.5-2.0% of revenue! The ratio of land rental value to national income is just below 10%. This proportion is low because high taxation depresses land values in a progressive, rather than a proportional way. The higher the taxation, the more land values are depressed. OECD figures show that tax receipts as a percentage of GDP are, for the UK and Denmark respectively, 34.1% and 51.6%. Denmark is more highly taxed than the UK by about 50%. Land rents would be more than 50% higher in Denmark if the economy was taxed at the same level as the UK. A cross-check with data from Finland (whose land values are provided in Appendix 2) reveal relationships consistent with our hypothesis.

Thus, the depression of land values in Denmark can be confidently assessed as more than 50% of the UK position. This allows us to take a figure of *more than* 15% of national income as land rent for Britain. Taking into account *Costing the Earth* estimates, we have used a figure of 17.5% of National Income to assess the potential impact of rent on tax reduction policies.

NB There will be a number of factors that tend to increase this figure in addition to those mentioned elsewhere in this chapter. One is mortgage interest on the land element of a property. We have taken, as an average, a figure of 35% as the land element. The inference is that 35% of all mortgage interest is for land. Since this interest depresses land values, it is safe to say that, when this payment is no longer necessary, the value of land will rise by an equivalent sum. Mortgage interest on the land element is land rent! The Bank of England figures at the end of October, 1997, show that *all* balances on Residential Mortgages came to £428 billion. Taking the land element of this figure as 35%, and an average interest rate of 7.5%, this land rental would be in excess of £10 billion. This is equivalent to council tax collection in 1996.

With National Income at about £675 billion in 1996, the annual land rental at 17.5% would be about £118 billion.

The main sources for a valuation figure for land values in the United Kingdom are *Costing the Earth* (Banks 1989); *The Chaos Makers* (Jones 1997); Nationwide Building Society, Housing Finance Review, Issue 11, October 1997; *The OECD Observer*, Paris, No. 206, June/July 1997; Inland Revenue Directorate, Copenhagen, Personal Communication, December 1997; and data provided in Chapters 6 and 7 of this book.

of land values. Thus, although we exercise extreme caution in our calculation, we are left with a figure which suggests that natural resource rents in Britain were at least £118 billion in 1996 (*see Box 5.II*).

The next question that confronts us is this: what are the expenses that legitimately need to be defrayed by all citizens, acting together in community? The answer emerges if we engage in an exercise, starting by taking one's mind back to the feudal era. In those times, expenditure for the common good came directly from the land. The services provided were, in effect, made available by the landlord, in return for which he charged rent. Modern political theory makes it clear that for a 'State' to be recognized, there needs to be sovereign control of the land. For this, common services for the enforcement of law and order and defense are required. The services provided today for the common good, not those that could be purchased privately if people were able to afford them, are summarized in Table 5:III A (page 130). The figure is £108 billion. This is *rent* for services provided by the supreme landlord - the state. Now, if one were to add this *rental* figure of £108 billion to the figure we have identified as land rental in the economy of today (£118 billion), *with all the tax depressed values in place*, we have a total land rent of £226 billion. This is 33% of the National Income of £675 billion! **This is sufficient to wipe out all taxes!**

But that is not the end of the calculations. If we *did* abolish taxes (with some exceptions), the wealth of the nation would increase dramatically: the deadweight loss turns into the Rent Revenue Dividend. How this occurs for the UK is explained in Chapter 6 and highlighted in Tables 6.I and 6.IVg. The conclusions given in Chapter 6 are based on the assumption that the rent revenue policy is fully operative. The order-of-magnitude gains from the rational public finance dramatically illustrates the damage inflicted by the tax regime on the people of Britain over the course of two centuries of industrial society. If rent had been treated as public revenue, the Net Domestic Product would today be nearly *double* what it is!

The calculation of the Rent Revenue Dividend by Tideman and Plassman is a leap into the future. It assumes that the transitional phase has been completed. Our projections for the UK are more conservative, and they take into account what is likely to happen during the transition.

Our proposed tax reductions for the first year amount to just over one-half of the taxation that could, realistically, be a target for abolition. We moderate the figures in Table 6.I (where the UK economy is shown to operate at 55% efficiency) and Table 6.IVg (where excess burden is shown as 40% of NDP) to take into account the damage from the remaining tax

Box 5:II
Land valuation & Taxation

A COMLETE valuation of land in the UK must be undertaken. Judging from experience in Denmark and from the two Whitstable (Kent) surveys conducted by Hector Wilks in 1963 and 1973, this valuation would take two years, including appeals. As both experiences show, valuing land alone is much easier than valuing land and property together. A bonus point is that, with buildings and structures free from tax of any sort, there is no "snooping". The tax authorities do not try to find out if a new garage has been built. It is proposed that the Inland Revenue be responsible for the valuations. Valuations take into account the value of the site as if it were unimproved. There must be no attempt to discount the value by deducting the cost of replacing the existing structure. This is still common practice that seriously underestimates the value of land.

After the completion of the valuations, including appeals, the Budget following should announce the collection of all land values, converted to annual values. We have used a figure of 7.6% to calculate this conversion, which is an average for *all* types of land value. It should be noted that residential land accounts for over 50% of all land value in the UK. This is one reason why income tax reductions are prime targets in the proposals offered here.

Simultaneously, the corresponding tax reductions should be announced. The impact should be neutral: the increase in rental income offsetting the reduction in revenue from wages and people's savings. Land rentals are *not* extra income for the exchequer. They are the *virtuous replacement* for taxation. From the time of a White Paper, through the valuation process to implementation, three years will have elapsed. People, businesses, companies, financiers will have the time to make the adjustments that are necessary to take advantage of the coming "tax free" society.

The same procedure would be recommended for the UK as for Denmark - the annual valuation of land. It is the only way that the distortions to the economy from dealing in, and speculating and profiting from, land can be forestalled. The alternative, to value every five years or so, would allow profit from land transactions, thus militating against the virtuous benefits of our policy, and severely restrict the possibility of continuing tax reductions that would otherwise occur if land rentals were collected annually.

The experience of Canberra in the 1920s is a warning. A policy of leasehold only on a greenfield site was instituted to ensure that no-one would be barred from becoming an occupier within the new Australian capital. The rent reviews were every twenty years! As land values rose, the leases acquired a capital value, which was traded in the normal way. At the end of twenty years, the rent increases were so draconian that they led to protests and a government scandal. The rent increases were canceled. *Annual valuations are the only way to stop all land speculation and allow continuing tax reductions.*

take and the time required for the economy to adjust. A conservative estimate of the UK's *additional* national income, using 50% only of those figures in the tables, would be in the region of £152 billion and £135 billion respectively. The UK's *new* national income for 1996 would, therefore, have been a minimum of £810 billion. A 33% land rental would produce sufficient revenue to meet all relevant government expenditure, and with a surplus with which to play.

The general proposition, then, is that in a tax free, or relatively tax free, economy, land rentals would approximate one-third of National Income. For the purpose of the present study, however, we shall begin our assessment of reforms to the budget based on rents that are visibly measurable under the current tax regime. The starting point is the cautious estimate for rental income of £118 billion - which, as it happens, was the figure that was originally estimated for 1990 (Table 5:I, col I). How much fiscal justice would this sum permit? Before we can answer that question, we also have to determine what constitutes legitimate *private* expenditure that is currently financed with the public sector as intermediary. The reader may wish to engage in this exercise by answering the following question: *If taxes were abolished tomorrow, which services would he or she choose to buy through the public sector?*

In answering the question, a key consideration needs to be taken into account. How much of the refunded tax revenue would a wage-earner be able to retain (to spend on family needs) and how much would have to be paid out as rent? The answer affects the outcome of deliberations provoked by the first question.

Assume that, as a result of a radical change in taxation, we can enjoy long-term economic stability, and no-one's wages would fall below the level required to buy the goods and services that elevates all families above the poverty level. Now we can expect interesting answers to the foregoing question.

In a thriving economy the whole population, for the first time, would be able to make private decisions over the disposal of their incomes, rather than have the State make those decisions for them. The "Welfare State" emerged because of the injustice of legal and institutional constraints, which prevented a significant number of people from earning enough to pay for all their basic needs, such as health, pensions and education. Given a "level playing field" and a socially just economic system, government expenditure on welfare would most likely be required only for those in dire need resulting from a personal tragedy, and, with a thriving economy, the provision for those people could be very generous indeed. Communal expenditure, such as that for law and order, defense, fire brigade, etc, would be sufficient to provide the best public services.

Table 5:II summarizes government spending in 1995. If all taxes were abolished, which of these items would be retained as activities that people had to finance on a communal basis? Which items would be withdrawn as services that people would choose to buy direct from suppliers in the private sector?

In a fully employed, prosperous society where these conditions would prevail on a sustainable basis, the high probability is that most people would choose to divide current public services into the two groups shown in Table 5:III

Table 5:II
General government expenditure 1995

	£ billion
General public services, including Public administration, Finance & Tax collection, External relations, etc.	13.504
Defense	23.154
Public order & safety, including police, Fire service, Law Courts and Prisons	15.320
Education	38.330
Health	40.842
Social security & welfare	102.483
Housing & community amenity, of which	10.468
Housing	4.607
Water & sewerage	0.290
Other	5.571
Recreational & cultural affairs	4.289
Fuel & energy	2.224
Agriculture, forestry, fishing & food	3.487
Mining & mineral resources, manufacturing & construction	1.427
Transport & communication	9.127
Other economic affairs & services	5.845
Other	33.377
General government expenditure (GGE)	**303.877**

Source: ONS (1996: 15, Table 2:2)

Table 5:III
Possible reductions in Government Expenditure - 1995
(£billions)
A: Retained expenditure areas

General public services	13.504
Defense	23.154
Public order & safety	15.320
Water & sewerage	0.290
Community amenity, other	5.571
Fuel & energy	2.224
Transport & communication	9.127
Other economic affairs & services	5.845
Other	33.377
Total	**108.412**

B: Expenditure areas for reduction

Education	38.330
Health	40.842
Social security & welfare	102.483
Housing	4.607
Recreation & Culture	4.289
Agriculture, etc	3.487
Mining & mineral resources, etc	1.427
Total	**195.465**

The group A services are necessary as social functions that individuals could not secure directly from the private sector. This is more obviously so for some items (defense of the realm, law and order) than others (such as transport and water services, much of which has now been privatized in Britain). Nevertheless, there are clear benefits from a community agreeing to pool resources and funding certain services on a social basis.

The group B activities, however, were driven into the public sector largely because, over the course of the 19th century, too many people were excluded from earning the incomes to buy those services themselves. The emerging democratic conscience, crystallized in the Liberals' People's Budget (1910), began the first steps towards the largest-ever insurance policy: the Welfare State. Deprived people were rescued by a system in which benefits were shared on a universal basis. Unfortunately, as events turned out, for many people this merely meant a shift from deprivation to dependency. But although self-esteem suffered, at least there was the hope of banishing material shortcomings. This did not prove to be the case, which is why the time has now come to contemplate the one reform that would finally release every person from private exploitation and social dependency.

In a carefully planned and controlled transition, public sector responsibility for education, health, social security and housing could be severely reduced, perhaps by as much as half. Those expenditures on recreation and cultural affairs, agriculture etc, and mining could be almost eliminated. Taking the savings on the social provisions as 50%, some £97 billion could be expunged from government expenditure and returned to income earners.

We have to remind ourselves that, with our policy fully operational, providing a growing economy that is "tax free", or relatively so, and with all the "tax led" distortions eliminated, the need for much state assistance or provision of services would disappear. This is not so much the dismantling of the "welfare state", rather the liberation of a people's desires to make decisions about health and education for themselves *because they can afford to do so*. In this way, the "welfare state" will begin to wither away; progressively, as people felt their way forward into the new society.

If we take the figures in column B and divide by two - the suggested 50% - we are left with social expenditure of £97 billion to add to the expenditure in A of £108 billion. This leaves us with a total government expenditure of £206 billion. Taking National Income figures for 1995 at £641 billion, and total government tax revenue of £270 billion, we can add at least 50% of the tax take to the National Income figures (which is a modest proportion of the estimate in Ch. 6). This results in a new National Income of £777 billion. Necessary taxation of £206 billion, as we have now defined it, is 26.5% of National Income.

We have already cautiously identified a land rent of 17.5% of National Income under the existing tax regime, which depresses land values as well as national income. In a society that progressively reduced taxes to deliver rising national income and full employment, land values and rentals would rise, certainly yielding more than 26.5% of National Income, and would be sufficient to cover government expenditure, as land rentals adjusted up to the one-third ratio.

We propose the retention of taxes for purposes of health and ecology, such as those on tobacco products, alcohol and petrol. Although not retained for revenue purposes, these taxes, nevertheless, produce a large amount of revenue (£32 bn: 1996). In addition, vehicle excise duties may well need to be retained so that policies towards the "car", that awkward possession that produces so many problems, can be flexible. The figure just quoted represents some 15.7%, a significant proportion of the necessary taxation shown above of £206 billion.

2. The virtuous circle of growth

BY BEGINNING to collect land rentals and simultaneously *detaxing* private enterprise and labor, the boost to the income of the nation would be remarkable. The tax reforming budget could increase national income by about £60 billion over a period of two years. Some 50% or more of this would surface as higher land rents that could be tapped at each succeeding budget for even more increments of tax reductions and a further increase in national income to be shared among wage earners, savers and the government. Within five years, all taxation, except that retained for health and ecology, could be abolished.

All the tax-led distortions would evaporate like the early morning mist receding in the heat of the rising sun. How we get from here to there is discussed in this section

The taxation revenue for the same year as the figure for National Income in Box 1 are given in Table 5:IV. (Figures rounded from HM Treasury, Table S24, The finances of general government). Those starred (*) are the suggested targets for reduction or elimination in year one. The targeted figures, some of which are reduced by 50%, amount to £116.7 billion. This is adequately covered by the existing conservatively estimated rental revenue of £118 billion.

Table 5:IV
UK Government Revenue : 1996/7
(£ billions)

Income tax	69.5*	Corporation tax	27.6*
Capital gains tax	1.1*	Inheritance tax	1.6*
Stamp duties	2.3*	Social security	47.3*
Business rates	15.3*	Council tax	10.1*
Vehicle excise duties	4.2	VAT	46.7
Petrol tax	1.8	Fuel duties	16.9
Tobacco duties	8.0	Alcohol duties	5.6
Betting duties	1.4	Air passenger duty	.4
Insurance premium tax	.7	Landfill tax	.1
Customs duties	2.3	Oil royalties	.7
Other taxes	7.8		
Total (Figures rounded) **£271. 4 bn**		***[£175.1 bn]**	

Table 5:V
Target sectors: proposed tax cuts

		Cost: bn
Income tax	**50%**	34.8
Capital gains	**100%**	1.1
Stamp duties	**100%**	2.4
Business rates	**100%**	15.3
Corporation tax	**100%**	27.7
Inheritance tax	**100%**	1.6
Council tax	**100%**	10.1
Social security	**50%**	<u>23.7</u>
Total		**116.7**

For companies, the abolition of corporation tax will have enormous benefits. Despite any asset value loss due to the obligation to pay land rent, values of companies will rise. Much of the loss of land value in their books will be offset by the abolition of the uniform business rate. Capital gains tax abolition will have beneficial effects on the value of buildings or structures on their books. There would be a freedom about untaxed "real" capital assets. The business community, including the financial sector, would no longer have to calculate the tax effects on any part of their business. The abolition of the employers' national insurance contributions would enable employers to use the savings in a number of ways, including the hiring of more people as labor costs were reduced, and the use of rising company values, either through the stock market or through negotiations with their financiers.

For wage earners, the results would be electrifying. New and rising employment possibilities and the opportunity for increased earnings with low income tax (and no income tax at all within a few years) would transform the labor market. With the understood prospect that these tax cuts were the first of many, with the expectation that the economy and national income would grow, with the knowledge that capital gains tax and inheritance tax would be abolished, people would be able, for the first time, to use their ingenuity and enterprise to maximize their incomes and savings in a way that would gradually reduce their current dependence on many of the welfare benefits. Provision would be guaranteed for those in real need with the prospect of having those needs met in a generous and caring way.

Companies producing real wealth - as opposed to speculating in capital gains from land - would be net beneficiaries. Their attention would be concentrated on their core businesses, freed from the distractions of the "sterile" land asset that prejudice the activities of many entrepreneurs. Their main concern about land and value would be to ensure that their location is exactly where it should be for maximum profit, paying for no more "public location value" than they need. An office in the city center may be necessary, but there would be little need for most companies to have an office at street level, where shops trying to attract customers would be located.

Those companies that rent or lease their premises will derive the largest immediate benefits. If they are paying the full rack rent, they will pay no more for their properties and yet their tax savings will be substantial. (Their rents to the landlord are likely to rise by the amount of the business rates, but the land rentals will be borne solely by the landlord). Their ability to use untaxed profits, together with the other tax cuts, for expansion and increased competitiveness will increase the value of the company. Shareholders will be among the beneficiaries as share prices rise. For companies with freehold properties, there will be a one off adverse effect on their balance sheets. But the tax cuts will offer sufficient compensation.

Inefficient companies that rely on their property assets to keep them afloat will be hard hit. They will be in a similar position to those businesses after the First World War that were on 99 year leases, inherited from the Victorian era, without rent reviews. As the value of money depreciated, rent became extremely low in relation to the value of the property occupied. Inefficiency was encouraged and a valuable site was not used for its most efficient purpose. Businesses closed down as leases came to an end, because the new rents were too high for their level of productivity. Redevelopment could take place and new lease holders found at the market rack rent for the property, leading to more efficient use of sites.

A more recent illustration of this phenomenon was the "asset stripping" of the 1950s and 1960s, associated with people such as Jim Slater. Companies that were inefficient but possessed valuable assets, mainly property, were targeted for takeover. This led to high-value locations being used in a more appropriate and efficient manner. Alas, the "unearned increment" went to the predators rather than to the public, whose communal efforts are siphoned off in land profits by the few. This virtuous consequence - the use of valuable locations in an efficient manner - is one of the results of the "land rent as public revenue" policy, and will put inefficient companies under pressure to reorganize their business on a more profitable basis.

The only "losers" are likely to be those companies that deal purely in land. Even here, however, the elimination of taxation on profits, no employers' national insurance contributions, no capital gains tax, no inheritance tax and no business rates, would mitigate losses and encourage developers to seek tax free revenue out of development. Those who deal in property as a whole will enjoy the removal of taxes on their buildings. Their position would be similar to those sectors of the economy that lose for any number of reasons: coal mines becoming redundant as power generators switch to other forms of energy; spat makers and hat makers redundant because of a change in fashion; tobacco workers and companies losing because of taxation and the influence of the anti-smoking lobby, etc. There is no longer a job for life, as inventions and changes in taste take hold and companies and their employees confront a new economic reality. In the very short term, the possible losers from our policy are in no different a situation - except that our policy, when fully implemented, has a once-for-all effect; and it creates so many opportunities for tax free profit and earnings, with the exception of profits from land.

Owners and "renters out" of residential property will have to pay the land rent. Since the council tax, normally paid by the tenant, will be abolished, there will be some leeway for rent increases to the limit of the tenant's saving on council tax. No tax will be payable on rental income from the hiring out of buildings.

Landlords may try to heap the whole land rental on to the tenant, as they do the council tax. Any attempt, however, to pass on the land rentals to the tenant will be frustrated. The virtuous pressure of payments of the land rentals will result in a rush to use residential property efficiently. Redevelopment or refurbishment will be the order of the day as owners of property seek to maximize their income. The number of residential units for rent will increase, thus promoting more competition in the renting business, thereby moderating rents. This would make it difficult, if not impossible, for landlords to pass on the land rentals to tenants. Any attempt to draw up rental agreements with the intention of avoiding payment of the land rentals by landlords will be frustrated by the legislation. The payers of the land rentals will be those who enjoy the benefits of a particular location. If the tenant is paying the full market rent for that location to his landlord, he will not be willing to pay a penny more, except for the slight adjustment for council tax abolition. The landlord will be liable for the whole of the land rental. Where full market rents are not being paid, the land rent liability will be assessed on the pro-rata basis of how much the tenant and landlord share the benefits of the location.

The tax reductions for landlords are substantial. With no corporation tax or a much reduced income tax, reinforced by abolition of inheritance tax, capital gains tax and stamp duties, there is a fair amount of compensation. The ability to reorganize and plan for a tax free future should excite landlords, despite the one-off effect on the asset value of land. In particular, the abolition of capital gains tax will mitigate the problem in which people use land and collateral for loans. There will need to be some accommodation between lender and borrower. The buildings are still there, free of any tax. The tax reductions produce an increased value in the development and should be taken into account by lender and borrower alike. The "capitalization" of such tax reductions should offset the perception of asset loss.

The value of companies in general will increase, and this increased value can be used, perhaps through the use of debentures, to calm the fears of lenders who see the collateral value of land eliminated.

There would be a similar perception within pension fund and insurance company investment management where there is an imbalance of property to production shares in portfolios. The rewards are in the tax cuts, resulting in increased portfolio values and all the potential for the future of Britain's economy.

The markets could adjust to the new situation speedily. The initial perception of asset value loss would be offset by lower risks and higher profits from the new economy. Businesses have always complained that they have to carry the burden of collecting revenue, such as income tax, for the Government. The cost of that burden would be cut dramatically. Within as short a time as four years, income tax could be abolished altogether, thus relieving all employers of the need for a large department to cater for the demands of the Inland Revenue.

3. Attractions for investors and financiers

FOREIGN companies would flock to Britain! Their only expense would be in locating in the right place, paying the land rent, and either leasing or developing their site to the appropriate level, with as high a building to land ratio as permitted under the planning laws.

This implies possible problems with other European Union members and the Commission in Brussels. The cry will be that of "unfair competition" as companies relocate in the UK from elsewhere in Europe. The UK can give appropriate notice of its intention to implement this policy and cite "overriding national interest" as the justification. In any event, there should be nothing to stop other EU countries from harmonizing their revenue policies with Britain for the benefit of *their* citizens.

It will be obvious to investors in the City that without the tax burden, and with increased profits, the potential for investment in British companies is enormous. The reduction of 50% of income tax would have consequences on dividend payments, mainly giving companies more flexibility in the handling of their profits. Companies might decide to take into account the net effect of dividend payments to shareholders and reduce the gross dividend to retain profits for expansion and investment.

The book value of collateral assets would be reduced to the extent that financiers had treated land as security for loans. This is something that the financial sector has actually come to expect, on a cyclical basis. Since 1945 there have been repeated cuts in asset values as the economy slumped from one crisis to the next. There are, however, some distinctive differences from the loss of value incurred through our proposed reform.

(i) The treatment of rent as public revenue would terminate *the "boom and bust" cycle*. So the asset value effect would be the last one; because people would no longer be encouraged to *speculate in land* with funds provided *by* banks. The financial institutions would continue to finance the construction and purchase of buildings, but they would be freed from financing the land element. They would be released to finance the productive capital projects that increase growth. And as the economy geared up to the new economic "dynamism" - a faster rate of growth, higher levels of output, lower costs - the banks would emerge as welcome partners in the creative process; rather than being viewed, as they too often are now, as mere money-milking machines.

(ii) Loss of asset value is partially if not wholly offset by the tax cuts - not just corporation tax, but the other tax cuts that would make economic activity more profitable, generating higher corporate and personal profits which then lead to increased savings deposits in banks. This would have an effect on interest rates, most probably downwards, thereby making it easier for people to start new companies with affordable bank loans.

(iii) Residential lending is only slightly different, and that due to the sheer numbers of mortgages in existence. The borrowers are still as creditworthy - even more so with immediate tax cuts and the prospects for future income with no tax to pay at all. Lenders will see some of their collateral written out of their books, borrowers will perceive a loss of some of their asset value. An accommodation between lender and borrower will be necessary, facilitated by government. Any real problems will arise *on occasion*, making solutions possible on a staggered basis.

The asset value issue will loom particularly large for the house building sector. At first sight it might appear that developers would be disadvantaged.

There would be a one-off adverse effect on the accounts. At the end of the transition to the rent-based budget, the land banks held by building firms (usually equal to two or three years worth of needs) would count for naught except the opportunity to use that land on which to build houses. Nonetheless, builders would also be among the winners.

Under the existing tax regime, the trauma of seeing asset values wiped out is something that has been inflicted on hundreds of thousands in recent years. Families saw the value of their homes (more accurately, the value of their land) crash in the "negative equity" crisis of the early 1990s. Their houses were worth less than the mortgages that they owed banks and building societies. The scale of this household financial crisis began to diminish in the mid-1990s, but - without rational reform to public finance - it will repeat itself ten years into the new millennium.

Building companies are at the forefront of a leading sector of the economy. They lead the way into slumps, and they lead the way out of slumps. They would have a great deal to celebrate as a result of being relieved of the continual struggle to find land that could be afforded by their prospective customers - the families that need the new homes.

Under the new fiscal system, profitable companies would not renege on their commitments to their financiers. This is because profitable opportunities would multiply: after an initial boom - to satisfy some of the pent-up demand - the construction sector would settle down to a stable path of growth in the provision of new houses and the construction and renewal of commercial and industrial properties. Profit would depend on entrepreneurial skill and productivity rather than speculating on trends in land prices; and that profit would be tax free.

As part of the transitional program, construction companies would use their land banks as quickly as possible and make arrangements with their financiers, perhaps rescheduling loan repayments. It may be necessary to allow a period of grace for the payment of the annual land rental while development took place. This grace period should be short, perhaps only six months, which may be necessary for all developments. New land acquisitions would be costless in capital terms, there being only an obligation to pay the annual land rental.

4. Self-financing social infrastructure

PUBLICLY FINANCED infrastructure has been a drain on the public's private purses when, all the time, the economically viable projects were self-financing!

The figures cannot, at this stage, be calculated as accurately as we might wish but the "unearned increment", as Churchill called it, is the legitimate source of finance for these projects.

This proposal has been mooted in the past. One suggestion in the latter part of the last century concerned the financing of New York's subway. It was suggested that the construction costs be financed entirely out of the increased land values that would surely follow the construction of such a system. Even more radical was the suggestion that travel on the system should be free of charge, thus further increasing the land values to pay for the running costs as well! The proposal was that the City should borrow the financing and pay back the loans by collecting the increased land rental values. That was a real "public transport initiative"!

The proposal has actually been implemented in Hong Kong, where land rent has been used for public revenue. The extension of the Metro was financed by such increases in land values (Harrison 1983: 222). The "unearned increment" was used by the government for the public's benefit. The same principle ought to apply to all publicly financed infrastructure projects.

Public investment projects, today, have as their main "indirect" consequence the giving of immensely increased values to the owners of properties in the affected vicinity of the project. The shortcomings of this outcome are illustrated by the two bridges across the Severn Estuary, which reveal the inherent flaws in Britain's "Private Finance Initiative". Private interests receive the tolls; users of the bridges pay heavily for the privilege; increased land values remain in the hands of the owners of those properties in areas benefiting from the construction.

Another example is the new road between the M5 and M4, the dual carriage way A419, by-passing Cirencester, Stratton St. Margaret (near Swindon) and several other villages. This shows yet another Private Finance Initiative that leaves untapped the "unearned increment" for property owners in the area. In this scheme, the road belongs to the investors and the government *pays a toll* for every vehicle using that road. This does not make financial or moral sense!

Public investment gives value to location. The most important element in this value is the amount spent from general taxation - specifically for infrastructure projects, like roads, bridges, public lighting, pavements, tunnels; and publicly provided services like schools, universities, hospitals, enforcement of public health standards, defense, police, etc.

In the UK today, there is yet another factor that has the same effect - the National Lottery. The Millennium Commission is making grants for local infrastructure projects. These include the complex at Greenwich, where it is reported that increased land values in the area have dramatically improved the balance sheets of several companies; a large grant to the City of Bath for improving its Spa facilities, where the local response is almost ecstatic, businesses and property owners alike knowing that their prospects for increased income is much improved; another large grant to the Kennet and Avon Canal for much needed restoration work, where local reports suggest that some 2,000 jobs will be created, many businesses saved and many more created. It would seem that lottery winners are not the only beneficiaries of the National Lottery, however. In addition to those causes and charities that receive grants, there is yet another, hidden, set of "winners" - the fortunate owners of land in the areas where lottery money is spent. The casino economy has but a few direct winners - but many more who gain from windfalls from a gamble in which they have not even had to risk a stake! This process offends all principles of equity and efficiency, and needs to be addressed through a People's Budget.

The economics that underpin sound public investment were analyzed by the 1996 Nobel prize winner, William Vickrey (*see Box 5.III, page 144*).

5. Of Farmers and Families

SOME PEOPLE will complain that the payment of rent will make their lot harder. That will be the claim from some farmers. Farmers *should* be assessed for payment of the land rent. They have been exempt from rates or taxes on their farmland since 1929, although they have paid property taxes on certain of their buildings, mainly their dwelling. This exemption was a grant or subsidy to working farmers. That subsidy was then capitalized into higher land prices, so that subsequent generations of farmers found they were not exempt from the rates at all: instead, they paid the money to their landlords.

Tenant farmers would not be affected unless they were not paying the full market rent for their farmland.

The Common Agricultural Policy of the European Union has created problems for the farm community. Current (1998) proposals for reform ought to include the fiscal dimension. The valuation of farmland is inaccurate in that it takes account of the subsidy factors within the CAP. Without the subsidy, farmland would be valued lower. There is also the problem of set-aside land where the EU, through its CAP, *pays* for land to be unused. If that payment represents the annual rental value of that land, is that not the annual land rent that should be assessed and claimed for the exchequer?

Should any further subsidy be considered necessary, best practice would be by direct payment out of the public purse, properly accounted for in the published accounts, and available for all to see for future reconsideration. This practice would concentrate the mind, especially when owners of vast landed estates, presently on a concealed subsidy, apply for open subsidies! As Lord Douglas of Barloch stated: "The arguments in favor of allowing some privileged persons to profit out of public values must indeed be overwhelming if they are to prevail" (Barloch 1936).

The offsetting advantages for the farmer are connected to the tax reductions and the market response. The taxes paid on buildings would be abolished. The owners of vast landed estates would also not pay taxes or rates on their buildings. Add to this the reductions in general taxation, and the perceived burden of rental payments by owner-occupiers would not be justified.

Unused land would be brought into use as well as poorly used land to better use. It would be an expensive luxury or indulgence to keep land out of use or poorly used when an annual land rent has to be paid. This would encourage the reduction of rents in line with demand. Planning controls over the use of farmland for ecological or social reasons would be commensurately reflected in the reduced rental liabilities of the affected sites.

The great landed estates would benefit from the abolition of inheritance tax on assets such as works of art, stocks and shares, etc. With the land element taken out of the asset equation, inheritance tax would produce a much lower figure than at present and should be scrapped. With public value being collected for the public good, there is no reason to "raid" a person's private wealth on death. Businesses could be passed down in the family without taxation. The same applies to capital gains. Without a land element, there is no sound reason why a capital gains tax should be levied. These two taxes have, in the past, collected a large amount of increased land values, but not in a way that helped the economy. In fact, they distorted decisions over investment, business planning, savings, and life assurance.

The rental liability of farmland, of course, would vary on the basis of different grades and quality. The higher the quality, the higher the price - except when other factors enter the equation, such as the land's proximity to local markets, excellent transport facilities, together with the potential for development within the framework of existing planning laws. Even poorer quality farmland benefits from these factors and is valued at a higher rate by users

The poorest of farmland, with no benefit from other factors, would be assessed at zero rent liability. Freehold or leasehold, the valuation would be low or nil, and yet that farmer would benefit from the abolition of rates or taxes on buildings, *and* the reductions in general taxation that would increase the real disposable value of people's income. The Danish experience is again of some import here. In that country, the small farmers were largely responsible for ensuring that the land tax policy was adopted.

Among families, the overriding sentiment will be one of huge excitement at the prospect of sustainable earnings at low or no income tax, and at the chance to make choices in the disposal of those earnings, tailored to their individual needs. The one area of possible disaffection is in the perception of a one-off asset loss in the value of their land.

A number of factors need to be considered. There is already a loss of asset value under the present taxation system through the inheritance tax. This produced, in 1994/5, £1.4 billion and should be abolished. It is a small sum and would be reduced even further through the fact that the land element in any property sale would not be taken into account in valuing the estate. The council tax reduces asset value as well.

Children and others benefiting from a will would be in a different position from their parents. In fact, the scope for further progression is much enhanced under the new funding of public expenditure. Together with the abolition of the council tax, house purchase would be easier and cheaper. Mortgages would reflect only the value of the house, not the land, and interest would not be payable on borrowing for land purchase. Parents should be delighted that their children would be in an even more advantageous position due to this reform, rather than focus on the perception of a partial loss in the value of one asset (offset by increased savings from untaxed earnings generated by the other assets). Parents would be bequeathing their children the legacy of a better economic world.

Tax reductions made possible by the collection of rental values leads to *real tax reductions*, not just *tax shifting* as occurred during the Thatcher years. The people on lowest incomes would notice the effect most immediately, in a variety of ways. The tax reductions should be targeted, in the first place, at people with welfare needs - the unemployed, the homeless, etc. Spending taxes should be a priority for the next stages of tax reductions, together with further income tax reductions, as these will be of most benefit to those with low or no incomes, and who need the maximum self-help incentives. The taxes cut in the first phase of the reform will have an effect on these low income families by giving the opportunity for earning from employment, stemming from the drop in unemployment. The reduced demands for welfare payments by government will enable those needing help to receive more generous treatment.

British economic history shows that taxes on employment, such as the employers' national insurance contributions (effectively a payroll tax), and income tax, especially the pay-as-you-earn scheme, increase *un*employment some 12 to 15 months after a rise in the rate of tax. Conversely, a cut in those tax rates leads, again after about 12 to 15 months, to a rise in employment. The complete abolition of the employers' national insurance contributions and a 50% reduction in income tax would revolutionize the jobs market by increasing employment markedly and reducing government expenditure on involuntary unemployment.

Those on lowest incomes should gain most, in relative terms, because they have traditionally been excluded from an equity stake in land or property. They would enjoy the first net gains. Welfare spending can be contained and the boost to employment would reduce the need for unemployment benefits. The needs of the really disadvantaged could be met with a care and generosity, unimagined by those people today.

6. Conclusion

THE FISCAL feasibility of the rent-as-public-revenue policy for the UK economy has been demonstrated. Certain issues require further examination before we can accurately quantify some of the benefits and costs. A fuller treatment is given in a forthcoming book (Banks 1998). The object of this chapter has been to establish the "big picture" so that the full advantages of the policy can be clearly seen. This is especially important for the Blair Government in its enquiry into reform of the welfare state. In late 1997, the Government found itself under considerable pressure from backbenchers, a number of Cabinet members and two of Labour's European Members of Parliament (who were expelled from the party in January 1998) to ease off on welfare reforms that decreased benefits to those in need. The Blair Government will find no better way *(in fact, no other way at all)* of providing for those in need at a generous level of care without bankrupting the state, other than by adopting the policy outlined here.

We need to be acutely alert to the cases of hardship. Solutions can be devised without vitiating the virtuous consequences of our reform. We can, for instance, use a proportion of the rent revenue dividend for additional tax cuts, and the balance to defray transitional costs. Implementing the policy in this way means that *all* the land rentals collected are available for the tax cuts we have identified. With national income growing apace, and people and businesses able, for the first time, to ignore any tax implications in their earning capacity, the stage will be set for a rise in land values, increased rental collection and further tax cuts. A virtuous circle!

Box 5:III
The Economic Theory behind the financing of Social Infrastructure

THE LATE William Vickrey of Columbia University, New York, was awarded the Nobel prize for economics after describing the optimum conditions for investment in public infrastructure. For example, he explained: "If the landlords of New York knew what was good for them, they would vote enthusiastically for an added tax on site values to be devoted to lowering subway fares, especially for off-peak and for shorter trips, and improving the frequency and quality of the service. Assuming that the subsidy would be used efficiently and not frittered away on administrative overheads, aborted or grandiose construction projects or overgenerous fringe benefits, this would increase the value New Yorkers get from their outlays on subway service, increasing the attractiveness of the city and in the long run *raising site rents by more than the tax"* (Vickrey 1995: emphasis added).

This draws out the interplay between the factor markets and public policy. If government ordains a change in, say, tax policy or institutional arrangements in the labor market, which result in greater efficiencies, the outcome is a rise in land values. Britain's Chancellor Lawson learnt that lesson the hard way following the deregulation of the financial markets in the 1980s. The greater efficiencies ended up boosting land prices - and therefore encouraged land speculation - which put the nail in his political coffin.

One way only exists to neutralize this rent effect to make sure that citizens are not shortchanged out of the benefits that should accrue to them, as a community: the rent should be paid into the public coffers. Most importantly, Dr. Vickrey showed that the collection of land-rents as public revenue would generate sufficient revenue to defray the capital costs of investment in infrastructure. This is how he put it:

"Collecting the rents attributable to the availability in a city of goods and services produced under conditions of economies of scale, priced a marginal cost for efficient allocation, would under competitive conditions be just sufficient to provide the necessary subsidies" (Vickrey, 1977).

The environment would be one of the winners. Dr. Vickrey illustrated this by his reference to the negative impact of the sprawling city on the countryside: "Site value taxation in the long run tends to diminish urban sprawl, increasing densities and site values at the center and usually diminishing them at the periphery".

Dr. Vickrey knew that his views, although they had enriched economic literature and were sufficiently acceptable among his peers to have earned him the presidency of the American Economic Association in 1992, were considered heretical by politicians in Washington's corridors of power. Just before Vickrey's death, House Speaker Newt Gingrich tried to brand him as "an obsolete socialist, representing all the values that collapsed with the Berlin Wall". His heresies, however, were not based on false economics: his theorizing was impeccable. He courted criticism, however, because he was willing to stray beyond the bounds of academic caution and into policy areas that challenged conventional political wisdom.

Dr. Vickrey's iconoclasm surfaced most forcefully in his attempt to instruct policy-makers on the nuances of public finance. As an illustration, take the example of fire protection. He wrote:

"Superficially it might seem that the cost of fire protection is to be charged to the combustible structures that benefit directly from the protection. From the standpoint of marginal social cost, however, nearly all of the cost of fire protection is properly charged against site value. The cost of providing a given grade of protection to a given area is only slightly affected by the number of structures in the area. There is the wear and tear on the equipment used and the risk of injury to personnel during the actual fighting of fires, plus the possibility that response time to a second fire may be longer if the local unit is out fighting a first fire and a unit must be brought from further away. Although dense development is associated with traffic congestion that may lengthen response times of fire companies, this cost is to be charged directly to the traffic and not the property improvements."

Similar reasoning requires that the cost of other public services - water, gas, electricity, mail delivery - ought to fall primarily on the rental value of land. Wrote Dr. Vickrey:

"The fact that the occupant [at a given location] does not make direct use of one or more of these facilities should not excuse the owner from contributing to the cost of carrying these services past his property, any more than one can expect to get a reduction in a car rental charge because one will not be using the headlights, the windshield wipers or the back seat. As matters now stand, electric and gas bills include the cost of carrying the services past the tennis courts and disproportionate shares of the cost of carrying the services past rows of houses and two-acre lots. The results are thus not only inefficient but regressive. In addition, land rents and land prices are higher by reason of the availability of these services, but not by as much as if they were available at marginal cost".

Treating the rent of land as public revenue had the reverse effect of taxes on earned incomes. As Dr. Vickrey put it: "Ultimately a shift to land value taxation, by attracting additional activity to the city, is likely to increase the net market value of the land". In other words, while other taxes bear down on the fiscal base, the treatment of land-rent as public revenue *expands* the base. That is the secret of virtuous growth: environmentally benign and socially sustainable!

Although he specialized in public infrastructure problems, Dr. Vickrey was emphatic about the benefits of the correct policy for families in the private sector. For example, land prices and rents would no longer be an obstacle to acquiring homes or creating small businesses. Following the fiscal reform, assured Dr. Vickrey, "Transactions in property at lower market values are easier to finance".

Chapter 6

Taxed Out of Work and Wealth:
The Costs of Taxing Labor and Capital

Nicolaus Tideman and Florenz Plassmann

1. Introduction

MOST OF THE TAXES that nations customarily levy are economically destructive. This destructiveness is not just that taxation makes people poorer. It is that most customary taxes entice people to be less productive by offering a lower tax bill to anyone who agrees to produce less. In particular, when people are taxed on their earnings or spending, they find work less rewarding and they work less. When they are taxed on their savings, or on the return from their savings, they save less. As a result of these destructive consequences of taxation, economies are much smaller than they could be. There are sources of public revenue that do not have these destructive consequences, namely public collection of rent for exclusive use of land and other natural opportunities. To have an economy that is as efficient as possible, a nation should obtain as much public revenue as possible from these non-destructive sources, and tax labor or capital only as a last resort. We estimate that the G7 economies had levels of output in 1993 that were only 52 percent to 77 percent of what they could have been if they had followed such policies, while continuing to have public sectors of the sizes that they had. Our estimates of changes in the sizes of economies by country are shown in Table 6.1 below. (Our estimates are based on figures for 1993, because that is the latest year for which we had tax information for all G7 nations. We report all our estimates in U.S. dollars, employing exchange rates based on purchasing power parity to

146

convert from national currencies.) All of our estimates are made considering just the potential of economies in terms of the factors of production - land, labor and capital - that are available to them. The estimates take no account of any financial difficulties of the transition to a new system of public finance, or of the need to expand the money supply to accommodate the greater level of production.

Table 6.I
Gain in output and per capita income from switch to public collection of rent

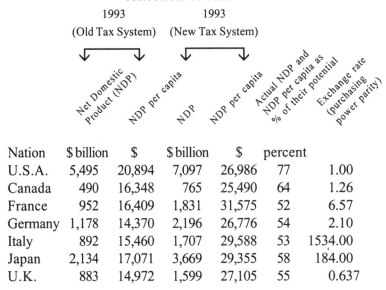

Nation	Net Domestic Product (NDP) $ billion	NDP per capita $	NDP $ billion	NDP per capita $	Actual NDP and NDP per capita as % of their potential percent	Exchange rate (purchasing power parity)
U.S.A.	5,495	20,894	7,097	26,986	77	1.00
Canada	490	16,348	765	25,490	64	1.26
France	952	16,409	1,831	31,575	52	6.57
Germany	1,178	14,370	2,196	26,776	54	2.10
Italy	892	15,460	1,707	29,588	53	1534.00
Japan	2,134	17,071	3,669	29,355	58	184.00
U.K.	883	14,972	1,599	27,105	55	0.637

As Table 6.I shows, we estimate that a shift to public collection of rent as the principal source of public revenue in the U.S. in 1993 would have increased the output of the U.S. economy by $1,602 billion above its actual level for 1993, implying that the U.S. economy is producing only 77 percent of what it could produce with a better tax policy. The other G7 economies are operating at even lower percentages of their potentials, because they currently have higher taxes.

Public finance economists have long known about the destructive effects of taxation, and use several phrases to refer to it. Sometimes it is called the "excess burden" of taxation, that is, the burden over and above the taxes paid. Sometimes it is called the "deadweight loss" of taxation, suggesting an uncooperative load that we must collectively carry as we produce. Sometimes it is called the "welfare cost" of taxation, referring to the reduction in aggregate well-being that is entailed in taxation. While any of the names would do equally well, here we will use the phrase "excess burden" of taxation.

The loss that people suffer because of harmful taxes is properly measured not by the change in the size of output, but by excess burden, because people need to work harder to achieve the higher output. We estimate that for the U.S. economy in 1993, the reduction in excess burden of taxation that would have been possible by relying primarily on rent for public revenue was $784 billion or 14 percent of net domestic product. In terms of the 1998 economy in 1998 dollars, this is an increase of about $1 trillion (that is, 1,000,000,000,000) in the well-being of citizens as a result of better public revenue policies. The reductions in excess burden as percentages of net domestic product are even greater for the other G7 economies, because of their higher current taxes. We also estimate that by replacing taxes on capital with public collection of rent, these nations could increase their savings rates by factors of between 2.4 and 2.9 in the first year after the change. The savings rates would be not nearly so high in subsequent years, because the incentive to save diminshes as capital accumulates. Still, stocks of capital would increase by between 18 percent and 106 percent over five years. These results are shown in Table 6.II.

Table 6.II

Reduction in excess burden and increase in the capital stock from improved public revenue policies

Nation	Reduction in excess burden (EB) in 1993	Reduction in EB as % of NDP	Savings rate in 1993 with existing taxes	Savings rate in 1993 with alternative taxes	Percent increase in the capital stock from 1993 to 1998 with alternative taxes
	$ billion	%	%	%	%
U.S.A.	784	14	3.4	8.2	31
Canada	141	29	5.6	14.6	29
France	457	48	7.2	18.8	31
Germany	531	45	15.2	38.6	60
Italy	451	51	9.3	20.3	18
Japan	699	33	19.6	57.4	106
U.K.	352	40	3.8	10.0	19

In Section 2 we identify in more detail the sources of public revenue that not only have no excess burden, but often improve economic efficiency when they are employed. In Section 3 we describe the parameters of an economy that must be used to estimate the value of using these beneficial sources of public revenue, and our beliefs about these parameters.[1] Section 4 presents tables that show our estimates of what the G7 economies could achieve with these alternative sources of public revenue. Finally, in Section 5, we offer some concluding comments.

2. Source of Revenue Without Excess Burden

IF ALL TAXES had the same excess burden per dollar of revenue, then economists would only be able to counsel that the magnitude of the excess burden of taxation should be taken into account when deciding on the size of the public sector. But taxes do not all have the same rate of excess burden per dollar of revenue. In recent years there has been renewed interest in making the economy more productive by introducing a flat (or flatter) income tax. Flattening the income tax increases a nation's productivity because the excess burden of a tax is roughly proportional to the square of the marginal tax rate. Thus if eliminating exemptions and deductions makes it possible to cut the marginal tax rate in half, the excess burden will be cut by three-fourths. Economists have also discussed reasons why taxes on capital have an even greater excess burden per dollar of revenue than taxes on labor. Taxes on capital reduce a nation's growth rate and add to the costs that people face in providing for their retirement. The reduction in the amount of capital relative to labor lowers the productivity of labor, and thus lowers wages.

These initiatives to reduce the excess burden of taxation are valuable. But it would be even more valuable to use revenue sources that have no excess burden. And there are such sources. The revenue sources with no excess burden are charges for the use of economic resources that were created by nature or by public action rather than by private economic activity. Some examples of these revenue sources are:

- Taxes on land
- Fees for exclusive use of portions of the frequency spectrum
- Severance fees for extraction of natural resources
- Pollution charges
- Congestion charges
- Public parking charges

---

[1] A Technical Appendix explains our methodology in more detail.

- Fees for catching fish
- Water use fees
- Airport landing fees
- Other public service fees

With each of the named revenue sources, there are conditions that must be observed to keep the particular revenue source from generating an excess burden. In the case of a tax on land, the tax must not vary with how productively the land is used. It must be based on an assessor's estimate of the rental value or selling price that the land would have in an unimproved condition (or, in the case of agricultural land, if there is no such thing as unimproved land, then land in the least improved condition in which land is customarily found). Similarly, charges for exclusive use of the frequency spectrum must be based on the market value of that exclusive use, and not on the profit that a particular user receives.

Severance fees for the extraction of natural resources should be based on estimates of the social cost of reduction in the stocks of resources. Some provision must be made to offer suitable rewards to those who discover new stocks, if discoverers are not given free rein to deplete what they discover.

Pollution charges improve the economic efficiency of an economy when the charge does not exceed the harm that is done by pollution. The same is true of congestion charges - for crowded tunnels, bridges, thoroughfares or downtown areas. Parking charges improve economic efficiency when they do not exceed the lowest level at which vacant places are rare.

Fees for catching fish promote economic efficiency when the charge is no more than the social cost of the consequent reduction in fish stocks (or, alternatively, the market value of permission to catch fish, if it is easier to know the right quantity than the right price). Similarly, a charge for water use improves economic efficiency when the charge is no more than the social cost of reduced water reserves (or, alternatively, the market value of water, if a fixed quantity is available). This fee would only be for the cost of using up the reserves of water; any delivery costs would need to be added.

When there is more demand for take-off and landing slots at an airport than the airport can offer, a fee for taking off or landing that allocates the available total number of slots will generate revenue while improving economic efficiency.

Finally, for any public service, the collection of a fee for the use of the service, equal to the marginal cost of providing the service, will raise revenue while improving economic efficiency.

The efficiency with which land and other natural opportunities are used increases when they are taxed. There are two different paths by which this occurs. The first is by preventing the waste that occurs when a resource is overused. If individuals are not required to pay for the use of a scarce natural opportunity (for example, fishing or polluting or driving on crowded city streets), then they will use that opportunity excessively, in ways that are not worth the true cost of use. This leaves the economy with excessively depleted fish stocks, excessively dirty air and water, excessively crowded streets, and without benefits that would justify these costs. Charging for the use of scarce natural opportunities can prevent these inefficiencies.

A second way in which taxing these natural opportunities improves efficiency arises when exclusive rights to natural opportunities have been assigned to particular individuals without an obligation to make continuing payments to the public treasury. This applies to the ownership of land, airport take-off and landing rights, fishing rights, water rights, etc. The private ownership of such rights prevents the waste of overuse, but it creates a risk of waste from underuse.

If markets were perfect, these rights would always flow into the hands of those to whom they are most valuable. But markets are not perfect. Because there is uncertainty about the future value of land, much land is held speculatively, in an unproductive condition, particularly when taxes on holding vacant land are minimal. This can be seen in almost any large city, where numerous one- and two-story buildings, and even vacant land, can be found in the shadows of skyscrapers. Such uneven development is a waste of urban infrastructure and generates an artificial scarcity of land. It is privately profitable because individuals profit from being the ones who own land at the time when everyone else becomes aware that it has previously unrealized potential, that is, individuals profit by speculating in land. But there is generally no corresponding social benefit to land speculation. The possibility of a speculative gain draws people to the land market who have little incentive or ability to use land productively and only want to hold it for the possibility of a gain. This creates an artificial scarcity of land. While the speculator waits decades for his dream, the land goes underused. The same can happen to ownership of other natural opportunities. Taxing the ownership of natural opportunities reduces or eliminates the potential for speculative gain, thereby eliminating this source of economic inefficiency.

While all of the revenue sources mentioned are worth pursuing as substitutes for existing taxes with excess burdens, the most significant potential source of public revenue without excess burden is land.

3. Estimating the Impact of Removing Taxes with Excess Burdens

THERE IS VERY LITTLE data that provides evidence about the public revenue that might be obtained from the sources that have no excess burden. In their models, most economists aggregate land and capital together, as if there were no significant differences between the two, when actually the fact that land is provided by nature and capital is provided by human effort is crucial for evaluating alternative taxes.

It is extremely important to understand how much more productively economies could operate if they used more efficient sources of public revenue rather than the ones that are now in use. Without adequate data, only initial rough estimates can be made. Yet because these initial rough estimates are as startling as they are, we are bold to offer them, hoping we will provoke others to improve on our work.

We begin by developing a characterization of each of the G7 economies by using published facts about the economy - output, share of output going to employee compensation, tax rates, tax revenues, saving, etc. We treat government pension schemes as half tax and half investment for future income.

The model incorporates parameters that characterize the way a nation's economy operates. Some of the parameters are "elasticities." An elasticity measures the percentage change in some affected economic quantity that results from a 1 percent change in a causative factor. For example, the elasticity of the supply of shoes with respect to the price of shoes is the percentage increase in the supply of shoes that results from a 1 percent rise in the price of shoes.

To develop the consequences of alternative tax regimes, we use an aggregate production function that specifies the output of an economy as a function of the inputs of land, labor, and capital. The form of production function that we use is a "constant elasticity of substitution" or "CES" production function. A CES production function incorporates the assumption that, for any two factors of production, A and B, when the ratio of the price of A to the price of B falls by 1 percent, the ratio of the quantity of A to the quantity of B used in production increases by σ percent, where σ is the elasticity of substitution. For all parameters that we use, we show the effect on our estimates for the U.S. economy of using somewhat higher and lower values. In the case of the elasticity of substitution, our favored value of σ is 1.5, but we also consider values of σ of 1.25 and 2.0. Our belief that σ must be greater than 1.0 is based on the fact that if σ were less than 1.0, then the share of output going to land would have increased as the quantities of labor and capital increased, and we believe that the share of output going to land has been declining.

We estimate that one-third of the income that is not labor income is a return to land or some other natural opportunity. In the U.S., this amounts to 10.3 percent of Net Domestic Product (NDP). We also explore the consequences of assuming that this fraction is one-fourth or one-half, rather than one-third.

One might think that if 10 percent of NDP is a payment for the use of land and other natural opportunities, then 10 percent of NDP is an upper limit on the revenue that could be obtained from these sources. But that is not so. The revenue from land would increase if taxes were removed from labor and capital. There are two reasons for this. The first is that if taxes were removed from labor and capital, people would work more and save more. The increase in these variable factors would increase the value of each unit of land and other natural opportunities.

The contribution of land would also increase as a result of the elimination of the speculative demand for land. With land going into the hands of people who wanted to use it more productively, land would contribute more to production, both because individual sites would be used more productively and because the increased concentration of economic activity would raise the value of urban land. Our model incorporates an estimate of the amount by which the rental value of land would increase from the combination of these two effects. Our main estimate is based on the assumption that only half of the potential services of land are now used, though we also provide alternative estimates, based on one-third and two-thirds of the potential services of land now being used.

One of the most important parameters we employ is the elasticity of the effective labor supply with respect to the wage after taxes. Our estimate of this parameter is based on the work of Martin Feldstein and others that he cites.[2] They observed how much more taxable income U.S. taxpayers reported when the U.S. lowered its marginal income tax rates in the 1980s. Their work suggests that the elasticity of the effective labor supply with respect to the marginal wage after taxes is 1.0. An elasticity of 1.0 would mean that if workers' pay after taxes on the last hour worked rises by 1 percent, then workers will deliver 1 percent more labor effort than previously. However, this value is so large compared to what most economists expect, and we need to apply the number over so great a

---

[2] Martin Feldstein, "The Effect of Marginal Tax Rates on Taxable Income: A Panel Study of the 1986 Tax Reform Act," *Journal of Political Economy* 103 (1995), pp. 551-572.

change in the marginal wage after taxes, that we reduce the value to 0.75, while also considering values of 0.5 and 1.0.

Another parameter is the elasticity of savings with respect to the interest rate after taxes. Economists understand that it is an oversimplification to suppose that there is some general elasticity of savings with respect to interest. The impact of a change in the interest rate will vary in particular with a person's age. An older person will probably save more when the interest rate rises, because the rise in the interest rate implies that future consumption is now less costly than current consumption. This effect also applies to a younger person, but for a younger person the chance to earn compound interest at the new higher rate can add so much to the value of savings at the end of life that the younger person may decide not to save as much, because the amount already saved would yield a superfluity of income in old age. The incorporation of such effects would require a more complex model than we had time to develop. Therefore we incorporate interest effects in our model in terms of the elasticity of savings with respect to one plus the interest rate (the amount of money that a dollar becomes when invested for a year). Our main assumption is that the elasticity of savings with respect to one plus the interest rate is 10, but we also consider values of 5 and 15. A value of 10 implies, roughly, that if the interest rate rises by one percentage point, the quantity of saving will rise by 10 percent.

Saving is also related negatively to a person's assets. Holding income and other characteristics fixed, a person will save less when his assets are greater, because the assets provide for the future, so he can spend more in the present. This is particularly relevant to proposals to collect public revenue from land and other natural opportunities, because such a proposal has a substantial redistributive effect across generations. Under existing institutions, people are born with a right to only a fraction of what they produce and no rights to land. A reduction in taxation of labor increases the share of what a person produces that the person owns. The introduction of public collection of the rent of land transfers the value of ownership of these opportunities from current title holders to the recipients of the benefits of future public expenditures. In other words, a shift to public collection of the value of using natural opportunities makes younger generations and those who are yet to be born richer, and makes older persons among those now alive poorer. Unless there is a perfect appreciation among the living of the benefits to those who are yet unborn, this reduction in the value of the assets of the living leads to an increase in the savings rate. We assume that the elasticity of savings with respect to the value of the assets of the living is -1, but also consider elasticities of -0.5 and -1.5.

The high nominal levels of taxation on capital in several G7 nations make it hard to understand how any saving occurs at all. A large part of the answer is that countries motivate a substantial amount of saving by special devices that exempt particular kinds of saving from taxation - investment tax credits, local development incentives, special rules for pension saving, and so forth. To model this phenomenon, we introduce the effective tax shelter rate for savings, as a parameter. We use a tax rate on savings which is the tax rate otherwise computed, multiplied by one minus this parameter. Our main assumption for this parameter is 0.5, with alternatives of 0.25 and 0.75.

One parameter for which we use just one value is the rate of technological improvement in the economy. We assume that this rate is 1 percent per year.

4. Tables

Our favored and alternative parameter values are shown in Table 6.III below:

Table 6.III
Parameter values

	Character	Favored value	Low	High
Elasticity of substitution	σ	1.5	1.25	2.0
Current land efficiency	ρ	0.5	0.33	0.66
Share of land in asset income	γ	0.33	0.25	0.5
Labor supply elasticity	λ_2	0.75	0.5	1.0
Elasticity of savings with respect to assets	δ_2	-1.0	-1.5	-0.5
Elasticity of savings with respect to one plus the after-tax interest rate	δ_3	10.0	5.0	15.0
Effective tax shelter rate for savings	ϕ	0.5	0.25	0.75
Rate of technical change	g	0.01	-	-

Table 6.IV (below) shows the results based on our first choices for all six parameters. It shows the economic performance in 1993 under existing taxes, and for each country and for each year from 1993 to 1998, it shows the paths of various economic indicators under the assumption that public collection of the rent of land had been introduced on January 1, 1993. The level of government revenue per capita that existed in 1993 is maintained, with any deficiency from taxing land made up by a proportional tax on labor.

The indicators shown are total output, output per capita, the savings rate, the average and marginal tax rates on labor and capital, the change in excess burden in billions of dollars and as percent of 1993 output, the quantities of capital, land, and labor employed in production, the implied labor efficiency, government revenue from taxing land, other government tax revenue, and total government tax revenue.

The principal effect of the shift to public revenue based on the use of natural opportunities occurs in the first year. Output increases between 29 percent and 92 percent in the first year, and then increases more slowly. These increases can be attributed to the doubling of the effective land input and the increases by factors of between 1.3 and nearly 2.7 in the effective labor input. Capital increases only as saving occurs. The savings rate in the first year after the change increases by a factor of between 2.2 and 2.9, and then diminishes as the stocks of assets rise. The decrease in excess burden in the first year varies from 14 percent to 51 percent of. output in 1993. All nations need a continuing tax on labor to maintain existing government revenues.

Applying variations in the parameters to the U.S. yields the following effects. Reducing the elasticity of substitution to 1.25, as shown in Table 6.V.a, increases the labor and savings responses, and therefore increases output and lowers the needed tax on labor. Increasing the elasticity of substitution to 2.0, as shown in Table 6.V.b, has opposite effects. Reducing the estimate of current land efficiency to one-third, as shown in Table 6.VI.a, increases the labor and savings responses, increasing output and reducing the needed tax on labor. Increasing the estimate of current land efficiency to two-thirds, as shown in Table 6.VI.b, has opposite effects. Reducing the estimate of the current share of land in asset income from one-third to one-fourth, as shown in Table 6.VII.a, reduces land inputs, reducing the output and efficiency effects of the tax change. Increasing the estimate of the current share of land in asset income to one-half, as shown in Table 6.VII.b, has opposite effects. Reducing the estimate of the elasticity of the labor supply with respect to the wage from 0.75 to 0.5, as shown in Table 6.VIII.a, reduces the labor response accordingly and increases the tax rate on labor that must be used to maintain the existing public sector. Increasing the elasticity of the labor supply to 1.0, as shown in Table 6.VIII.b, has opposite effects. Reducing the elasticity of savings with respect to assets from -1.0 to -1.5, as shown in Table 6.IX.a, increases the savings response by about 50 percent. Increasing the elasticity to -0.5, as shown in Table 6.IX.b, decreases the savings response by 37 percent. Reducing the elasticity of savings with respect to one plus the interest rate from 10 to 5, as shown in Table 6.X.a, cuts the increase in savings in half. Increasing it to 15, as shown in Table 6.X.b, increases the savings response by 50 percent. Reducing the current effective tax shelter rate for savings from 0.50 to 0.25 means that removing taxes from saving will be even more effective; as shown in Table 6.XI.a, the savings response rises by about 20 percent. Increasing the current tax shelter rate to 75 percent has opposite effects.

5. Conclusion

The removal of taxes from labor and capital and substitution of public revenue from charges for exclusive use of natural opportunities improves economic efficiency through a number of different paths. First, allowing people to keep their full earnings (or at least a larger fraction) induces people to produce much more than they produce now. Second, the removal of taxes from capital, and from the income from capital, induces people to save more. Third, public charges for the use of land and other natural opportunities induces people to economize appropriately on the use of these opportunities when there has been excessive use. Fourth, where natural opportunities have been privatized, public collection of the value of exclusive use improves efficiency by ending the opportunity to gain by speculation. This encourages people to use productively the land and other natural opportunities that have been underused because of speculation.

Table 6.IV.a
U.S.A.

	1993(O)	1993(N)	1994	1995	1996	1997	1998
Output (NDP) ($ bn)	5,495	7,097	7,308	7,468	7,635	7,798	7,961
Output per capita ($)	20,894	26,986	27,508	27,828	28,142	28,432	28,713
Savings rate	0.034	0.082	0.079	0.077	0.074	0.072	0.070
Average tax rate on labor	0.289	0.137	0.132	0.128	0.125	0.122	0.119
Marginal tax rate on labor	0.390	0.137	0.132	0.128	0.125	0.122	0.119
Average tax rate on capital	0.255	0.000	0.000	0.000	0.000	0.000	0.000
Marginal tax rate on capital	0.300	0.000	0.000	0.000	0.000	0.000	0.000
Decrease in excess burden ($ bn)		784	804	817	829	839	848
as percent of 1993 output		0.14	0.15	0.15	0.15	0.15	0.15
Capital services ($ bn)	14,334	14,334	14,915	15,487	16,053	16,613	17,169
Land services (Efficiency units)	9,538	19,076	19,076	19,076	19,076	19,076	19,076
Labor services (Efficiency units)	282	366	378	386	394	403	411
Implied labor efficiency	1						
Government land tax revenue ($ bn)	147	862	879	891	905	917	930
Other government tax revenue ($ bn)	1,383	668	667	670	674	678	683
Total government tax revenue ($ bn)	1,530	1,530	1,545	1,561	1,578	1,595	1,613

Table 6.IV.b
Canada

	1993(O)	1993(N)	1994	1995	1996	1997	1998
Output (NDP) ($ bn)	490	765	792	814	836	857	878
Output per capita ($)	16,348	25,490	26,150	26,600	27,024	27,427	27,810
Savings rate	0.056	0.146	0.137	0.129	0.123	0.117	0.112
Average tax rate on labor	0.415	0.165	0.157	0.151	0.146	0.142	0.138
Marginal tax rate on labor	0.470	0.165	0.157	0.151	0.146	0.142	0.138
Average tax rate on capital	0.297	0.000	0.000	0.000	0.000	0.000	0.000
Marginal tax rate on capital	0.404	0.000	0.000	0.000	0.000	0.000	0.000
Decrease in excess burden ($ bn)		141	143	145	147	148	150
as percent of 1993 output		0.29	0.29	0.30	0.30	0.30	0.31
Capital services ($ bn)	1,786	1,786	1,895	2,000	2,103	2,203	2,302
Land services (Efficiency units)	1,189	2,349	2,349	2,349	2,349	2,349	2,349
Labor services (Efficiency units)	21	37	38	39	40	41	42
Implied labor efficiency	0.709						
Government land tax revenue ($ bn)	16	97	99	101	103	105	106
Other government tax revenue ($ bn)	128	85	84	84	84	85	85
Total government tax revenue ($ bn)	182	182	184	186	187	189	191

Table 6.IV.c
France

	1993 (O)	1993 (N)	1994	1995	1996	1997	1998
Output (NDP) ($ bn)	952	1,831	1,883	1,928	1,972	2,014	2,055
Output per capita ($)	16,409	31,575	32,360	33,037	33,676	34,283	34,863
Savings rate	0.072	0.188	0.174	0.162	0.152	0.144	0.136
Average tax rate on labor	0.410	0.079	0.073	0.069	0.065	0.061	0.057
Marginal tax rate on labor	0.630	0.079	0.073	0.069	0.065	0.061	0.057
Average tax rate on capital	0.303	0.000	0.000	0.000	0.000	0.000	0.000
Marginal tax rate on capital	0.392	0.000	0.000	0.000	0.000	0.000	0.000
Decrease in excess burden ($ bn)		457	459	460	461	462	462
as percent of 1993 output		0.48	0.48	0.48	0.48	0.49	0.49
Capital services ($ bn)	4,927	4,927	5,254	5,567	5,867	6,156	6,436
Land services (Efficiency units)	3,278	6,834	6,834	6,834	6,834	6,834	6,834
Labor services (Efficiency units)	34	81	83	85	86	87	89
Implied labor efficiency	0.658						
Government land tax revenue ($ bn)	31	248	253	257	261	264	268
Other government tax revenue ($ bn)	231	94	91	88	85	83	80
Total government tax revenue ($ bn)	343	343	344	345	346	347	348

Table 6.IV.d
Germany

	1993 (O)	1993 (N)	1994	1995	1996	1997	1998
Output (NDP) ($ bn)	1,178	2,196	2,301	2,391	2,472	2,547	2,617
Output per capita ($)	14,370	26,776	27,989	29,002	29,907	30,731	31,494
Savings rate	0.152	0.386	0.326	0.285	0.255	0.232	0.214
Average tax rate on labor	0.491	0.103	0.092	0.084	0.078	0.072	0.067
Marginal tax rate on labor	0.512	0.103	0.092	0.084	0.078	0.072	0.067
Average tax rate on capital	0.192	0.000	0.000	0.000	0.000	0.000	0.000
Marginal tax rate on capital	0.290	0.000	0.000	0.000	0.000	0.000	0.000
Decrease in excess burden ($ bn)		531	535	538	540	541	542
as percent of 1993 output		0.45	0.45	0.46	0.46	0.46	0.46
Capital services ($ bn)	5,378	5,378	6,128	6,809	7,438	8,029	8,588
Land services (Efficiency units)	3,579	7,674	7,674	7,674	7,674	7,674	7,674
Labor services (Efficiency units)	45	102	105	107	110	112	114
Implied labor efficiency	0.545						
Government land tax revenue ($ bn)	24	291	300	308	315	321	327
Other government tax revenue ($ bn)	253	150	141	135	129	124	119
Total government tax revenue ($ bn)	440	440	442	443	444	445	446

Table 6.IV.e
Italy

	1993 (O)	1993 (N)	1994	1995	1996	1997	1998
Output (NDP) ($ bn)	892	1,707	1,741	1,771	1,801	1,830	1,859
Output per capita ($)	15,460	29,588	30,086	30,529	30,960	31,380	31,789
Savings rate	0.093	0.203	0.195	0.188	0.182	0.176	0.171
Average tax rate on labor	0.509	0.044	0.040	0.037	0.033	0.030	0.027
Marginal tax rate on labor	0.503	0.044	0.040	0.037	0.033	0.030	0.027
Average tax rate on capital	0.287	0.000	0.000	0.000	0.000	0.000	0.000
Marginal tax rate on capital	0.338	0.000	0.000	0.000	0.000	0.000	0.000
Decrease in excess burden ($ bn)		451	451	452	452	452	452
as percent of 1993 output		0.51	0.51	0.51	0.51	0.51	0.51
Capital services ($ bn)	9,203	9,203	9,543	9,877	10,205	10,527	10,844
Land services (Efficiency units)	6,124	12,809	12,809	12,809	12,809	12,809	12,809
Labor services (Efficiency units)	18	48	49	50	51	51	52
Implied labor efficiency	0.413						
Government land tax revenue ($ bn)	21	292	296	299	302	306	309
Other government tax revenue ($ bn)	179	42	40	37	35	32	30
Total government tax revenue ($ bn)	334	334	335	336	337	338	339

Table 6.IV.f
Japan

	1993 (O)	1993 (N)	1994	1995	1996	1997	1998
Output (NDP) ($ bn)	2,134	3,669	3,943	4,152	4,328	4,485	4,627
Output per capita ($)	17,071	29,355	31,447	33,003	34,296	35,421	36,427
Savings rate	0.196	0.574	0.405	0.322	0.272	0.238	0.213
Average tax rate on labor	0.281	0.067	0.056	0.049	0.043	0.039	0.035
Marginal tax rate on labor	0.478	0.067	0.056	0.049	0.043	0.039	0.035
Average tax rate on capital	0.263	0.000	0.000	0.000	0.000	0.000	0.000
Marginal tax rate on capital	0.344	0.000	0.000	0.000	0.000	0.000	0.000
Decrease in excess burden ($ bn)		699	705	707	709	709	709
as percent of 1993 output		0.33	0.33	0.33	0.33	0.33	0.33
Capital services ($ bn)	5,824	5,824	7,421	8,758	9,935	11,001	11,987
Land services (Efficiency units)	3,875	7,749	7,749	7,749	7,749	7,749	7,749
Labor services (Efficiency units)	107	210	218	225	230	235	240
Implied labor efficiency	0.671						
Government land tax revenue ($ bn)	59	411	431	446	459	470	480
Other government tax revenue ($ bn)	393	176	157	144	133	124	116
Total government tax revenue ($ bn)	587	587	589	590	592	594	596

Table 6.IV.g
United Kingdom

	1993 (O)	1993 (N)	1994	1995	1996	1997	1998
Output (NDP) ($ bn)	883	1,599	1,630	1,657	1,684	1,711	1,737
Output per capita ($)	14,972	27,105	27,564	27,973	28,370	28,756	29,132
Savings rate	0.038	0.100	0.096	0.091	0.088	0.084	0.081
Average tax rate on labor	0.348	0.070	0.066	0.063	0.060	0.057	0.054
Marginal tax rate on labor	0.480	0.070	0.066	0.063	0.060	0.057	0.054
Average tax rate on capital	0.276	0.000	0.000	0.000	0.000	0.000	0.000
Marginal tax rate on capital	0.392	0.000	0.000	0.000	0.000	0.000	0.000
Decrease in excess burden ($ bn)		352	353	354	354	354	355
as percent of 1993 output		0.40	0.40	0.40	0.40	0.40	0.40
Capital services ($ bn)	3,828	3,828	3,984	4,136	4,283	4,427	4,568
Land services (Efficiency units)	2,547	5,096	5,096	5,096	5,096	5,096	5,096
Labor services (Efficiency units)	35	76	77	78	79	80	81
Implied labor efficiency	0.558						
Government land tax revenue ($ bn)	26	205	208	210	213	215	217
Other government tax revenue ($ bn)	168	74	72	71	69	67	66
Total government tax revenue ($ bn)	280	280	280	281	282	282	283

Table 6.V.a
U.S.A., elasticity of substitution σ = 1.25

	1993 (O)	1993 (N)	1994	1995	1996	1997	1998
Output (NDP) ($ bn)	5,495	7,028	7,154	7,233	7,319	7,403	7,487
Output per capita ($)	20,894	26,723	26,929	26,952	26,978	26,992	27,005
Savings rate	0.034	0.000	0.000	0.000	0.000	0.000	0.000
Average tax rate on labor	0.289	0.150	0.147	0.145	0.144	0.142	0.141
Marginal tax rate on labor	0.390	0.150	0.147	0.145	0.144	0.142	0.141
Average tax rate on capital	0.255	0.000	0.000	0.000	0.000	0.000	0.000
Marginal tax rate on capital	0.300	0.000	0.000	0.000	0.000	0.000	0.000
Decrease in excess burden ($ bn)		760	779	789	800	809	818
as percent of 1993 output		0.14	0.14	0.14	0.15	0.15	0.15
Capital services ($ bn)	14,334	14,334	14,336	14,337	14,339	14,340	14,342
Land services (Efficiency units)	9,538	19,076	19,076	19,076	19,076	19,076	19,076
Labor services (Efficiency units)	282	362	371	377	384	390	397
Implied labor efficiency	1						
Government land tax revenue ($ bn)	147	806	818	825	833	841	848
Other government tax revenue ($ bn)	1,383	723	727	736	745	755	765
Total government tax revenue ($ bn)	1,530	1,530	1,545	1,561	1,578	1,595	1,613

Table 6.V.b
U.S.A., elasticity of substitution σ = 2.00

	1993 (O)	1993 (N)	1994	1995	1996	1997	1998
Output (NDP) ($ bn)	5,495	7,186	7,320	7,403	7,495	7,584	7,674
Output per capita ($)	20,894	27,324	27,552	27,585	27,624	27,650	27,678
Savings rate	0.034	0.000	0.000	0.000	0.000	0.000	0.000
Average tax rate on labor	0.289	0.121	0.119	0.118	0.117	0.116	0.116
Marginal tax rate on labor	0.390	0.121	0.119	0.118	0.117	0.116	0.116
Average tax rate on capital	0.255	0.000	0.000	0.000	0.000	0.000	0.000
Marginal tax rate on capital	0.300	0.000	0.000	0.000	0.000	0.000	0.000
Decrease in excess burden ($ bn)		814	829	838	846	854	861
as percent of 1993 output		0.15	0.15	0.15	0.15	0.16	0.16
Capital services ($ bn)	14,334	14,334	14,336	14,337	14,339	14,341	14,342
Land services (Efficiency units)	9,538	19,076	19,076	19,076	19,076	19,076	19,076
Labor services (Efficiency units)	282	371	381	387	394	401	408
Implied labor efficiency	1						
Government land tax revenue ($ bn)	147	933	941	946	952	958	964
Other government tax revenue ($ bn)	1,383	597	604	615	626	638	649
Total government tax revenue ($ bn)	1,530	1,530	1,545	1,561	1,578	1,595	1,613

Table 6.VI.a
U.S.A., current land efficiency ρ = ¹/₃

	1993 (O)	1993 (N)	1994	1995	1996	1997	1998
Output (NDP) ($ bn)	5,495	7,765	7,996	8,173	8,356	8,534	8,712
Output per capita ($)	20,894	29,526	30,098	30,455	30,800	31,116	31,421
Savings rate	0.034	0.087	0.083	0.079	0.076	0.074	0.071
Average tax rate on labor	0.289	0.092	0.087	0.084	0.082	0.080	0.078
Marginal tax rate on labor	0.390	0.092	0.087	0.084	0.082	0.080	0.078
Average tax rate on capital	0.255	0.000	0.000	0.000	0.000	0.000	0.000
Marginal tax rate on capital	0.300	0.000	0.000	0.000	0.000	0.000	0.000
Decrease in excess burden ($ bn)		1,200	1,214	1,222	1,229	1,235	1,239
as percent of 1993 output		0.22	0.22	0.22	0.22	0.22	0.23
Capital services ($ bn)	14,334	14,334	14,998	15,647	16,285	16,913	17,533
Land services (Efficiency units)	9,538	28,614	28,614	28,614	28,614	28,614	28,614
Labor services (Efficiency units)	282	387	399	407	416	425	433
Implied labor efficiency	1						
Government land tax revenue ($ bn)	147	1,047	1,068	1,084	1,100	1,115	1,131
Other government tax revenue ($ bn)	1,383	483	478	478	479	480	482
Total government tax revenue ($ bn)	1,530	1,530	1,545	1,561	1,578	1,595	1,613

Table 6.VI.b
U.S.A., current land efficiency ρ = ²/₃

	1993 (O)	1993 (N)	1994	1995	1996	1997	1998
Output (NDP) ($ bn)	5,495	6,683	6,883	7,033	7,191	7,345	7,499
Output per capita ($)	20,894	25,412	25,907	26,208	26,504	26,779	27,048
Savings rate	0.034	0.080	0.077	0.075	0.073	0.071	0.069
Average tax rate on labor	0.289	0.168	0.162	0.158	0.154	0.150	0.147
Marginal tax rate on labor	0.390	0.168	0.162	0.158	0.154	0.150	0.147
Average tax rate on capital	0.255	0.000	0.000	0.000	0.000	0.000	0.000
Marginal tax rate on capital	0.300	0.000	0.000	0.000	0.000	0.000	0.000
Decrease in excess burden ($ bn)		525	550	565	580	593	605
as percent of 1993 output		0.10	0.10	0.10	0.11	0.11	0.11
Capital services ($ bn)	14,334	14,334	14,865	15,391	15,914	16,433	16,950
Land services (Efficiency units)	9,538	14,307	14,307	14,307	14,307	14,307	14,307
Labor services (Efficiency units)	282	352	364	371	380	388	396
Implied labor efficiency	1						
Government land tax revenue ($ bn)	147	752	767	778	790	801	812
Other government tax revenue ($ bn)	1,383	778	779	783	789	795	801
Total government tax revenue ($ bn)	1,530	1,530	1,545	1,561	1,578	1,595	1,613

Table 6.VII.a
U.S.A., share of land in asset income γ = 0.25

	1993 (O)	1993 (N)	1994	1995	1996	1997	1998
Output (NDP) ($ bn)	5,495	6,707	6,910	7,065	7,226	7,385	7,545
Output per capita ($)	20,894	25,502	26,010	26,324	26,636	26,927	27,212
Savings rate	0.034	0.071	0.069	0.067	0.066	0.064	0.063
Average tax rate on labor	0.289	0.197	0.190	0.185	0.181	0.176	0.172
Marginal tax rate on labor	0.390	0.197	0.190	0.185	0.181	0.176	0.172
Average tax rate on capital	0.255	0.000	0.000	0.000	0.000	0.000	0.000
Marginal tax rate on capital	0.300	0.000	0.000	0.000	0.000	0.000	0.000
Decrease in excess burden ($ bn)		611	640	659	677	693	709
as percent of 1993 output		0.11	0.12	0.12	0.12	0.13	0.13
Capital services ($ bn)	14,334	14,334	14,813	15,289	15,764	16,239	16,712
Land services (Efficiency units)	6,133	12,267	12,267	12,267	12,267	12,267	12,267
Labor services (Efficiency units)	282	346	358	366	374 ·	383	391
Implied labor efficiency	1						
Government land tax revenue ($ bn)	110	622	635	644	654	664	673
Other government tax revenue ($ bn)	1,420	908	911	917	924	932	940
Total government tax revenue ($ bn)	1,530	1,530	1,545	1,561	1,578	1,595	1,613

Table 6.VII.b
U.S.A., share of land in asset income γ = 0.5

	1993 (O)	1993 (N)	1994	1995	1996	1997	1998
Output (NDP) ($ bn)	5,495	7,852	8,082	8,255	8,432	8,603	8,772
Output per capita ($)	20,894	29,856	30,420	30,759	31,080	31,368	31,640
Savings rate	0.034	0.119	0.111	0.105	0.099	0.095	0.090
Average tax rate on labor	0.289	0.027	0.024	0.023	0.022	0.021	0.020
Marginal tax rate on labor	0.390	0.027	0.024	0.023	0.022	0.021	0.020
Average tax rate on capital	0.255	0.000	0.000	0.000	0.000	0.000	0.000
Marginal tax rate on capital	0.300	0.000	0.000	0.000	0.000	0.000	0.000
Decrease in excess burden ($ bn)		1,096	1,099	1,100	1,100	1,098	1,096
as percent of 1993 output		0.20	0.20	0.20	0.20	0.20	0.20
Capital services ($ bn)	14,334	14,334	15,232	16,095	16,931	17,744	18,537
Land services (Efficiency units)	21,441	42,881	42,881	42,881	42,881	42,881	42,881
Labor services (Efficiency units)	282	402	414	422	431	439	448
Implied labor efficiency	1						
Government land tax revenue ($ bn)	220	1,382	1,409	1,429	1,450	1,469	1,488
Other government tax revenue ($ bn)	1,310	147	136	132	129	126	124
Total government tax revenue ($ bn)	1,530	1,530	1,545	1,561	1,578	1,595	1,613

Table 6.VIII.a
U.S.A., labor supply elasticity $\lambda_2 = 0.5$

	1993 (O)	1993 (N)	1994	1995	1996	1997	1998
Output (NDP) ($ bn)	5,495	6,688	6,864	6,993	7,128	7,259	7,391
Output per capita ($)	20,894	25,428	25,835	26,055	26,272	26,467	26,656
Savings rate	0.034	0.080	0.077	0.075	0.072	0.070	0.069
Average tax rate on labor	0.289	0.154	0.149	0.146	0.143	0.140	0.138
Marginal tax rate on labor	0.390	0.154	0.149	0.146	0.143	0.140	0.138
Average tax rate on capital	0.255	0.000	0.000	0.000	0.000	0.000	0.000
Marginal tax rate on capital	0.300	0.000	0.000	0.000	0.000	0.000	0.000
Decrease in excess burden ($ bn)		674	693	704	715	724	733
as percent of 1993 output		0.12	0.13	0.13	0.13	0.13	0.13
Capital services ($ bn)	14,334	14,334	14,863	15,385	15,901	16,412	16,918
Land services (Efficiency units)	9,538	19,076	19,076	19,076	19,076	19,076	19,076
Labor services (Efficiency units)	282	335	345	351	357	364	370
Implied labor efficiency	1						
Government land tax revenue ($ bn)	147	828	843	853	864	875	885
Other government tax revenue ($ bn)	1,383	702	703	708	714	721	728
Total government tax revenue ($ bn)	1,530	1,530	1,545	1,561	1,578	1,595	1,613

Table 6.VIII.b
U.S.A., labor supply elasticity $\lambda_2 = 1$

	1993 (O)	1993 (N)	1994	1995	1996	1997	1998
Output (NDP) ($ bn)	5,495	7,533	7,783	7,979	8,181	8,379	8,578
Output per capita ($)	20,894	28,644	29,295	29,729	30,154	30,552	30,938
Savings rate	0.034	0.085	0.082	0.079	0.076	0.073	0.071
Average tax rate on labor	0.289	0.121	0.116	0.112	0.108	0.105	0.102
Marginal tax rate on labor	0.390	0.121	0.116	0.112	0.108	0.105	0.102
Average tax rate on capital	0.255	0.000	0.000	0.000	0.000	0.000	0.000
Marginal tax rate on capital	0.300	0.000	0.000	0.000	0.000	0.000	0.000
Decrease in excess burden ($ bn)		896	917	930	943	953	962
as percent of 1993 output		0.16	0.17	0.17	0.17	0.17	0.18
Capital services ($ bn)	14,334	14,334	14,972	15,600	16,220	16,835	17,444
Land services (Efficiency units)	9,538	19,076	19,076	19,076	19,076	19,076	19,076
Labor services (Efficiency units)	282	399	413	424	434	445	456
Implied labor efficiency	1						
Government land tax revenue ($ bn)	147	897	916	932	947	962	978
Other government tax revenue ($ bn)	1,383	633	629	630	631	633	635
Total government tax revenue ($ bn)	1,530	1,530	1,545	1,561	1,578	1,595	1,613

Table 6.IX.a
U.S.A., elasticity of savings with respect to assets δ_2 = -1.5

	1993 (O)	1993 (N)	1994	1995	1996	1997	1998
Output (NDP) ($ bn)	5,495	7,097	7,328	7,504	7,684	7,857	8,028
Output per capita ($)	20,894	26,986	27,583	27,961	28,321	28,647	28,956
Savings rate	0.034	0.106	0.099	0.092	0.087	0.082	0.078
Average tax rate on labor	0.289	0.137	0.131	0.127	0.123	0.120	0.117
Marginal tax rate on labor	0.390	0.137	0.131	0.127	0.123	0.120	0.117
Average tax rate on capital	0.255	0.000	0.000	0.000	0.000	0.000	0.000
Marginal tax rate on capital	0.300	0.000	0.000	0.000	0.000	0.000	0.000
Decrease in excess burden ($ bn)		784	805	818	830	841	850
as percent of 1993 output		0.14	0.15	0.15	0.15	0.15	0.15
Capital services ($ bn)	14,334	14,334	15,057	15,748	16,414	17,058	17,683
Land services (Efficiency units)	9,538	19,076	19,076	19,076	19,076	19,076	19,076
Labor services (Efficiency units)	282	366	378	386	395	404	413
Implied labor efficiency	1						
Government land tax revenue ($ bn)	147	862	880	894	908	922	935
Other government tax revenue ($ bn)	1,383	668	665	667	670	673	677
Total government tax revenue ($ bn)	1,530	1,530	1,545	1,561	1,578	1,595	1,613

Table 6.IX.b
U.S.A., elasticity of savings with respect to assets δ_2 = -0.5

	1993 (O)	1993 (N)	1994	1995	1996	1997	1998
Output (NDP) ($ bn)	5,495	7,097	7,292	7,437	7,591	7,743	7,897
Output per capita ($)	20,894	26,986	27,446	27,713	27,981	28,232	28,481
Savings rate	0.034	0.064	0.063	0.063	0.062	0.061	0.061
Average tax rate on labor	0.289	0.137	0.132	0.129	0.126	0.123	0.121
Marginal tax rate on labor	0.390	0.137	0.132	0.129	0.126	0.123	0.121
Average tax rate on capital	0.255	0.000	0.000	0.000	0.000	0.000	0.000
Marginal tax rate on capital	0.300	0.000	0.000	0.000	0.000	0.000	0.000
Decrease in excess burden ($ bn)		784	804	816	827	837	846
as percent of 1993 output		0.14	0.15	0.15	0.15	0.15	0.15
Capital services ($ bn)	14,334	14,334	14,795	15,260	15,730	16,205	16,685
Land services (Efficiency units)	9,538	19,076	19,076	19,076	19,076	19,076	19,076
Labor services (Efficiency units)	282	366	377	385	393	401	409
Implied labor efficiency	1						
Government land tax revenue ($ bn)	147	862	877	889	901	913	925
Other government tax revenue ($ bn)	1,383	668	668	672	677	682	688
Total government tax revenue ($ bn)	1,530	1,530	1,545	1,561	1,578	1,595	1,613

Table 6.X.a
U.S.A., elasticity of savings with respect to one plus the after-tax interest rate $\delta_3 = 5$

	1993 (O)	1993 (N)	1994	1995	1996	1997	1998
Output (NDP) ($ bn)	5,495	7,097	7,295	7,444	7,600	7,753	7,906
Output per capita ($)	20,894	26,986	27,460	27,737	28,012	28,267	28,517
Savings rate	0.034	0.069	0.067	0.065	0.064	0.062	0.061
Average tax rate on labor	0.289	0.137	0.132	0.129	0.126	0.123	0.120
Marginal tax rate on labor	0.390	0.137	0.132	0.129	0.126	0.123	0.120
Average tax rate on capital	0.255	0.000	0.000	0.000	0.000	0.000	0.000
Marginal tax rate on capital	0.300	0.000	0.000	0.000	0.000	0.000	0.000
Decrease in excess burden ($ bn)		784	804	816	828	838	846
as percent of 1993 output		0.14	0.15	0.15	0.15	0.15	0.15
Capital services ($ bn)	14,334	14,334	14,822	15,308	15,793	16,276	16,759
Land services (Efficiency units)	9,538	19,076	19,076	19,076	19,076	19,076	19,076
Labor services (Efficiency units)	282	366	377	385	393	401	410
Implied labor efficiency	1						
Government land tax revenue ($ bn)	147	862	878	889	902	914	926
Other government tax revenue ($ bn)	1,383	668	668	672	676	682	687
Total government tax revenue ($ bn)	1,530	1,530	1,545	1,561	1,578	1,595	1,613

Table 6.X.b
U.S.A., elasticity of savings with respect to one plus the after-tax interest rate $\delta_3 = 15$

	1993 (O)	1993 (N)	1994	1995	1996	1997	1998
Output (NDP) ($ bn)	5,495	7,097	7,323	7,496	7,674	7,848	8,020
Output per capita ($)	20,894	26,986	27,564	27,932	28,287	28,614	28,927
Savings rate	0.034	0.099	0.094	0.089	0.085	0.082	0.079
Average tax rate on labor	0.289	0.137	0.131	0.127	0.124	0.120	0.117
Marginal tax rate on labor	0.390	0.137	0.131	0.127	0.124	0.120	0.117
Average tax rate on capital	0.255	0.000	0.000	0.000	0.000	0.000	0.000
Marginal tax rate on capital	0.300	0.000	0.000	0.000	0.000	0.000	0.000
Decrease in excess burden ($ bn)		784	805	818	830	840	849
as percent of 1993 output		0.14	0.15	0.15	0.15	0.15	0.15
Capital services ($ bn)	14,334	14,334	15,022	15,691	16,346	16,988	17,621
Land services (Efficiency units)	9,538	19,076	19,076	19,076	19,076	19,076	19,076
Labor services (Efficiency units)	282	366	378	386	395	404	412
Implied labor efficiency	1						
Government land tax revenue ($ bn)	147	862	880	894	908	921	935
Other government tax revenue ($ bn)	1,383	668	666	668	671	674	678
Total government tax revenue ($ bn)	1,530	1,530	1,545	1,561	1,578	1,595	1,613

Table 6.XI.a
U.S.A.,effective tax shelter rate for savings φ = 0.25

	1993 (O)	1993 (N)	1994	1995	1996	1997	1998
Output (NDP) ($ bn)	5,495	7,097	7,318	7,486	7,661	7,831	8,001
Output per capita ($)	20,894	26,986	27,543	27,895	28,237	28,553	28,858
Savings rate	0.034	0.092	0.089	0.085	0.082	0.079	0.076
Average tax rate on labor	0.289	0.137	0.131	0.128	0.124	0.121	0.118
Marginal tax rate on labor	0.390	0.137	0.131	0.128	0.124	0.121	0.118
Average tax rate on capital	0.255	0.000	0.000	0.000	0.000	0.000	0.000
Marginal tax rate on capital	0.450	0.000	0.000	0.000	0.000	0.000	0.000
Decrease in excess burden ($ bn)		784	805	817	829	840	849
as percent of 1993 output		0.14	0.15	0.15	0.15	0.15	0.15
Capital services ($ bn)	14,334	14,334	14,982	15,618	16,244	16,862	17,474
Land services (Efficiency units)	9,538	19,076	19,076	19,076	19,076	19,076	19,076
Labor services (Efficiency units)	282	366	378	386	395	403	412
Implied labor efficiency	1						
Government land tax revenue ($ bn)	147	862	879	893	907	920	933
Other government tax revenue ($ bn)	1,383	668	666	668	672	675	680
Total government tax revenue ($ bn)	1,530	1,530	1,545	1,561	1,578	1,595	1,613

Table 6.XI.b
U.S.A.,effective tax shelter rate for savings φ = 0.75

	1993 (O)	1993 (N)	1994	1995	1996	1997	1998
Output (NDP) ($ bn)	5,495	7,097	7,300	7,452	7,612	7,768	7,925
Output per capita ($)	20,894	26,986	27,477	27,769	28,056	28,322	28,582
Savings rate	0.034	0.073	0.071	0.069	0.067	0.065	0.064
Average tax rate on labor	0.289	0.137	0.132	0.129	0.125	0.123	0.120
Marginal tax rate on labor	0.390	0.137	0.132	0.129	0.125	0.123	0.120
Average tax rate on capital	0.255	0.000	0.000	0.000	0.000	0.000	0.000
Marginal tax rate on capital	0.150	0.000	0.000	0.000	0.000	0.000	0.000
Decrease in excess burden ($ bn)		784	804	816	828	838	847
as percent of 1993 output		0.14	0.15	0.15	0.15	0.15	0.15
Capital services ($ bn)	14,334	14,334	14,855	15,370	15,881	16,389	16,894
Land services (Efficiency units)	9,538	19,076	19,076	19,076	19,076	19,076	19,076
Labor services (Efficiency units)	282	366	377	385	394	402	410
Implied labor efficiency	1						
Government land tax revenue ($ bn)	147	862	878	890	903	915	927
Other government tax revenue ($ bn)	1,383	668	668	671	676	680	686
Total government tax revenue ($ bn)	1,530	1,530	1,545	1,561	1,578	1,595	1,613

Technical Appendix

THE RESULTS in the chapter were derived from a general equilibrium model for the economies of the G7 countries. Because we examine only a simultaneous tax shift in all countries, and because it proved to be too difficult to obtain reliable data for an eighth sector that would represent the rest of the world, we decided not to incorporate labor and capital flows among the countries into our model, but to treat each economy as a separate entity. This appendix describes the economic model and the method of calibrating the model parameters to fit the real-world data.

A.1. The model

Each economy is assumed to consist of a private sector that produces, consumes, and saves, and a public sector that imposes taxes on the factors of production to finance public consumption.

The private sector uses three factors of production (land services, T, labor services, L, and capital services, K) to produce the homogenous output Q according to the production function[3]

$$Q = g(aT^\alpha + bL^\alpha + cK^\alpha)^{\frac{1}{\alpha}}. \qquad (6.1)$$

where g is a factor that symbolizes technology and it is used to introduce exogenous growth into the model.

The returns to the three input factors (the rent of land, R, the wage, W, and the interest rate, I) are obtained as the first derivatives of the production function with respect to the three factors. For example, the wage is given by

$$\frac{dQ}{dL} = g(aT^\alpha + bL^\alpha + cK^\alpha)^{\frac{1}{\alpha} - 1} bL^{\alpha - 1} = W. \qquad (6.2)$$

The share of output that is paid to each factor can be calculated by multiplying each of the derivatives by the factor of production; for example, the share of output that is paid to labor, s_L, can be determined as

$$s_L = L\frac{dQ}{dL} = \frac{bL^\alpha}{(aT^\alpha + bL^\alpha + cK^\alpha)}Q. \qquad (6.3)$$

The demand function for each factor is derived by setting the derivatives in equations of the form of equation 6.2 equal to zero and then solving the equations for T, L, and K, respectively.

A certain stock T_0 of land services is available in each economy, yet the

---

[3] This production function has a constant elasticity of substitution between any two of the three factors of $\sigma = 1/(1-\alpha)$.

incentive to put land into production rather than to withhold its services from the market for speculative reasons depends on the marginal tax on land, $MTAX_T$, that is levied on land. The amount of land that is put into production is determined according to

$$T^S = T_0 \cdot e^{-\tau(1+MTAX_T)} \ .$$ (6.4)

If land is not taxed, the proportion $(1-e^{-\tau})$ of the total services are withheld from production, and only $e^{-\tau}$ percent are made available. If 100 percent of the value of land services is collected as taxes, then the total stock T_0 is put into production. The value of τ is calculated by assuming that the current property tax produces a ratio of currently used land services to potential land services equal to ρ, a parameter of the model.

The supply of labor depends on the after-tax wage $W(1 - MTAX_L)$, and is given by

$$L^S = \lambda_1(W(1- MTAX_L))^{\lambda_2} \ .$$ (6.5)

Time constraints and the lack of suitable data for all countries prevented us from using a more realistic labor supply function that would make an individual's labor supply decision the outcome of an intertemporal maximization of a function of consumption and leisure.

While the stock of capital is fixed at the beginning of each period, the supply of capital for the next period is determined by the savings function. Output can be either consumed or saved (transformed into new capital), and the decision to save depends on the after-tax interest rate, on output, and on the stock of assets, A, which is calculated as the sum of the stock of capital and the market value of land. The market value of land is the after-tax rent of land, discounted by the difference between the after-tax interest rate and the rate at which land grows in value over time, which is assumed to be 2 percent. We assume that the elasticity of saving with respect to output is equal to 1 and with respect to assets equal to δ_2, which permits us to calculate net saving (saving beyond the amount that is necessary to replace the capital that has been used up during the production process) as

$$S = \delta_1 QA^{\delta_2}(1+ I(1- MTAX_K))^{\delta_3}.$$ (6.6)

At the end of each period S is added to the stock of capital.

Government revenue is calculated as the sum over factors of the total return to the factor, multiplied by its average tax rate, and it is assumed to grow at the rate of population growth. Government pension schemes are treated as half a tax, and half investment for future income.

The change in the excess burden of taxation is calculated as the difference between the additional output that is produced after the taxes on labor and capital are removed or reduced, and the integral of the supply price over the additional amounts of labor and capital that were used to produce the additional output.

A.2. Data and calibration of the model

To evaluate the model we collected data regarding the stock of land, labor, and capital, output, consumption, labor supply, savings, government spending, and average and marginal tax rates for each country, and used this information to calibrate the ten model parameters a, b, c, α, τ, λ_1, λ_2, δ_1, δ_2, δ_3.

Data collection

Data for the Gross Domestic Product, capital consumption allowances, private consumption, public consumption, the capital stock in the U.S. and the compensation of employees in each country are available from the OECD.[4] Information about net savings and labor force and demographic data for each country were obtained from the World Bank.[5] All values that were expressed in national currencies were converted into U.S. dollars on the base of OECD estimates of the purchasing power parities between the national currencies and the U.S. dollar.[6]

The average tax rates on labor and assets were calculated from the OECD revenue statistics.[7] We determined the average income tax and the average sales tax as the ratios of income tax revenue and sales tax revenue to net domestic product (NDP), the average payroll tax as the ratio of payroll tax revenue to labor income, and the average property tax as the ratio of tax revenue to asset income. The sum of the individual income tax, the payroll tax, and the sales tax yielded the average tax on labor, and the sum of the corporate income tax, the property tax, and the sales tax yielded the average tax on assets. Because countries try to stimulate saving by making certain assets tax exempt, we multiplied the

---

[4] OECD, *National Accounts*, 1995.
[5] The World Bank, *World Development Indicators*, 1997.
[6] OECD, *Purchasing Power Parities and Real Expenditures*, 1993.
[7] OECD, *Revenue Statistics*: 1965 - 1996, 1997.

average tax rates on assets by $(1-\phi)$, where ϕ is the fraction of taxes that are avoided. We assume that ϕ is equal to 0.5, but we also experimented with $\phi=0.25$ and $\phi=0.75$.

To estimate average marginal tax rates for labor and assets we first calculated the average household income as NDP per household, by assuming that the average household consists of 2.5 persons. We then used each country's income distribution[8] to divide the economies into population quintiles, and determined the gross income for each quintile. To obtain taxable income we assumed that the average household can claim deductions and exemptions of one-third of its gross income. From the information in Coopers and Lybrand about different tax brackets for various income levels we obtained the average marginal federal and local tax rates for each quintile, as well as information about social security and other payroll taxes.[9] The total marginal tax on labor for each quintile was then calculated as the sum of the federal and local income taxes, sales taxes, payroll taxes, and half of social security, and the total marginal tax on assets was calculated as the sum of the federal and local income taxes, the sales tax, and the property tax.[10] Taking account of the fact that excess burden is roughly proportional to the square of the tax rate, the effective average marginal tax rates could now be obtained as the square root of the sum of the squares of the marginal tax rates for the quintiles, weighted by the share of labor income and asset income, respectively, of the quintile. We obtained the income shares by calculating each quintile's asset income from the economy's total asset income and the distribution of wealth within the economy;[11] the labor income was then determined as the difference between the quintile's total income and the quintile's asset income.

Parameter calibration

A. The parameters of the production function

Because it is reasonable to assume that all countries have the same production function when inputs are properly measured, we calibrated the

---

[8] The World Bank, *World Development Indicators*, 1997.

[9] Coopers and Lybrand International Tax Network, *International Tax Summaries*, New York: John Wiley & Sons, Inc (1993).

[10] The marginal and average tax rates for sales taxes and property taxes are identical because neither tax is progressive.

[11] Because the distribution of wealth was available only for the U.S. and Canada, we used the average of these two distributions for each country. This information reflects 1983 and 1984 data, and can be found in Edward N. Wolff, *Economics of Poverty, Inequality, and Discrimination*, Cincinnati, OH: Southwestern College (1997), p.387.

production parameters a, b, and c for the U.S., and used them for all seven economies. Similarly, we initially assumed a uniform value of 1.5 for the elasticity of substitution, σ, which results in $\alpha = 1/3$, but we also investigated the effects of $\sigma = 1.25$ and $\sigma = 2$.

Labor supply L was computed as the product of the population between ages 15 and 64, the labor force participation rate, the hours worked per year, and the productivity of labor. This productivity was set to 1 for the U.S., and the productivity of labor in the other countries was set to match Net Domestic Product (NDP) in each country, given a, b, c, and the share of output going to labor. From the National Accounts we obtained a measure of the stock of capital services for the U.S. and the share of output that is paid to labor in each country; we assumed that the proportion γ of the remainder is paid for the services of land and $(1-\gamma)$ for the services of capital. Our favored estimate of γ is one-third, but we also tried $\gamma = 0.25$ and $\gamma = 0.5$.

This information enabled us to calculate the selling price of land in the U.S. as the present value of the return to land, discounted at the after-tax return to capital minus the rate at which land grows in value over time (2 percent). Equations of the form of equation 6.3 could now be solved for the parameters a, b, and c, and equations of the form of equation 6.2 yielded the marginal return to each factor.[12]

With the shares of factor payments, the three output parameters, and the estimate of NDP in each country, it was now possible to determine the stocks of capital, the flows of land services, and the labor efficiencies for the other countries from equations of the form of equation 6.3.

B. The parameter of the supply of land services function.

To determine the values of τ we calculated an implicit asset tax rate as the ratio of the government's asset tax revenue to the sum of the pre-tax returns to land and capital for each country. We initially assumed that only $\rho = 0.5$ of the potential land services are currently used, so that $T_0 = 2 \cdot T$, which enabled us to determine τ for each country from equation 6.4. We also investigated the possibilities that one-third or two-thirds of land services are currently used, and changed our estimates of τ accordingly.

C. The parameters of the supply of labor function.

The elasticity of labor supply can be derived from what Martin Feldstein

---

[12] NDP was known for each of the seven countries, and from equation 6.1 it follows that $(a T^{\alpha} + b L^{\alpha} + c K^{\alpha}) = \text{NDP}^{\alpha}$.

has called the elasticity of pre-tax income with respect to the after-tax rate. This elasticity, η_M, is defined as $\partial M/\partial X \cdot X/M$, where M is gross income and X is the share of income that is not taken by federal income taxes at the margin. The following algebraic transformations convert the expression for the elasticity into an equation for the change of labor supply L as a result of a change in X:

$$\frac{\partial M}{M} = \eta_M \frac{\partial X}{X}$$

$$\Leftrightarrow \quad \frac{\partial L}{L} + \frac{\partial W}{W} = \eta_M \frac{\partial X}{X}$$

$$\Leftrightarrow \quad \frac{\partial L}{L} + \frac{\partial W}{\partial L} \frac{L}{W} \frac{\partial L}{L} = \eta_M \frac{\partial X}{X} \tag{6.7}$$

$$\Leftrightarrow \quad \frac{\partial L}{L} (1 + \eta_{DL}) = \eta_M \frac{\partial X}{X}$$

$$\Leftrightarrow \quad \frac{\partial L}{\partial X} = \eta_M \frac{L}{X(1+\eta_{DL})},$$

where η_{DL} is the elasticity of the wage with respect to labor supply. Note that the marginal tax rate on labor in equation 6.5, $MTAX_L$, is the sum of the federal income tax rate X and the state and local income tax rate H, and can be written as $X + H$. The first derivative of equation 6.5 with respect to X is $\partial L/\partial X = \lambda_2 \, L/(X-H)$, which can be used in equation 6.7 to yield an expression of the elasticity of labor supply:

$$\lambda_2 = \frac{\eta_M (X - H)}{X(1+\eta_{DL})}, \tag{6.8}$$

where the only unknowns are the elasticities. The wage elasticity of labor demand can be determined by calculating the derivative of the wage equation 6.2 with respect to a change in labor demand, and by multiplying the result by L/W. Our estimate of η_M is based on the results of Martin Feldstein, who estimates elasticities between 1.04 and 1.48, based on comparisons of different groups. We extrapolated from his comparison of persons with medium and high marginal tax rate to estimate an elasticity of income with respect to the after-tax rate of 0.94 for the average tax payer in the U.S.

The resulting estimate for the wage elasticity of labor supply, λ_2, was 0.9911 for the U.S. Because we did not have any estimates of the tax elasticity of income for countries other than the U.S., we decided initially to set λ_2 equal to 1 in all countries. When we saw what large increases in labor supply that implied for high-tax nations, we lowered the estimate of the labor supply elasticity to 0.75. Knowing the wage rate, the marginal tax rate, and λ_2, we could determine λ_1 for each country so that equation 6.5 would yield the labor supply as calculated in part A.

D. The parameters of the savings function.

A reasonable guess of the elasticity of savings with respect to assets, δ_2, seemed to be -1, so that an increase in an economy's assets of 1 percentage point would result in a reduction of the amount of saving of 1 percent. We also calibrated the model with $\delta_2 = -1.5$ and $\delta_2 = -0.5$. Similarly, we initially assumed that the elasticity of savings with respect to the interest rate, δ_3, is equal to 10, so that an increase in the interest rate of 1 percentage point leads to an increase in net saving of 10 percent. We repeated the analysis with $\delta_3 = 5$ and $\delta_3 = 15$. With these values for δ_2 and δ_3, our estimate of each country's stock of assets, and the data about each country's NDP, we could calibrate δ_1 for each country to match the observed amount of savings.

- The spreadsheets used for these analyses are available on the internet at http://www.econ.vt.edu/tideman/taxedout.htm

Chapter 7

The Philosophy of Public Finance

Mason Gaffney

1. Organic Theory of the State

THE TREATMENT of rent as public revenue is part and parcel of an organic theory of the State.

In the contractual theory, government is a kind of business which extends services to landowners. They only need pay for benefits received, which are construed in the narrowest possible terms.

In the organic theory, landowners hold title to land as a privilege. In return, they owe the State - acting on behalf of the community - certain obligations. The entire value of land is regarded as a benefit received from government. This is in keeping with the definition of land as "Public Value" offered by Alfred Marshall, the distinguished Victorian economist.

Land and its value is the joint product of at least three things:

- nature, which created it;
- government, which acquired it from other sovereigns and protects it from other powers and extends public works for the public's benefit; and
- synergism, which is the increment to value that spills over from social and economic activity in the neighborhood of each parcel of land.

Value stemming from all these elements is regarded as unearned by the individual landowner. It is the product of outside forces and therefore a fit object of taxation.

Along with this goes a Puritan ethic or productivity theory of distribution. Private receipt of land income is regarded as non-functional, since no incentive is required to create land. Incentive is only required to turn land to its highest use. A tax on land that is based only on capacity to serve, and does not vary with use, has the property of socializing rent while sharpening the incentive to turn land to the highest use permitted under the law.

Critics of site value taxation sometimes argue that socialization of rent would impair the allocative incentive. This is seldom heard today. Now the criticism is more likely to be the opposite. Land taxes are disliked precisely because they do force land into its highest use as defined by the market. One may not agree with the values of these critics, but their analysis of cause-and-effect is accurate.

The philosophy of site value taxation distinguishes sharply the land from the landowner. It says that taxes on land value are paid out of income which the land earns. They are not paid by the owner as a person unless we regard him as having a prior right to own the land free of any liability for taxes. But if no such right was part of the original land grant, then it is the land that pays the tax rather than the person who holds title. *No sovereign that I know of has ever alienated land without reserving the right to tax it, condemn it, police it, and so on.*

A legal counterpart of this philosophical position is that land taxes are *in rem*, that is, they are levied on a thing, the land, rather than the person who owns it. In case of nonpayment, it is the thing, the *rem* that is forfeited and not the *corpus personae*, as with the income tax. Again, tax liability is based on characteristics of the thing, regardless of the personal circumstances of the owner. In the eyes of many people, this is a shortcoming of site value taxation (and all property taxation). In the philosophy of site value taxation, this is not a drawback but an advantage.

Another philosophical rationale for a site value tax is stewardship. The idea is that land titles stem from the Crown which represents all citizens. Titles were transferred to private hands to facilitate the use of land for the benefit of everyone. Those not holding land were excluded from a sort of charmed circle. New generations and young people coming along are always excluded unless they inherit land, and modern medicine makes that a long wait. Taxes on land value are viewed as a counterpoise to this exclusion, in three ways.

(1)   Money is raised for public purposes.
(2)   The owner is pressed to use his land in such a way as to render service to others.
(3)   The owner has to hire labour.

It is consistent with this philosophy that lands which are open to public access are exempt from property taxes. Open access is accurately perceived as negating the need for compensation because there is no exclusion. It would be compatible with site value tax philosophy to exempt "open space" from the property tax provided the open space was not fenced and was truly open for use. The philosophy is, however, incompatible with passive fencing, that is, exclusion of people.

Consistent with this concept, site value tax philosophy enables us to exempt public right-of-way and even utility rights-of-way, in certain circumstances: provided they carried the obligation to serve everyone on a common carrier basis; provided they were sized somewhat ahead of demand, so that marginal costs fell below average costs; provided they were regulated so that rates might not exceed marginal costs; and provided the rights-of-way were not excessive. As to owner-occupied residences and their curtilages, nothing is so private and exclusive as they are, so there is little reason to exempt them, possibly except for a minimum pied-a-terre. Lands used for commerce and to some extent industry are "open to the public" in significant ways that private residential lands are not. The philosophy of assessing residential use at lower rates than business and commercial use is a movement away from site value taxation. The idea that "commercial" is a dirty word is alien to the site value tax philosophy.

The idea that "ability to pay" should be the sole criterion of taxation is alien to the site tax philosophy. An individual owning land is obviously better able to pay taxes than the same individual without the land, true. But people may be able to pay because of earned as well as unearned income, and site value tax philosophy would clearly consider unearned income to be the more eminently taxable. The fact that unearned income is more highly concentrated than earned would be important to many.

"Ability-to-pay" in practice often stresses short-run liquidity more than long-run wealth or permanent income. Many people find this attractive in payroll taxation and sales taxation, for example. Site value tax philosophy, on the other hand, is more inclined to make a virtue out of taxation to put a cash-flow bind on owners of under-utilized land. It would deplore an emphasis on liquidity: the percentage of people's assets held in cash and near-cash declines with their total wealth.

But the core idea is to preserve incentives. The philosophy is a logical extension of the productivity theory of distribution where people are to be rewarded according to their contribution to the joint products of the economy. Work should not be discouraged by taxes which dilute the rewards of effort.

Finally, there is the function which I shall call "social auditing." The landholder is regarded as a trustee, presiding over resources in which the community has a paramount sovereign interest. Each year a payment is assessed against him based on the capacity of the land to serve society.

The demand for this payment is a kind of social audit, a way of asking the Biblical question: "What have you done with the talents with which we have entrusted you?"

2. The Citizen's Obligations

THE RIGHTS that citizens claim are matched by corresponding obligations. Much of political philosophy is about how to establish the character of these rights and obligations, and how to balance them in a practical way.

Rent is the cement that binds these together, when that income is paid by the individual to the community that articulates and protects the rights.

How the state and the citizen meet their obligations reveals a great deal about governance; and about the collective attitudes of citizenry.

Site value taxes are sometimes identified with the idea of socializing land rent or unearned increments, but several other taxes already do that: examples include taxes on corporate profits, the mining tax and income tax applied to land income. All of these are based, at least in part, on the value of unproduced land, and they do not lower its supply. However, they differ from the site value tax in an important way: they depend on the owners taking action, and realizing something from a cash sale. They are taxes that "shoot anything that moves." One consequence is that they help to keep land from its best use.

The difference in incentives to the taxpayer is sharp. The site value tax adds nothing to the variable costs of developing or using land. The result is that the landowner will develop the "intensive margin" of his land more fully. In respect to mineral deposits, for example, we often hear that the imposition of a royalty, based on gross production, causes "high grading". That is, the royalty adds to the marginal cost of extracting low quality ore and so it raises the cut-off grade. A site value tax applied to mines, on the other hand, would be based on the value of reserves that are in place, and levied at a constant annual rate regardless of the amount of ore extracted in a given year. It would not raise the cut-off grade.

The exemption of urban buildings from the property tax likewise lowers the cut-off grade. It results in owners adding marginal increments of size and quality which would have been submarginal if they were taxed.

Aside from the tax on new buildings, which ought to be abated, most taxes other than the site value tax are synchronized with the taxpayer's liquidity. The site value tax is not so designed, either in philosophy or application. It is in vain to criticize it because it is inconvenient for some landowners to raise the cash to pay it. It is not supposed to convenience such landowners; and the inconvenience it causes does not suppress useful activity; quite the reverse. Its philosophy is that the landowner owes society something for the privilege of holding a piece of the limited surface of this small planet, and an annual required cash payment is calculated to inconvenience him into using his land so as to render service to others and offer employment to others, many of whom may not own land. One may subscribe to that philosophy or not, but that is the issue rather than the issue of convenience to the taxpayer.

Untaxing improvements and untaxing activity on land encourages higher uses; taxing land as a positive step adds pressure to utilize land. It is more than permissive. It is not absolutely mandatory, but it does apply steady pressure. The combination undoubtedly pushes or pulls, as you will, land into higher uses.

Site value taxation is oriented towards encouraging and goading landowners to use land more economically. It implies the inclusion of a "succession premium" in the tax base. The succession premium has two elements: a current latent capacity to serve in a higher use than the present one; and an unripe capacity expected in the future. I will refer to the capacity-to-serve premium as the "ripe premium" and the succession premium as the "green premium" to underscore this distinction.

The succession of land from a lower to a higher use could and should take place in an orderly, peaceful fashion, but it rarely does. Zones of transition ("ecotones") become "combat zones". Land value in these zones develops a green premium in anticipation of conversion. It is sometimes referred to as "speculative". That is misleading, for "speculative" suggests that conversion to higher use is uncertain when, in fact, it may be more certain than a repeat of the present use. It is rather, simply, a green premium because the time is not yet ripe to change the use.

Including the succession premium in the tax base is often criticized on the grounds that it is inequitable; inconvenient; and finally inefficient because it forces premature conversion to the higher succeeding use. Let us consider these points in order, beginning with a review of how land is transacted under the current fiscal regime.

Outside Britain , the capital value of land is almost always used as the tax base, for several reasons:

- The market evidence for assessment is more available because land normally trades that way. A capitalized value is paid for the transfer of fee simple title. Ground rents are paid here and there, in large cities particularly, but are much scarcer than deed recordings and are likely to be long term contracts which do not give accurate information about current values.

- Land prices, as they trade, are based on highest potential use of land, while existing rents are based, in part, on current uses that may be less than the best use.

- Rents often are multi-partite, consisting of a fixed annual amount plus a fraction of sales plus a bonus or "key money" that is paid up front. Capitalized values in the market are usually easier to compress into a unitized figure.

- Residential and recreational properties which yield no cash flow to the owners still have fee simple values which are the capitalization of imputed service flow. This fact serves to head off the fallacy that residential and recreational land yield no "income," or just yield values too ethereal to be weighed in the balance with something as prosaic as money. The cash value of deeds to residential property is one of the more accurate economic measures we have. Every man may not have his price but every land parcel does, especially if it is liable for annual taxes that increase with the price demanded.

Now, capitalized value adds to the tax base the premium value caused by anticipation of future use. As the poet Thomas Campbell (1777-1844) wrote in *Lochiel's Warning*: "Coming events cast their shadows before them." These shadows develop a present value that is bought and sold today. The premium goes by a confusing variety of names like floating value, speculative value, urban shadow value, development value, and so on. I will call it "succession premium." Whether and how to include succession premium in the tax base is a controversial topic in taxation, whether under a site value system or the present general property tax system. It warrants close attention.

The equitable argument for including succession premia runs as follows. The premium is the discounted present value of future income and as such tends to increase yearly along a compound interest curve, growing like money in the bank. This annual increment in value is income. According to Canada's Carter Commission, which was in the tradition of Professors Haig and Simons, unrealized accruals of value are and should be treated as current income. The annual accrual of value is, in a perfect market, proportional to the value. So is the property tax.

Therefore the property tax is proportional to the income. Thus a tax on the green value is a way, probably the only practical way, of taxing that income at the appropriate time, which is when it accrues.

It is indeed the only sure way of taxing it at all. If we look at an alternative like the Ontario speculation tax, it is levied only at the time of sale. That means that a person wanting land in the future could buy it today, hang on for 30 years, and finally realize its unearned increment by use, never becoming liable for the tax.

Residential land is not taxed in any other way. A person whose residence succeeds to higher use is uniquely favored by income tax law. His capital gain is mostly or entirely tax-free, now and forever. This unpre-empted tax base lies waiting to be tapped.

Turning to inconvenience, it is undoubtedly inconvenient for land-owners to pay taxes on succession premia. The argument for inconvenience cited in respect to ripe premia holds no water in respect to green premia, but rather the contrary. We do not want a policy that inconveniences landowners into converting land to succeeding uses prematurely.

It is not likely that assessing and taxing succession premia would indeed have this effect. If a landowner were prematurely to convert land to a higher use, one of two things would happen, both bad. One, the might lose money for the first several years since the market is not yet there for the premature improvement, or two, the owner may, in order to avoid the first problem, inadequately develop to meet future demand. In this second case the land will soon move into a future where land taxes are based on a higher use than it is improved to meet. This is assuming that the assessor continues to increase the assessed value each year, as the capability of the land increases with time, as we are proposing.

The only circumstance I can imagine in which assessment and taxation of a succession premium would cause premature conversion would be if the taxpayer anticipated, correctly or not, that the assessor was going to freeze the land assessment at the low level corresponding to the premature under-improvement. It is the valuer's job and every official's job to broadcast the fact that such freezing will not occur.

As a general rule, the anticipation of future taxes during the ripening period and thereafter will be capitalized into lower present values. Beginning from this lower base, the growth path of the green value is steeper, up to its value at time of conversion to the future use. The growth path is steeper because the value will grow at a rate equal to the interest rate plus the land tax rate. Thus the growth in value is at a rate high enough to pay both interest and land taxes, without changing the optimal time of conversion. This capitalization effect takes away a substantial part of the premium which is the tax base. In addition to being the tax base this premium is the market value on which interest is computed (either cash or imputed interest). Reducing this premium value therefore reduces both the temptation of individuals to sell prematurely to developers, and that part of carrying cost which is interest.

THERE IS A tendency for people to attribute their actions to taxes in order to divert responsibility onto the shoulders of the tax authorities. This may be why we hear that land is being developed prematurely "because of taxes".

As to efficiency, we have discussed this in part in connection with inconvenience, but there is more to it. Site value taxation, we have seen, has a developmental tendency. It strengthens the higher use *vis-à-vis* the lower use at every margin of decision, be it the extensive or the intensive margin; be it at the fringe of cities or on under-developed land that permeates the cores of every city. From observation, it is my judgment that under present circumstances the major effect of site value taxation would be to encourage infilling and redevelopment of older central cities. *There is so much land there on the verge of renewal which would be pushed over the margin by the exemption of new buildings from the property tax and the application of fiscal inconvenience to landowners.* In addition, there would be an enormous synergistic effect from the replacement of older buildings by new.

Frequent reassessment is of the essence. In the normal course of events buildings and other capital depreciate with time in contrast with land, which often appreciates. Any movement in the direction of more frequent reassessment, therefore, is a move towards site value taxation and *vice versa*.

There is a tendency in many jurisdictions to treat the issue of a building permit as either a taxable event or an assessable event. New buildings, in an inflationary period, thus come on the rolls at inflationary price levels. If land is not reassessed annually, it quickly becomes seriously under-assessed relative to new buildings. As to old buildings, practice varies. In some jurisdictions they are "factored" upwards from time to time to keep pace with inflation of replacement cost. Since land has no replacement cost, this kind of factoring may omit land.

If land is not reassessed frequently then the assessable event in the life of land is likely to be subdivision or other improvement, and what is called a land tax becomes a sort of increment to the tax on new buildings. Under site value taxation the assessed value of raw land would increase annually with its market value so that actual subdivision would occasion no great jump, if any, in assessed values.

3. Rent: the fiscal base

SOCIAL POLICY is generally best served by defining rent as the highest latent opportunity cost of land. Ideally, this rent would be charged against all land uses so as to eliminate all marginal extensions of land holding, in space or time, whose marginal service flow fell short of the marginal social cost.

There is a lingering tradition of regarding rent as a "residual." This makes of rent a waste basket for the mistakes of managers and the slothfulness of heirs. Landowners dealing with lessees are more importunate: rent is due periodically with the passage of time, regardless of land use. Owner occupants leasing land from themselves need to apply the same principle. If an owner fails to profit from good land, it is not the land's fault. For social as for private accounting, land should be imputed the highest available latent opportunity cost. Like the lawyer, its time is its stock in trade. Land-time is worthy of its hire that is rent. Land as such is passive and unresponsible. It yields its service flow by being available. It is always an input to its owner's economy, regardless of output. Actual use is a function of possession and management.

Neither should land be regarded as a risk-bearing agent. Land is a flow resource, not a fund of circulating capital which can be depleted to meet losses. Land is best regarded as a hired factor, like daily labor, to which the capitalist employer advances "subsistence". The owner demands regular payment, in advance of product completion and consumption. Knut Wicksell (1901; 1893) nailed down this point. Landowners who lease land to building owners on long terms for level annual payments - the most common arrangement - confirm the point.

The reason that common parlance and perception often confuse the landowner function with the capitalist function is that the functions are usually joined in the same person. Imputation of rent requires a functional analysis, however. Functionally, the owner of capital hires land and advances rent. Capital then carries the product over time, absorbing risk for better or worse. It is capital that is embodied in a product irreversibly, losing any scrap value commensurate with its previous value, while land retains a scrap value in general equal to its previous value. It is capital whose return is meaningfully "residual."

These definitional details assume great importance when we ask how best to tax "rent," and what effects to expect. They assume great importance when we ask how much of urban property income is "rent." If the above definitional detail be used, the estimates of urban rent and land value made by Goldsmith (1955: 12; 1962: 186, 234, 238) and Kurnow (1959: 834), often cited and relied upon, are meaningless. The allocation between land and buildings made by most tax assessors is meaningless. *If rent is the latent opportunity cost of land, then most current operating income from property in older central cities is rent.*

Land income is much greater than the current cash flow, for the following reasons.

a. Appreciation is current income

The income of depreciable capital is cash flow less depreciation. The income of appreciable land is cash flow plus appreciation. That is quite a difference: they move in opposite directions!

With land held for appreciation there is no cash flow to disclose the high values and the steady accrual of gains in wealth. This quality of "silent accrual" is found in land surrounding cities, or growing retail centers, as well as in land that is considered potentially mineral-bearing. Other land is valued for expected higher future cash flows in its present use, or some higher use to come. Some land is valued for future "plottage" increments from assembly, or "negative plottage" from subdividing.

Professors Haig and Simons have given their names to the standard definition of income which includes unrealized appreciation of durable assets like land and corporate shares as current income. Stock brokers and real estate brokers habitually do the same thing for the trade. They may appear to question it when lobbying for tax breaks, at which time some say it is "double taxation" to tax both current cash flow and appreciation. When selling stock or real estate, however, unrealized appreciation is unequivocally touted as current income, and correctly so.

Some even deny that appreciation should be taxable income at all. Yet, no one denies that depreciation should be a deduction from current taxable income. This asymmetry and glaring contradiction generally passes unremarked. It could only survive if never challenged in the profession, which apparently it is not. "Land," with its tendency to appreciate, is not in the abridged lexicon.

b. Landowning yields large non-cash service flows

Land income also includes service flows other than cash. Because of its versatility, and fundamental character, land often yields service flows in kind that never pass through the market place. For example, land used for homes and owner-recreation yields no cash flow at all, but has high value.

It is common for economists to write of the "imputed income of durable consumer capital", especially owner-occupied houses, and occasionally to persuade some political candidate to advocate including their imputed income in the income tax base, or at least to end the deduction of interest and property taxes paid on house values. Those making such proposals, unfortunately, fail to exercise reasonable care in distinguishing houses from land. Much or most of the non-cash service flow received from consumer capital proper is not income at all, but two other things: a return from operation, maintenance, and upkeep; and a return of capital. Depreciation and expenses offset more than half the service flow from most owner-occupied houses, especially middle-aged buildings on the steep slope of the depreciation curve. The service flow from land, on the other hand, is pure income.

The measure of this imputed land income is not subjective nor fuzzy. It is interest on the market price of the land, a measure of its opportunity cost. Alternatively, it is the periodic ground rent on comparable lands. This could easily be included in the base of the present income tax, converting it in one stroke into a national land tax.

Forest land yields cash only once in decades. Some land is valued mainly for ancillary benefits like the preferential access it gives to adjoining lands for grazing, recreation, water rights, waste disposal, information gleaned from mining, etc. Other land is held for its contingency value, for example for possible future expansion. Some is held pre-emptively to freeze out competition, and some is used (under current US income tax laws) to yield non-cash tax shelter benefits.

Part of farmland value is an amenity, especially of course in pleasant places. The value of lands held for the owner's recreational pleasure is noncash. Part of the value of media ownership - especially through control of the radio spectrum - is power and prestige. Business sites in Newport Beach give access to water recreation; in Cambridge, Mass., to intellectual stimulus and hobnobbing. The list of non-cash service flows from land is much longer. As the 15th Earl of Derby wrote 1881:

> The objects which men aim at when they become possessed of land in the British Isles may, I think, be enumerated as follows: (1) political influence; (2) social importance, founded on territorial possession, the most visible and unmistakable form of wealth; (3) power exercised over tenantry; the pleasure of managing, directing and improving the estate itself, (4) residential enjoyment, including what is called sport; (5) the money return - the rent (cited in Douglas 1976: 17).

In Ireland, during rent wars, boycotts, etc., landlords "had long decided that Ireland would yield few of the spiritual delights of land ownership." This resulted in lower prices for Irish than English land.

c. Land income is a large share of national income

Throughout history the prime business of national governments has been to gain and keep land, mainly by force and threats. The prime business of politics has been to apportion lands among the winners. A third business is then to subsidize them in various ways. It is most inconsistent, then, when the winners of all three battles counter tax proposals by pleading poverty, saying their land has little value. How little value it has may be gauged by playing "what if?" What if the English, with all their capital, were removed to Antarctica? What would be their national income?

Less drastically, we might just ask what the owners would sell England for?

A common way to trivialize land values is to play "what if the owners tried to sell it all at once?" What if, instead, we went to buy it all? Much of it has been off the market for centuries, with reservation prices effectively infinite.

Consuming land means pre-empting its time. To consume most goods and services is to use them up. Land is not used up. "Consuming" land must have some other meaning, therefore, than the intuitive and common idea that consuming means turning-to-waste. To consume land is rather to pre-empt its service flow without impairing its substance. To consume land is to occupy it for a time-slot, which may be as brief as beating a red traffic light on the highway or (rarely) as long as the pyramids last. After us life goes on, on the land once left to us which we then leave to others. "Time-sharing" was not invented by the holiday industry but is inherent in the nature of land and life.

How shall we measure land-consumption by owners, where no rent is paid? Is it purely subjective? Does it vary with the owner's mood and health? It is simpler than that, and fully practicable. The essence of consuming land is pre-empting the time-slot from others. Thus, holding land without using it, or using it below capacity, is a form of consumption. The measure is the market opportunity cost of land, i.e. the price multiplied by the interest rate. Holding an urban site has been likened to holding a reserved seat at a play, sporting event, or concert. The ticket holder properly helps pay for the event, whether or not he is there to enjoy it. As a result, very few paid customers fail to show up. Likewise, people who pay cash rent for land seldom leave it vacant. Doubtless if people paid regular cash taxes to hold land, they, too, would consume (pre-empt) less.

Proponents of "consumer taxation" almost universally overlook this point. I am not aware of one who has proposed including land-consumption in the tax base. Aaron and Galper (1985: 76), propounding a "cash-flow tax," explicitly allow for letting each succeeding owner rewrite off the purchase of land as a cost of production, effectively exempting land rents from taxation 100%. Robert Hall and Alvin Rabushka (1995: 62), authors of *The Flat Tax* (the flat taxers' bible), propose the same.

Theirs, and other proposals, and consumer taxes actually imposed now and in the past, bear heavily on the necessities of median income families. We deride the salt tax of the French ancient regime, and of pre-Ghandian India. We recognize them as instruments of tyranny and class warfare, even as we tolerate modern legislators who impose comparable burdens on ourselves, and economists who rationalize such taxes by belittling the necessities of life.

In doing so, they compound the deception in the label "consumer taxation". Much of what is taxed in the name of taxing consumers is actually used for capital formation: human capital formation. The same economists who say human beings are or contain capital, turn around and tell us to tax the formation and maintenance of such capital, by calling it "consumption." Coupling this with their proposed exemption of land-consumption we have the ultimate victory and application of semantic cleansing.

It follows from the above that land's rent is its opportunity cost, regardless of use. This means land rent is a much larger share of national income than national accounts presently show. Land income is a prior claim to the joint product of combined resources. To consume land economically is merely to pre-empt a time-slot from others, regardless of what one does with it. The unreaped harvests of idle land flow like water wasting through a desert into a salt sea. Lost water may sometimes be useful downstream; lost time never returns. To keep others from using a time-slot is to consume it.

A great deal of land in fact is not allocated to its highest and best use. The value of pre-empting this land is the highest and best use that might have been made of the land pre-empted. That is the economic cost. The land is not responsible if the manager fails to realize its value at optimal capacity. Neither are the persons who are excluded. Only the pre-emptor is responsible, as a manager. This person is the residual imputee who deserves credit for performing above par and blame for falling below.

Most economic theorizing has failed to bring out this point. The tendency is to treat ground rent as a residual, a waste basket for all the errors and dereliction of responsible economic actors. Too many economists who make much of "choice" and "opportunity cost", fail to apply that properly to land, when estimating its value. This has resulted in greatly understating the value of land relative to other factors of production. Institutional and social factors, too, often obscure the opportunity cost of land. Of course, definitions are arbitrary and one may define rent as he pleases - and many economists do. However, as a proponent of a tax on land rent, it is my right and duty to define the word "rent" as intended in the proposal.

This is a case where theorizing lags behind practice. In dividing value between land and a building affixed to it the standard practice of appraisers, and speculative buyers too, is the "building-residual method." The land is appraised as though vacant; the building gets the remaining value, if any. The building, once attached to a specific site, loses the mobility of place and form that fluid capital possesses and has no opportunity cost but scrap value, which is often negative. Land, always lacking mobility of place, retains mobility of reuse because of its versatility, permanence, and irreproducible location.

4. The concept of ATCOR

ALL ECONOMIC PRINCIPLES must be tried and proved at the margin. On marginal land there is no surplus above non-land costs, hence there is no taxable capacity of any kind. Any tax on marginal land, or people, or buildings, or outputs on marginal land, renders it sub-marginal (Ricardo 1821: Ch.11).

Seligman (1913: 66-99) faulted land taxation on the score that marginal communities could have no local tax base. But that is true of any tax. The difference reveals something important about the exploitative character of taxes other than those that fall on the rent of land.

- Land taxes on marginal land are zero. This means that intra-marginal land has to fund public expenditure.
- Other taxes, if they are imposed on people who occupy marginal land, add additional costs of living on no-rent land. These have the effect of scorching and sterilizing that land, aborting its teeming fruits.

The taxable surplus in any jurisdiction can only be the excess value generated above the external opportunity cost of mobile labor and capital. This is identical with land rent. After-tax returns to mobile labor and capital seek a common level throughout the economy. Local land supply is inelastic; local labor and capital supply are elastic. Therefore, any tax nominally levied on buildings must reduce land rent. Conversely, lowering taxes on buildings must increase land rent by an equal amount. Taxable surplus is not lost or destroyed by untaxing buildings; it simply surfaces elsewhere. This is what is meant by the ATCOR concept: All Taxes Come Out of Rent.

When governments lease land to private parties, this relationship is even more obvious, and is understood by all. A lease contract contains several elements over which the parties negotiate. If one element is higher, then another must be lower to offset it. Thus a landowner may charge a lessee a low royalty for pumping oil. If the royalty is low, then the landowner lets the "bonus" bid, paid up front, be the "bid variable." The lower the royalty rate, the higher the bonus bids that come in. If the landowner is canny, and the bidders many, the landowner thus soaks up all the rent. Similarly, let us view tax payments as elements of rent paid to the Crown. *If sales and income taxes are less, then rent payments may and will be higher.*

Land is the equity interest in the municipal corporation. Rent is the earning on common stock, what remains after other costs. If the tax cost on buildings falls, land rent rises by the same amount, just as earnings on common stock would rise by the amount of any fall of interest on bonds. There is a Newton's Third Law in economics, a conservation of economic energy. This is nothing more than good book balancing: everything must be accounted for.

Suppose a locality could stop taxing buildings altogether and replace the revenue from outside grants. Does anyone doubt that this bonanza would raise local values? *Land rent would rise by the amount of the grants.* Now if the source of the "grant" is a tax on local land rent itself, the land tax simply takes rent which is simultaneously replaced by building exemption. If the total tax levy remains the same, there is no general invasion of the rent now privately collected. Some particular parcels may suffer and others may gain, as in any change of public policy. But the tax base remains intact.

The matter is obscured by the fact that the nominal tax rate must rise, in order to tap the rent in this new manner. I say "nominal" because the tax as a percentage of total real estate value will remain about the same (or, indeed, fall, if there is increased construction). But as a percentage of land value it must therefore rise.

Suppose the present rate on land value is at such a level as to take one-third of present ground rent (after building taxes). Exempt buildings and this same rate will take one-third of the added ground rent, that is, one-third of the former building taxes. To recoup the other two-thirds, the tax rate must rise.

To complete the example, suppose the original ground rent equaled the building taxes. Untaxing buildings then doubles ground rent. The original tax on land took one-sixth of this higher ground rent, the original building tax took three-sixths, so the new tax on land alone must take four-sixths.

Next, by how much must the tax rate rise to maintain the same levy?

Now we are juggling several factors. A simple case would be if land values were to remain the same. The tax rate must rise by the same proportion that the base falls. That proportion is the share of buildings in real estate value. If buildings are half, the rate must double.

But would not land values fall under this higher rate? Wouldn't the higher rate be capitalized into lower land values, leading to a further rise of the tax rate? If there were no change but a higher rate on land, "yes"; but when this accompanies lower rates on buildings, then "no." This is one of those unusual cases when algebra can clarify rather than muddle a point, so, let:

a = original annual ground rent (after building taxes but before land taxes),

i = interest rate, t = original tax rate, B = building value,

L = original land value,

L' = new land value when buildings are untaxed, and t' = new tax rate necessary to maintain same levy.

According to tax capitalization theory,

$$L = a/(i+t \tag{1}$$

$$L' = (a + tB)/(i + t') \tag{2}$$

Clearing denominators, and subtracting equation (2) from equation (1):

$$i(L-L') + tL - t'L' = -tB$$

To maintain the levy:

$$t'L' = t(L + B) \tag{3}$$

Substituting

$$L = L' \tag{4}$$

therefore, from equation (3),

$$t' = t(L+B)/L \tag{5}$$

Equation (5) takes account of tax capitalization. It leaves us with the surprisingly simple conclusion that *the new tax rate may be forecast on the basis of existing ratios of building to land*. Just multiply the present tax rate by the present base divided by land value - what the simple man would do anyway! But be sure to use true current land values estimated properly from current markets by a good mapper-assessor. Current assessed land values are much too low.

A corollary is that land values will remain unchanged by the tax shift, just as in the simple case before the algebra (above). The land tax simply extracts from ground rent the same amount which is added to it by untaxing buildings. There is no "confiscation," unless the levy rises.

A simple way to grasp how untaxing buildings raises land rents lies in the feudal basis of our law, which is good fiscal theory. The sovereign is a super-landlord administering the royal estate. He asserts his right in the land by collecting taxes, which he may do in various ways. But whatever the nominal base, these are alternative means of gathering rent from vassals on the royal estate. There is a limited taxable surplus, which he can destroy but not exceed. What he takes by one means he cannot take by another. He is always taxing the same real estate; he is just taxing it in different ways.

If equation (5) seems too simple to cover all factors, it is. Actually L' will be higher than shown in equation (2), for several reasons which I treat below under the rubrics of spillovers, excess burdens, and reallocation. Equation (2) accounts only for the removal of the tax on existing buildings, with no account of incentive effects. And in fact it even understates the impact of the one factor it does treat.

That is because of the timing of building taxes: high when a building is new, dropping towards nothing when it is old. Land value being defined as renewal value, it is more depressed by taxes that come early than late in building life. So the land value tax base, L', will rise more than shown by equation (2). The expression $t \times B$ is too simple and too low. It should be replaced by the present value of all future building taxes annualized by the capital recovery coefficient. To do so will increase L' a great deal, depending on particulars.

Limited space prevents full treatment here, but a simple approximation is possible. The building tax, tB, cuts into land values by almost as much as though it lasted at its peak for the full life of buildings. But it does not. For simplicity assume it lasts half the life of buildings and then stops and that this depresses land values as much as though it lasted the full life of buildings. Assume building ages are evenly staggered. Then half the sites yield no building taxes, yet all the land values are depressed by the capitalized value of the building taxes even though these are being collected from just half the sites! Thus, the building tax cuts the land portion of the tax base by double the value of the building base being taxed.

In a new city this factor would not amount to much. But in an old central city where 90% of the buildings are very old - that is, in Boston, Newark, and other crisis spots - untaxing buildings would suddenly multiply the tax base. As proof of this effect, note that tax exempt institutions pay a premium for their fiscal status. This premium raises land rents. The Chrysler Building in New York is tax exempt because it is owned by Cooper Union, so the lessee pays a ground rent premium equalling the unlevied taxes (Meyers 1969: 79). Any sale-leaseback deal by which a business borrows the tax exemption of a church, college, or public district exemplifies the same principle.

5. The Excess Burden of Building Taxes

THE ANALYSIS above treats only of taxes actually collected from existing buildings. It says nothing of how the threat of building taxes suppresses buildings and replacement and so destroys taxable surplus before it is created. But that, too, is important. After all, one of the main reasons for preferring the land tax is to avoid impairing incentives.

Taxes on buildings reduce the intensity of site improvement. Just as they sterilize marginal land, the "extensive margin," so they abort marginal intensification of superior or rentable land, the "intensive margin." The aborted outlays include increments to height, quality, perhaps coverage, and, most damaging, earliness of renewal.

A function of the land market is in the development of new areas, or redevelopment when new uses succeed old, to synchronize interdependent private investments that interact synergistically to produce a total community. Thus as a city expands, high land values at the perimeter put simultaneous pressure on all owners there to convert to urban use. Were this mechanism in good working order, planners could extend city services to compact increments of land, initially sizing utility lines and streets for ultimate demand, secure in the knowledge that the ultimate demand would be there in short order. Private builders could orient their plans to a more certain future, minimizing transition costs of, for example, shifting from wells and septic tanks to public water and sewers. Every private improvement could be less self-sufficient and more oriented to the prospect of a total community.

But the market is not in good working order. *Taxation intercedes in every land use decision.* Every piece of land is periodically mobile among uses - when there is some "sacrament" in its life, such as demolition and construction, sale, subdivision, or assembly. It is then in press among competing buyers, uses, densities, timings, parcel sizes, and so on. In every such press, taxation biases the choice in favor of the lighter taxed use. The real estate tax on building thus always favors old over new; gas stations over apartments; junk yards over factories; parking lots over parking structures; high income residences over low (high income residences are usually less intensive because of larger lots in neighborhoods of higher land value); billboards over offices; unused over improved land; waiting over acting. *This bias has half-destroyed the market as an arbiter among competing land uses, and as an agency promoting urban synergism.* It has lowered the density, retarded renewal, and broken up integral linkages of the central city, fostering in their place random scattering of new buildings at the outskirts. It has so far impaired the city's function of linking small independent industrial firms as to bear large responsibility for today's galloping merger movement in which a key word is - *synergism!* Firms seek through merger and vertical integration the access to services, labor, and supplies which in a well ordered city they could get from independent firms through the market.

The aborted outlays would have created new rents above cost and thus increased taxable surplus. To abort them is a deadweight loss, an "excess burden" from building taxation. It is not building exemption that truly threatens the tax base, but building taxation. The lagging rate of new taxable construction in the United States today dramatizes how serious the threat has become.

Referring back to equation (2), here is a second reason why it understates L', the land value tax base. The first reason is that tB understates the true gain in ground rent from untaxing buildings as shown above. The present reason is the removal of deadweight loss, or excess burden. We should add a term to the numerator for the rent added by intensification and renewal.

Anyone who has ever learned about diminishing marginal returns can duplicate the basic rationale of excess burden, so I will not labor it. Two special aspects do bear comment, however.

The first is economy of scale in buildings and rooms. As these get larger, diminishing returns do not take the form of higher cost per square foot of floor, for costs fall. What diminishes is the marginal demand of the individual buyer or renter. Taxing buildings is similar to reducing buying power, forcing everyone into smaller quarters. So it forestalls the realization of economies of scale in building. There is a trade-off of land for capital in supplying floor space. Expanding horizontally requires less capital per increment of floor, but requires more land than expanding vertically. To oversimplify, unit nonland costs fall (economies of scale) when one expands horizontally, but rise (diminishing returns) when one builds upwards.

Now, taxing buildings has the same substitution effect as raising building costs relative to land costs. It puts a premium on holding down building costs. One does this by spreading out rather than rising up, using more land to save on capital. It puts an artificial premium on achieving all economies that save on capital, including scale economies.

Building taxes do make buyers take less floor space than otherwise. But the reduced space they do take will be supplied with more relative emphasis on economies of scale from horizontal spread, because added floorage is gained with minimum added cost and hence minimum added taxable valuation.

There is still a net loss of scale economies. But the greater loss is in the capital-using third dimension (and the fourth, treated next). Land is used more extensively. The scale economy that this most impairs is the social economy of scale of city, market, and society. As each person adds his bit to the spatial barriers among people he worsens access among parts, raises area-sensitive costs, and shrinks the central market and cultural centers.

In terms of tax base, one might now guess that taxing buildings could add to land values by raising the demand for space for horizontal expansion. And this is one element in the picture. It raises the danger that untaxing buildings might reduce the demand for land and reduce the land tax base, as builders go up instead of out.

But economics always involves appraising the net balance of counter forces. In this case, there is a more powerful counterforce. It is true that taxing buildings adds to what a buyer would bid for, say, the hundreth front foot, but it lowers what he will pay for the first ninety-nine. That is because he cannot use the first ninety-nine as intensively. The optimal parcel becomes larger, but the unit rent will be smaller.

In graphic terms, visualize a plotting of land inputs (abscissa) against the marginal net (after all associated costs) product of land (ordinate). With no building taxes the curve arches high, then drops steeply. Impose building taxes and the curve flattens. It falls throughout, of course, because taxes add to associated costs. But it falls more on the left and center, less on the right.

The result is that while every land user bids less for land, bids for smaller units using more capital per front foot of land fall relatively more than bids for larger units. So units get larger. This resolves the paradox that building taxes raise demand for space but reduce ground rents.

Beginning from where we are now, untaxing buildings will add to what people bid for smaller parcels of ground, but will reduce the aggregate need. The demand for what is now the outer exurban fringe will be relocated to the upper floors of more central buildings, as well as to all floors of new buildings on the great reservoir of derelict land more central than the outer fringe. In this shift there may or may not be a change in aggregate ground rent. But there will certainly be a spectacular fall of public costs, the area sensitive costs of supplying infrastructure in the sprawling fringe. Thus, the need for a tax base will fall a great deal while the base may at worst fall a little, and at best will rise.

The second special aspect of excess burden is in the fourth or temporal dimension. There is an excess burden in the deferral of site renewal. Any tax which varies with the use to which land is put biases the owner in favor of the lighter taxed use. That means the building tax favors old buildings over new.

There are large areas in our central cities which would be renewed forthwith in the absence of the fiscal deterrent. In the 1960s I drew an "isovalic" contour map of Milwaukee County land values, based on several thousand actual sales either of vacant land or of land with old buildings on the eve of demolition. Comparing the bare land values with the combined values of land and old buildings, it was clear that in 25% or more of the city the bare or renewal value of land already nearly equaled the defender values. Remove the fiscal deterrent and the challenge values would have moved well above the defense values, bringing prompt private renewal. Thus, the fiscal deterrent played a primary role in blocking urban renewal. Today, land prices are much higher than they were then, and the buildings 30 years older.

Few would deny that the market has failed to renew our cities fast enough. For this the real estate tax, bearing differentially on new buildings, must shoulder much of the blame. The economical time for an individual to clear and renew land is when the current cash flow from existing or "defender" use ceases to yield a fair return on the "scrap value" of the site in the most eligible succeeding use (the "challenger"). This scrap value is the "discounted cash flow" (DCF), i.e. the present value of future income less the present value of future costs.

The land-based tax is neutral in this decision, because it is unmoved by renewal. It is the same on the defender as the challenger. The building-based tax is unneutral and inhibiting because it rockets upward when new succeeds old. It weakens the challenger *vis-a-vis* the defender, by the amount of tax increase. Not only is the new building valued higher than the old: often assessors seize this occasion to reassess the land upwards, adding to the bias against renewal.

The general qualitative direction of the bias is clear. Quantitatively, the number of years during which building taxes retard site renewal depends, among other things, on how the cash flow from old buildings drops off. If it plummeted off steeply, then renewal dates would be preordained by nontax factors, and tax policy would be unimportant. If it tails off gradually, a substantial tax bias against new buildings retards the renewal of each site regarded individually; and of neighborhoods and school districts even more, as the nonrenewal of each site robs neighboring sites of their renewability, and suppresses competition from new buildings which would pull tenants from old defenders.

A number of time series showing historical income experience of commercial buildings have been compiled and published by Leo Grebler (1955), Fred Case (1960), and Louis Winnick (1958). I have deflated them for price level changes. They are much affected by cycles of depression and war. The general time pattern and period of dropoff is clear enough, however. Real income from old buildings dwindles away slowly over many decades, in spite of depreciation and obsolescence. There is no sharp cutoff, no predestined date of demolition determined by technology or taste. Even when an old building has gone vacant, it may come back. After World War II, real income of many buildings rose sharply.

Another source of data is the Institute of Real Estate Management "Experience Exchange" among members of the N.A.R.E.B. In 1967, their 1,069 respondents reported on operating ratios (total expenses including real estate taxes divided by total actual collections) for apartment buildings classified by age groups. For elevator apartments the ratio rose gently from 45% for 1961-66 birthdays to 59% for all buildings over 47 years old, that is, pre-1920. For low-rise apartments it was from 41% to 58%; for garden apartments from 40% to 48%. In other words, almost half the gross collections from old apartments represents net income to the owner. A powerful factor that helps to hold down these operating ratios is that real estate tax expenses keep falling as a building ages.

Measured in years, therefore, the fiscal deterrent to urban renewal - the threat of increased taxes on new buildings - retards by decades renewal of the individual urban site.

The deterrence is greater than simple numbers show. Unwise taxes may defer private renewal not just for decades but indefinitely, because there are reverberating neighborhood effects, from deterioration of old buildings which progressively rob sites of their renewability. Unused and blighted land lies among used parcels and disrupts their symbiotic interactions, which are the heart of public land planning and the essence of urban civilization. With that in mind, cities are constantly intervening in the real estate market to subsidize renewal in various ways. For example, some Milwaukee suburbs, recognizing their fiscal and neighborhood interest in site renewal, have quietly entered the real estate market, bid on older houses, and willingly absorbed demolition losses, without federal subsidy, in order to accelerate renewal. They buy for the market, demolish, and resell land for a loss. They reckon that the present value of the augmented future tax stream is worth to them as tax collector at least the loss, even though they receive only part of the increased property taxes. (They are also motivated by shared state income taxes.) Recalling that the tax collector's meat is the taxpayer's poison, that suggests that the removal of fiscal deterrence would push the threshold of renewal clear out into high income suburbs, selectively. That is, the prospective future tax stream has to the challenger a high deterrent value. If taxes were unmoved by renewal, the bidding power of challengers *vis-a-vis* defenders would rise by that amount or more (whether by a rise in the former or a fall in the latter, or both) and renewal would occur without any subsidy of write-down.

Urban renewal is a social, synergistic phenomenon. The renewal of one site speeds the renewal of nearby sites in at least three ways. First, it raises the renewal or challenger value of nearby land. One new building gives heart to potential builders of others, who naturally prefer new buildings for neighbors. Slum environs can virtually destroy the renewal value of land. One or a few sound new buildings as *Inspiration* can support supplementary and complementary renewal in the neighboring area. The GM building on 5th Avenue, New York, at the southeast corner of Central Park, when new, was reported by *Fortune* to have doubled floorspace rentals across the street.

This, of course, raises the negative possibility that new buildings strengthen adjacent defender values as well as challenger values. There are frequent complaints that successful urban renewal projects, for example, raise the cost of nearby land for the next project. However, these higher land "costs" are merely asking prices and may be based on higher anticipated challenger values, plus the knowledge that federal funds are on tap to buy. They do not in general represent higher defender cash flow nearly as much as challenger values.

The reason is that new buildings pull tenants from old, which in general weakens defenders. This is the second way that renewal reinforces itself. It is especially true when the new buildings are at higher density than what they replace - something which building taxes also discourage - and represent net new supply.

Where tenants have a choice they move to newer quarters. The oldest defender filters down to be demolished. Its successor then pulls tenants from others, repeating the cycle. In the right conditions the reverberations from one new structure resound through several rounds of induced renewal (Box 7:I).

A third way that renewal reinforces itself is through the higher income that it brings. Renewal means capital inflow, construction payrolls, material sales, new jobs, and so on. This pushes up local income levels. Now new buildings are "superior goods." The higher the local income, the greater the premium paid for new over old floor space, and the stronger are challengers relative to defenders.

So neighborhood and aggregate effects multiply the good done by each new building; conversely, of course, they multiply the damage from the present tax policy, which defers renewal.

But neighborhood effects are not the whole of the story of multiplied effects from taxing challengers more than defenders. Consider that most building is done on borrowed money. We live in a world of credit ratings, cash flows, front money, cash squeezes, and leverage - matters too often underweighed in rarefied theoretical economic analysis. A tax on new buildings, coupled with low taxes on old, weakens the credit of challengers and strengthens that of defenders. It adds to challengers' needs for front money and reduces defenders' needs for any money at all.

A tax on new buildings is at its maximum in the early years, the time of tightest cash squeeze. A high property tax rate today, say at 4%, may take 30% of gross income from a new building. If other expenses take 30%, that is three-sevenths of the net operating income. If the entrepreneur is highly leveraged, as is standard, most of the rest of net operating income goes to debt service. The net cash remaining for the entrepreneur, especially during the early cash squeeze, is doubly leveraged, so a small rise in building taxes can wipe him out. His credit rating in turn is leveraged by the prospects for his equity position. It is a familiar fact that a small rise of mortgage rates causes a large drop in building. Loanable funds rush out of building, not just because borrowers balk at higher rates, but because lenders lower everyone's credit rating because of lower equity income. Real estate taxes on new buildings add to costs in the same way as interest rates - that is,

> **Box 7:I**
> **Chain Reaction from One Building**
>
> MILWAUKEE'S progress during the 1960s represented the ramifying effects that may flow from one new building. Through a series of historical accidents and legal technicalities, Wisconsin had an assessment freeze law that proved unconstitutional after being used essentially just once, in 1960, for the Marine Plaza - a high rise office and bank building. It was the first downtown building of consequence in thirty years. It pulled tenants from other buildings, forcing a wave of remodeling and renewal which changed the face of downtown Milwaukee. By general account, this one new competitor set off the chain reaction. There is a multiplier the like of which few other economic processes approach. The facts speak volumes.
>
> It is not that this one stroke alone was enough. The ripples died out, long before the job was fully done, but the point is this: if one original cause can ramify and drive a multiplier process so far, even though every induced new building was fully taxed, twenty original causes would transform a city, if every induced new building were to be tax free.

they are a fixed percentage of value. A 3%-of-true-value property tax rate hits new building with the impact of a rise of mortgage rates from 4% to 7%; except that the real estate tax is worse because the tax rate applies to the whole value, while mortgage rates apply only to the debt. The tax not only defers renewal by its simple direct impact, but additionally by its leveraged effect on entrepreneur net cash flow and thence on credit ratings.

So it is powerful medicine to convert the real estate tax base to the site value basis. In comparing challenger and defender values in Milwaukee County, I found that a small rise of challenger values over defender values would cause 20% of the central city area to be renewed forthwith; and that the large change resulting from a full exemption of buildings from real estate tax would cause some 50% to be renewed - if the labor and money could be found to do it. These results would be magnified by consideration of the neighborhood effects.

They would be magnified again by consideration of the positive effect of cash squeeze on defenders. So far I have written only of exempting new buildings, but the land basis of real estate taxation does more than that. It raises taxes on defenders. The result is a potent cash squeeze effect. Today's real estate tax puts the squeeze on buildings. The proposed land tax puts it on defenders, holdouts, and pre-emptors of land.

The economic time to renew a site is when the standing building ("defender") ceases to earn a return on the scrap value of the site, as imputed by the outstanding "challenger." But challengers pay much more taxes than do defenders. The scrap or renewal value of land is reduced by the full present value of future building taxes. This defers renewal. The unreaped rents of the deferred renewal period are a deadweight loss.

Land held unrenewed to avoid building taxes is yielding less taxes under present policy than it would under land value taxes.

Let us underscore here a basic point developed above, that has wider meanings. The ATCOR principle says that untaxing buildings will raise land rents by the amount of the tax that is abated. **That understates the matter by a large factor. Land rents and corresponding land values will rise by more than the abated taxes. The land tax base will rise by the amount of the abated taxes on the highest and best future building that might be put on a site.** Generally, that will be much more than the taxes yielded by the extant building.

6. The Synergy of Spillover Benefits
LAND RENT, as we have noted, has three basic sources: nature, public works, and the net benefits that spill over from private land uses to benefit others' land. There is constant grumbling about negative spillovers, leaving an impression that these outweigh the positive, but if they did there would be no cities, no clustering tendency at all. In fact, land values still rise sharply to the center of cities. And land values are continuous, because builders prefer to anchor onto viable neighborhoods.

Here is a fourth term for the numerator of equation (2). Untaxing buildings and taxing land stimulate building. They encourage compactness, pulling buildings in from scattered isolated outposts where they dissipate their benefits, and the value of teamwork is lost in overcoming the friction of space among the buildings. These policies let a city - and farmers and miners too - realize to the full the economies of spatial agglomeration. These economies are "synergistic," that is, the whole is worth more than the sum of its parts. The extra value adds to land rent and taxable surplus.

To scatter buildings is to waste synergistic surplus, prodigally. The surplus is a valuable social resource that a sage policy will husband and utilize for the public good.

Many economists have written on synergistic economies of agglomeration (*see Box 7:II*) The sources of its power are many. They include sharing common costs, pooling risk and raising load factors, widening markets and allowing greater specialization, spreading information, fostering innovation, whetting competition, widening choice, facilitating social contacts, and so

BOX 7:II
Synergy in Sydney

THE POWER of synergism in a specific city was graphically pointed out by *The Observer* (Sydney, 16 April 1960): "The record $51 a foot that the British E. Alex Colman group offered for the Sydney City Council's property at the top of Martin Place a couple of weeks ago seems to suggest that the Sydney land boom is far from over...Sydney's land prices have been rising since the war, but the past seven or eight years has been the most remarkable price period. And the most dramatic of the price rises have taken place in the northern part of the city, particularly that once-depressed section of old warehouses, State public service offices, and old insurance buildings between Hunter Street and Circular Quay. The coming of the Quay railway, the huge new buildings (Unilever, I.C.I., and, soon, A.M.P. and British Tobacco) that are spreading along the harbour at the north end of town, have stimulated a remarkable redevelopment of the northern city area....

"Back in Pitt Street towards Hunter Street there has been redevelopment aplenty. Insurance offices are no longer dull, brown, squat stone buildings dated 1890; they have become steel, concrete, and glass monsters. And there are plans for more changes...It is inevitable that with such interest in rebuilding and development city land values should rise. However, the pace of that rise in recent years has certainly been hectic...Will they keep up? One thing about high land prices and development is that they are self-generating. The growth of a big office sector near the Quay brings added demands to the area - for retail shops, for example...Certainly some sort of saturation point for office space will eventually be reached, at least the backlog of demand will be overcome, and only new pressures will need to be catered for. But this should not mean any falling in the city land prices, at least in the city's northern section."

Urban synergism has been described and in part analyzed in the following: Alfred Marshall, *Principles of Economics*, 8th ed. (London: Macmillan and Co., 1947), pp.794-804; Henry George, *Progress and Poverty* (New York: Modern Library, n.d.), bk. 4, ch. 2; Sargant Florence, "Economic Efficiency in the Metropolis," in *Metropolis in Modern Life*, ed. R.M. Fisher (Garden City, N.Y.: Doubleday and Co., 1955), pp.85-124; Robert Futterman, *Future of Our Cities* (Garden City, N.Y.: Doubleday and Co., 1961), Ch. 2; Wilbur Thompson, Preface to *Urban Economics* (Baltimore, Md.: The Johns Hopkins Press, 1965), chap. 1; Mason Gaffney, "Urban Expansion," *Land*, 1958 Yearbook of Agriculture (Washington, D.C.: U.S. Government Printing Office, 1958), pp.503-507; Mason Gaffney, "The Synergistic City," Real Estate Issues, *J. of the American Society of Real Estate Counselors*, Winter, 1978, pp. 36-61; and E. M. Hoover, *Location of Economic Activity* (New York: McGraw-Hill, 1948), Ch. 8.

on. Nothing less than many books can do justice to synergism. The *Yellow Pages* are Volume 1. Here I merely note it as a large addition to the land value tax base.

There is yet a fifth term for the numerator of equation (2). This is an increase of ground rent, a, that occurs as land changes hands from the credit-strong to the credit-weak. Daniel Holland (1966) and I have written on this elsewhere (Gaffney 1962).

Equation (2) involves the assumption of simple capitalization theory that realized ground rent remains the same as the land tax rate rises. This conventional assumption understates the tax base. In practice rent will certainly rise, as the land tax puts the squeeze on sleeping owners and speculators.

This is essentially a matter of credit rationing. Raising the tax rate on land works to substitute a tax cost for the interest cost of holding land. Interest costs are discriminatory, favoring the wealthy and established. Tax costs are more impartial, and if the assessor does his job right, they are completely impartial. Changing an interest cost into a tax cost therefore raises the holding costs of many present owners relative to alternative owners whose need for the land is greater and causes sales from less to more productive users.

Thus, land taxes are not fully capitalized on the lines of equation (2). As the rate rises, some land shifts to new owners who impute it a higher ground rent.

A parallel effect comes about from untaxing buildings. The building share in real estate is higher for the poor than for the rich. Untaxing buildings adds to everyone's power to bid for land (t x B in equation [2]). But it adds more to the power of those with higher ratios of building to land.

The combined effects of credit rationing and building taxation now act to pen up the poor and middle classes on a remarkably small share of the land in every city. Their potential demand for living space is suppressed. Since they have so little, the price elasticity of their demand for more must be greater than that of the rich, who have so much already. Removal of present barriers to the full expression of their demand should therefore result in a net rise of imputed ground rent.

Credit rationing is often perceived as a "wealth effect." We hear a lot about how the site value tax is economically "neutral," and leaves the market alone to do its work. In an important sense that is true. But tax theorists have long noted that taxes have two kinds of effects. There is the marginal effect, and the wealth effect. Land taxes have no marginal effect, that is, the marginal increment of capital applied to land is not taxed, and that is a great virtue. But land taxes do have a wealth effect. They drain wealth from holdouts and reduce their holdout power. It is not a small matter.

In some European colonies in Africa, the European governments once forced natives to work in the mines by levying a head tax. The natives, living happily in the bush, were forced to work in the mines to raise the money to pay the head tax - or else go to jail. That is a wealth effect. The land tax uses the same principle in favor of labor. It forces landowners to put land to use to pay the tax. But there is no jail in view. It is a carrot and stick phenomenon. The carrot is the option of building on land free of building taxes. The carrot and stick together get results. The carrot balances the stick in terms of equity. Everyone gains.

That might seem too obvious to spell out were it not that there exists an influential, highly reasoned philosophy that pretty well dismisses wealth effects. To this school of thought it does not matter who originally owns property or who begins the game with all the chips. Create good tenure rights, minimize transaction and information costs, and the market will lead to the same ideal results. For example, charging polluters an effluent tax leads to the same results as "bribing" them not to pollute so much. It is this kind of thinking that makes a tax on site value merely "neutral." There is far more in taxing the earth than is comprehended in this poor philosophy. In my opinion the wealth effects are at least as important as the marginal or trade-off effects.

7. Taxing Land Economizes on Public Capital
WHEN public works are extended, land assessments rise. This brings in private buildings to match the public, nicely synchronized with it and with each other. Planning needs such a tool. And here at last is a way to relieve people of tax - true tax relief achieved in the only possible way by economy in public spending, not by the childish dodge of substituting another tax and calling it relief.

Compact settlement reduces almost all public costs *per capita* since most of these, and many private costs as well, vary with the length of streets and lines. This important principle has been obscured in many comparative studies because they have lumped school costs with land-service costs. High density does not reduce school costs, except in small ways. It does reduce street improvement costs, capital budgets, linkage and distribution costs, and all the other costs that vary with area, like the costs of flood control and radio coverage, for example.

By stimulating rebuilding and new building and putting land to full use, the site value tax stimulates employment. This cuts down on welfare costs, which affords true tax relief.

This has to be viewed in the national perspective. Many people are preoccupied with viewing the property tax in provincial and particularistic terms, and they think of employment as a pestilence, inviting problems and especially school taxes into their enclaves. But here we are discussing the property tax as a national institution. The national effects of a national change in the character of the tax would be to increase the demand for labor nationwide, and abate the problem of unemployment and its derivative evils. It would not involve flooding any one particular jurisdiction with the rejects of the others.

Looking at it this way, you can see why some have thought that the site value tax might tend to accomplish the goal that we once hoped Keynesian policies would achieve, to wit full employment. Society has now allowed this utopian dream to be entertained, and even legislated it as a national goal in the Full Employment Act of 1946. The Keynesian approaches seem to have been pushed past their load limit, but perhaps at least it is permissible to dream some more. It was unrealistic of the old Georgists to expect local jurisdictions to solve the national unemployment problem with local tools. But now that we have a national Full Employment Act, and an Advisory Commission on Intergovernmental Relations that is concerned with the property tax, could we not begin to think of the property tax in part as a tool to help achieve full employment?

A sixth addition to equation (2) should be a dynamic growth factor. Untaxing buildings will attract capital and free a city to flourish. Growth prospects add to land values above and beyond current rents. As shown earlier, the resulting accrual of land value and of city borrowing power are current income.

My review of the philosophy of public finance has emphasised the efficiency aspects of treating the value of land as public revenue, rather than the justice issues. In fact, the two are interrelated - as in the arguments in favor of the income tax (*see Box 7:III*).

Box 7:III
Progressive & Regressive Taxation

THE INCOME TAX is defended by many because it is supposed to enable the tax authorities to levy progressively higher charges on the higher incomes.

The share of wealth that is land tends to increase with total wealth, making the land tax very progressive.

The use of land is regressive, making a land tax progressive relative to taxes levied on activity. The land tax may be as heavy as the community likes without driving away capital; in fact, the higher the tax, the more capital it will attract. *No other tax can make that statement.*

Housing taxes proportioned to housing values bear heavily on the poor. One reason is that a unit of shelter commands a minimum floor value, however miserable, simply because it enables a person to survive in a community. Above this floor, higher rents command higher quality out of proportion to the higher rent. A parallel reason is economies of scale in building. Double the cost and you may quadruple the space in a building.

For these reasons it is generally believed that housing values (and taxes based on them) do not rise in step with income, which severely limits possible property tax rates. Margaret Reid (1962) has challenged this view, and a debate rages. The resolution which the debaters have yet to see lies in the fact that outlay on buildings rises with income slower than outlay on land. The share of land in housing values tends to rise with value of house and lot together.

The plight of many people on marginal incomes in small houses sets an upper limit on the building tax rate. There is no such general limit on land taxes. While there are individual instances of poor people holding valuable land, this is almost a contradiction in terms. In general the land tax is progressive, for two reasons.

(1) It is not shifted, so only an owner and not a tenant bears it.

(2) The ownership of land is highly concentrated. As a consumer good, land is a superior good and a status symbol. As an investment, land promises capital-gains type income with minimal management problems, traits that attract the wealthy buyer.

Unlike most progressive taxes, land taxes do not suppress incentives or distort allocation. Therefore, there is no upper limit to the tax rate that may be applied to land, either on distributive or incentive grounds. Untaxing buildings removes the usual objections to raising property tax rates. It enables a community to socialize as much of its taxable surplus as is possible under any system of taxation.

Chapter 8

The Income-Stimulating Incentives of the Property Tax

Mason Gaffney and Richard Noyes

1. Reputation of the property tax

IT WAS common practice in the 1990s to proclaim the unpopularity of the property tax in the United States.

Unpopularity, of course, is generic with taxes. Property taxes are levied in relatively large sums once, twice or at best only a few times each year, an inconvenience that may aggravate the attitude more so than for taxes that are "candy coated". But is there something universally detrimental in this case? Or is the attitude fostered by the holders of large properties who find other taxes easier to escape? The architects of good government need to know.

The hard evidence supports the latter explanation. But whatever the explanation the electorate's prejudice, where it exists, is misconceived. The facts are clear enough. Where a large share of fiscal revenue comes from property taxes, individual income tends to be high. There is a clear propensity for the local economy to grow faster than in those states which are less dependent upon the property tax than on taxes linked to income or sales.

Our findings begin with an analysis of two states - New Hampshire and California - which differ in that choice.

New Hampshire shows a strong and stable aversion to taxes on income or consumption (Table 8:I), and a strong preference for the property tax. It is the only state in the Union where more than half of all government revenue, both state and local, comes from the property tax. In fact, nearly two-thirds of all state/local revenue is from that source.

But that is not the only distinctive feature about New Hampshire. For example, it has been growing twice as fast as its neighbors - such as Maine and Vermont - and that difference needs explanation. Could there be a connection between the property tax and prosperity?

California's use of the property tax has diminished sharply since the change known by its enactment: Proposition 13. Its tax history has been more typical of the 50 states as a whole, during the two or three decades when the "unpopularity" claim emerged. Limited sharply in property tax use, it has turned of necessity to taxes on both sales and income. Its once vigorous growth rate has been slowed. Could there be a connection between the decline of the property tax and the slump in the state's economic prosperity?

The two states differ in other ways, too, so we have looked at a wider number of states, grouping them by a range of differences, in search of valid conclusions.

As unpopularity was charged against the property tax, voters came to oppose it sharply enough to make political leaders propose, as alternatives, new taxes on labor, industry, trade and money flow. The property tax, once the principal source of money to fund state and local governments, dwindled in the latter half of the 20th century. Having "provided some 80% of all state-local revenue until the early 1920s, [it] was providing only 45% of that total in the mid-1950s" and had fallen to about 30 % at the start of the 1980s (Netzer 1983: 222).

Some states shifted away from it sooner than others. New Hampshire refused to make the shift at all. The results make it possible, by a comparison of tax structures in the 50 United States, to draw some conclusions about cause and effect.

California's basic state rate for sales taxes is 7% (1997), but counties may add to it. The top combined rate in San Francisco county is 8.5%. Ever since Proposition 13, sales taxes have risen to make up for the losses.

There is no clear pattern to the new taxes adopted by states as the property tax waned. Texas, Wyoming, South Dakota, and Washington are among states which have no personal income tax but do have general sales taxes. Oregon has no sales tax, but a personal income tax ranging from 5% to 9%. Several states have corporate income taxes. Most states have added many sundry "nuisance" taxes like a surtax on hotel rooms, tuition hikes at state universities, sin taxes, etc.

All things taken into account, New Hampshire's state tax burden is the lightest for any of the 50 states when measured as a percentage of *per capita* income. When local taxes are included, the total burden moves up a little in the rankings, but the essential fact is that those local taxes are on property. And by a number of different measures, the state is among the most prosperous states.

Table 8:I
Rates of Three Major Taxes Selected States, USA, 1992: %

	Individual income tax (range)	Corporation income tax (range)	General sales taxes
New Hampshire	(a)	8.0	0.0
California	1.0-11.0	9.3	6.0
Maine	2.1- 9.89	3.5-8.93	6.0
Vermont	(b)	5.5-8.25	5.0
New Jersey	2.0-7.0	9.0	6.0
New York	4.0-7.87	9.0	4.0
Pennsylvania	2.95	12.25	6.0

SOURCE: Tanzi 1995:21, Table 3-1, which drew from data furnished by the Advisory Commission on Intergovernmental Relations (ACIR).

Note (a): New Hampshire has only a twilight shadow of a personal income tax. A 5% tax on income from interest and dividends is a left-over from the earlier revision of personal property taxes on securities. Local assessors had found it hard to keep up-to-date information on them, so the state imposed the tax on income. The total income subject to it in 1995 was only 2.5% of all individual personal income.

Note (b): Vermont's income tax was pegged at from 28% to 34% of federal income tax liability.

Could this correlation be due to its heavy dependence on the property tax, coupled with a low dependence on other taxes?

California, by contrast, has been running down its use of the property tax as a revenue-raiser. Can we accurately see, as a result of this, the relative collapse of its economic prosperity and the quality-of-life of its citizens?

Figures published by ACIR in its two-volume *Significant Features of Fiscal Federalism* (SFFF) for 1994 provide some data that will help. They are for the year 1992.

Since the search is for evidence of cause and effect, it is necessary to be concerned with relationships. This explains the fact that many of the numbers in what follows are ratios: a measure of relationship.

It makes sense to examine the relationship between the property tax and all state and local taxes, taken together. We start at the top and at the bottom of the list, with New Hampshire and Alabama, comparing them with the average for the nation. And because the population of the 50 states varies so greatly, it is not total dollars that interest us, but dollars *per capita*.

Table 8:II
Taxes *per capita ($)*

	Property Tax	All state/ local taxes	Ratio
United States	699	2178	.32
New Hampshire	1344	2098	.64
Alabama	174	1435	.12

The top and bottom are highly suggestive. They accurately symbolize our more general findings. However, we need to look at the figures for more states, and to the ratios between more of the factors under consideration. We start by grouping those states with high ratios of property tax use and those states with low such use ratios, so as to compare those highs and lows, and other factors.

The top five states in this Property Tax/All Taxes ratio have higher *per capita* incomes than the bottom five states. It means extra columns; the three above, plus one for state/local tax burden in dollars per thousand and another for the *per capita* income ranking within the whole country.

The "New Hampshire five" have high property tax *per capita* as the sum of two reasons: first, higher taxes *per capita*; and second, a higher ratio of property tax to all state and local taxes. Of the two reasons, the second is stronger. Here are the ratios for the means above: first, 3091/ 1606 = 1.92; second, .41/.15 = 2.73

Do the top five levy higher taxes *per capita* because of higher *per capita* income? The ratio for the means here are 24.3/16.0 = 1.52. This direction of causation would require that a 52% rise of income *per capita* caused a 92% rise of all taxes, and a 173% rise of property taxes. That seems extreme, and therefor implausible. It is more plausible that the heavier dependence on property taxes caused the rise of personal income *per capita*. We explore this further below.

Table 8:III
States Ranked by Property Tax *per capita ($)*

	Prop Tax	All Tax	Income ratio	per cap ($000s)	Rank
TOP FIVE					
New Hampshire	1344	2098	.64	21.9	8
New Jersey	1268	2926	.43	26.1	2
Connecticut	1198	3061	.39	27.2	1
New York	1178	3534	.33	24.1	3
Alaska	1069	3835	.28	22.1	7
(Unweighted Mean)	1211	3091	.41	24.3	4.2
BOTTOM FIVE					
Louisiana	277	1654	.17	15.9	45
Arkansas	261	1518	.17	15.6	46
Oklahoma	243	1635	.15	16.4	42
New Mexico	217	1788	.12	15.5	49
Alabama	174	1435	.12	16.5	41
(Unweighted Mean)	234	1606	.15	16.0	44.6

Hypothesis 1

A high ratio of high property taxes to all taxes is associated strongly with high personal income per capita.

This is important enough so that we should complete the ranking by the ratio of property taxes to all taxes. The source of data is the same as above. The new columns at the right are personal income *per capita* and the ranking for that measure.

The mean personal income *per capita* ranking of the high eleven is 19.3, versus a ranking for the low eleven of 36.3.

The mean all-tax revenues are higher in the Top Eleven (Table 8:IV). This refutes the conventional argument that states like New Hampshire skimp on public spending (although New Hampshire itself is slightly below the United States mean of $2,178.)

The starkest contrast is between New Hampshire itself, with 64% of its state and local revenues coming from the property tax, and Alabama and New Mexico with only 12%. New Hampshire ranks eighth in personal income *per*

Table 8:IV
US States Ranked by Ratio of Property Tax to All Taxes

	Alltax	Proptax	ratio	rank	PI/cap	Rank
TOP ELEVEN						
New Hampshire	2098	1344	.64	1	21.9	8
Michigan	2173	950	.44	2	19.6	20
New Jersey	2926	1268	.43	3	26.1	2
Wyoming	2335	991	.42	4	18.2	27
Vermont	2283	954	.42	5	18.8	26
Rhode Island	2243	943	.42	6	20.3	18
Oregon	2096	864	.41	7	18.6	28
Montana	1770	707	.40	8	16.2	43
Connecticut	3061	1198	.39	9	27.2	1
Illinois	2205	849	.39	10	21.8	9
Texas	1857	730	.39	11	18.4	30
Mean	2277	982	.43	20.7	19.3	
BOTTOM ELEVEN						
Tennessee	1471	348	.24	40	17.7	35
North Carolina	1814	374	.21	41	17.9	34
West Virginia	1660	294	.18	42	15.6	47
Kentucky	1755	297	.17	43	16.5	40
Arkansas	1518	261	.17	44	15.6	46
Louisiana	1654	277	.17	45	15.9	45
Hawaii	2935	481	.16	46	22.2	6
Oklahoma	1635	243	.15	47	16.4	42
Delaware	2341	330	.14	48	20.7	14
Alabama	1435	174	.12	49	16.5	41
New Mexico	1788	217	.12	50	15.5	49
Mean	1819	300	.17	17.3	36.3	

capita. Alabama ranks as number 41. New Mexico ranks as number 49.

It would be a mistake not to take into account some of the non-statistical factors: geography, history, weather, for instance.

Alabama and New Mexico are in the fast-growing sunbelt, but they are not high growth states. New Hampshire is an old state in an old region - one of the original 13 colonies - but it is a growth state. Over the past several decades it has been the fastest growing state in the northeast.

Among eastern states, it is the only one except Florida in which more of its residents have moved into the state than those who were born there.

New Mexico is between Arizona and Texas, two of the fastest growing states, but New Mexico does not grow much. Nearby Utah, Colorado and Nevada all grow, but not New Mexico.

New Mexico is a border state, with a minority population which doubtless lowers its mean personal income. So, however, is New Hampshire. The immigrant Canadian fraction (Quebec is New Hampshire's neighboring province) of the New Hampshire population probably exceeds the immigrant fraction in New Mexico, and certainly that of Alabama.

New Mexico has attracted a number of very wealthy land buyers who hold ranches in the million dollar league. Ted Turner is well known; Robert Anderson of ARCO has long been another; Maurice Strong and his consortium of water-rights speculators are a third. The distribution of landownership in New Mexico is extremely unequal, as documented in Gaffney (1992), New Hampshire is at the other extreme, as shown in the same source.

We cannot attribute the higher property tax/all tax ratio of New Hampshire to higher incomes in that state, because its other taxes are much lower. It is, in fact, below the United States mean in all state and local taxes *per capita*. The conventional explanation on income is that it arises independently of tax expenditures, and taxes are a kind of consumption item, reflecting a consumer taste for state and local services. This blanks our minds to the possibility that a better tax system might raise incomes, and/or attract people of higher income.

New Hampshire is a rugged, mountainous, northern-tier New England state with harsh winters, no outstanding farm resources, or minerals, or fuels, or seacoast, or natural urban confluences. It is a summer vacational and winter ski-land. It has many old mill towns where obsolescent plants are still to be found, although computers and other technological industry has begun to multiply.

Its major natural or non-institutional "lucky break" advantage would seem to be its Boston suburban bedroom communities on the Massachusetts fringe, but it is doubtful if they make up a large share of its population much north of the border.

The mild winters of New Mexico and Alabama enable people to survive with lower incomes than are required to survive in New Hampshire. On the other hand, this factor tends to increase land values in the milder states, and should therefor make it easier to raise property tax revenues. This clearly has not been done in New Mexico and Alabama.

The most likely causal relationship, therefor, is from the tax system to the personal income. Let us, for that reason, pose a second hypothesis.

Hypothesis 2
Heavy reliance on property taxes, as opposed to others enacted in recent decades, tends to cause higher incomes per capita.

The data supports the hypothesis.

It will be helpful, as a cross-check, to rank states by personal income *per capita*. This will sort out the effect of personal income on taxes. States with higher personal incomes *per capita* will also have higher totals of all taxes *per capita*, because of income elasticity of demand for public services.

However, higher income will not cause higher reliance on the property tax. (If anything, it would cause higher reliance on the income tax.) Therefore, a finding of higher ratio for property taxes to all taxes in high income states indicates that the high ratio itself caused the higher incomes.

Summary of and inferences from Table 8:V
First, the U.S. means ratio of property taxes to all taxes is .32. Six of the Top Ten states are above it. The other four are Maryland with .28, Hawaii with .16, Arkansas with .28 and Nevada with .24. These exceptions are explained below. The unweighted mean for the Top Ten states is .35

Nine of the Bottom Ten states, on the other hand, are below the .32 ratio. The sole exception is Montana. The unweighted mean for the Bottom Ten is .21

In sum, a high ratio of property tax to all taxes is associated with the Top Ten, while a low ratio is strongly associated with the Bottom Ten. Thus a tax-mix that is rich in property tax is not the only cause of high incomes, but a tax-mix that lacks property taxes seems to guarantee low incomes.

Second, moving from the means of the Bottom Ten to the Top Ten:
- Personal income *per capita* rises from 15.8 to 23.4, a rise of 48%.
- All taxes rises from 1607 to 2751, a rise of 71%.
- Property tax rises from 344 to 940, a rise of 173%.

One might explain the rise of all taxes as an effect of the rise of income. There is nothing, however, about a rise of income that would explain a higher preference for the property tax over all other taxes. This leaves us with the more likely finding that the preference for the property tax explains the higher incomes.

A weaker statement is that high incomes permit higher use of all taxes, which acts as a brake on further rises, except that people learn to switch

Table 8:V
US States Ranked by Personal Income *per capita*

	PI/cap	rank	Alltax/cap	Proptax/cap	ratio
TOP TEN					
Connecticut	27.2	1	3061	1198	.39
New Jersey	26.1	2	2926	1268	.43
New York	24.1	3	3534	1178	.33
Massachusetts	23.7	4	2554	877	.34
Maryland	23.3	5	2332	653	.28
Hawaii	22.2	6	2935	481	.16
Alaska	22.1	7	3835	1069	.28
New Hampshire	21.9	8	2098	1344	.64
Illinois	21.8	9	2205	849	.39
Nevada	21.7	10	2031	488	.24
Mean	23.4		2751	940	.35
U.S.	20.1		2178	699	.32
BOTTOM TEN					
Alabama	16.5	41	1435	174	.12
Oklahoma	16.4	42	1635	243	.15
Montana	16.2	43	1770	707	.40
South Carolina	16.2	44	1584	451	.28
Louisiana	15.9	45	1654	277	.17
Arkansas	15.6	46	1518	261	.17
West Virginia	15.6	47	1660	294	.18
Utah	15.6	48	1701	461	.27
New Mexico	15.5	49	1788	217	.12
Mississippi	14.1	50	1323	357	.27
Mean	15.8		1607	344	.21

to a higher use of property tax in the mix because it is less of a constraint than other taxes.

Third, moving from the mean of the Bottom Ten to the Top Ten, the ratio of property taxes to all taxes rises from .21 to .35, a rise of 67%.

Fourth, the unweighted means of the Top Ten exceed the U.S. means as follows:

- Personal income *per capita* is 23.4, exceeding the U.S. mean of 20.1 by 16%.

- All taxes *per capita* total 2721, exceeding the U.S. mean of 2178 by 25%.
- The property tax mean is 940, exceeding the U.S. mean of 699 by 34%.

Fifth, the unweighted means of the Bottom Ten fall below the U.S. means as follows:

- Personal income *per capita* is 15.8, or 21% below the U.S. mean.
- The mean of all taxes is 1607, or 42% below the U.S. mean.
- The property tax mean is 344, or 51% below the U.S. mean.

Moving from the bottom state, Mississippi, to the top state, Connecticut, we see the following rises:

- Personal income *per capita* rises from 14.1 to 27.2, or by 93%.
- All taxes rises from 1323 to 3061, or by 131%.
- Property tax rises from 357 to 1198, or by 236%.

Another difference between the Top Ten and the Bottom Ten is that the latter states are more rural. There is no obvious reason, however, why being rural would create a preference for all other taxes over the property tax. A plausible hypothesis, however, is that a bias against the property tax would inhibit the growth of cities and commerce. New Hampshire is a state that has become quite urban in spite of its lack of any great natural urban confluence, whereas Louisiana, Mississippi and Alabama are all located on great waterways.

2. California: a sudden break

WHAT HAPPENS when a state abruptly changes its degree of dependence on the property tax? California provides the most obvious case study. A great many of the states have shifted gradually away from the property tax in the past several decades. California did it suddenly.

In 1978 the electorate was persuaded to support Proposition 13, which put a cap on the rates of the property tax. California's rank in personal income *per capita* dropped from seventh place in 1978 to twelfth place in 1992.

The drop in real personal income *per capita*, and especially in wage income *per capita*, is considerably greater. Both rents and housing prices soared after 1978, such that only ten years later, in 1988, one could not find an apartment for less than $600 a month. Between 1980 and 1989, according to reports in the press, real disposable income fell for a majority of the region's residents. The average household's income in 1985 was $26,500; in 1990, it was $50,800, but when we adjust for inflation those gains disappear. This was a gain of 91%. This compares with the consumer price index, which rose 64%; with median rent which rose 132%, from $274 a month to $635 a month; and with the median price of owner-occupied homes and condominiums which rose 163%, from $98,100 to $257,800. (These data are from *San Francisco Examiner*, September 27, 1991, page B-1.)

California's unemployment rate has become the highest in the United States, rising to over 9%, three percentage points above the national rate. It was "good news" when it fell to 8.5% in May, 1994 - high above the national rate of 5.6%. Its student/teacher ratio, grades K-12, deteriorated. Most telling of all, spending per pupil dropped from fifth place in 1965 to fortieth place in 1985. It is hard to see how a state can continue to win and hold the high-tech professionals required for California's high-tech industries to remain competitive, with one of the worst school systems in the nation.

California was one of three states where median household incomes fell by 2.1% in the two years from 1992 to 1994. California's poverty rate in 1994 was 17.9%, compared with the U.S. rate of 14.5.

The *Los Angeles Times* (October 11, 1995) chronicled the continuing decline. Colleen Kreuger, explaining a new Census Bureau report by Census staffer Kristin Hansen, on geographic mobility from March 1993 to March 1994, said a smaller fraction of people in the country as a whole were moving, possibly because of hard times. In California, however, the trend was reversed. There was a net outmigration from California to other states of 236,000. Out of a population of 31,000,000 that is .76%. Hansen told Kreuger, moreover, that more accurate "Census estimate" put the outmigration into other states at 426,000 people, or 1.37%, including international migration (which showed a net inflow). And worse yet, excluding international migration the loss ran even higher, at 2.3%. Most of the loss was from Los Angeles-Riverside, a "large metro area."

Economist Michael Boskin blamed defense cutbacks and government regulations. This turned attention away from Proposition 13 and its effects. Daniel J.B. Mitchell of UCLA, writing a forecast in the UCLA Quarterly, helped to shift the cause in people's minds by blaming a downturn in the "real estate industry," and predicting the creation of new jobs ahead.

California's counties lack funds to maintain existing stretched-out roads. Riverside County is responsible for 2,500 miles of roads. In the eight years to 1995 it repaved an average 19 miles per year. At that rate roads are repaved once every 130 years. It should be once every 20 years, according to industry standards, if roads are to be correctly maintained.

California's bond rating dropped to last among the states. Some cities and neighborhoods are especially devastated. In 1976, San Bernardino was an "All-American City," one of ten receiving the award as a "city on the go." But two decades later, and after the sharp turn away from the property tax, 40 % of its 185,000 residents were on welfare, up from 18% in 1985. Orange County, known as the epicenter of wealth and conservatism, actually went bankrupt in 1995, and some other counties are close to it.

Still, median home value in 1995 in San Bernardino was $94,000. High as that is, it is the lowest in southern California. A shack rents for $550. Absentee ownership and tenancy are rising, because in the 1980s speculators moved in from Los Angeles and Orange County, thinking values had to rise. (So thinking, they ruined neighborhoods and caused values to fall.)

Downtown Los Angeles remains a basket case. It was boom and bust carried to the nth degree, as has been the case in Hawaii. Federal tax breaks encouraged speculative office building. Then, floor space rents dropped over 50% from their peak, and values dropped even more.

Walkaways and bankruptcies multiplied.

Large parts of the San Fernando Valley are failing to renew themselves following the Northridge Earthquake of January, 1994. California was quickly rebuilt after many previous earth quakes. This time it is different.

It is too easy to "explain" California's recent fall by the ending of the Cold War, the loss of defense jobs, and cutbacks in aerospace. Many professional "explainers" seize upon these factors. The events of recent decades must be compared with the similar, but much more severe, external events after World War II. Wartime immigrants did not languish unemployed, then, or return home. They remained to create or join in a fantastic burst of growth.

Things went otherwise before the scuttling of the property tax. By the end of 1945, Los Angeles lost three quarters of its aircraft workers, and 80 % of its shipbuilders. Motion pictures went into a decline. Los Angeles was left without much of its former "economic base" of export industries.

Yet, during 1945-there was an increase in jobs (Jacobs 1969: 151-54). Los Angeles grew by replacing imports. It became remarkably self-contained, as large metropoles do. New local companies prospered.

One eighth of all new businesses started in the United States during those four years were in Los Angeles. Firms which formerly sold materials to Los Angeles opened branch plants there: Detroit auto-makers, for instance, and Akron time-makers.

What was different about 1945-49? Why did Los Angeles thrive then, but not now? The difference in which to look for cause and effect is in the fact that in those earlier years California was taxing property heavily, and land heaviest of all. Absentee land speculators, rushing in to free-ride on California's enterprise, were required to share in bearing its public costs. Holders of prime land were pressed to sell or use it to pay the taxes. Anecdotal evidence comes from executives of interstate firms, who commented on the greater pressure toward land performance in California.

The state's fall did not begin until 1978, with Proposition 13. It continues. When we compare California with other states that ranked high in property taxation in 1977 - Alaska, New Jersey, New York, Connecticut, Wyoming and New Hampshire - we see that they performed better.

3. New Hampshire: prospect for growth

NEW HAMPSHIRE can be seen as the stable element in this study of what happens as property tax use dwindles as a part of the state/local fiscal revenue mix.

It has stayed with the property tax, as other states have shifted steadily into an increasingly heavy dependence on sales, income or other taxes on labor and industry or cash flow.

As the northernmost of the 13 original colonies, and one of the smaller in both area and population from the start, it has had a relatively fixed position in economic terms, near the center of the cluster. It lost population for a few years in the middle of the 19th century, as the continent was being opened up, but for the most part has kept pace.

It was not until the start of the national disenchantment with the property tax that the state's place began to move up.

In 1967 it stood exactly in the center - in 25th place - on the best indicative measure: all state and local taxes *per capita*.

The only major change in tax policy, during the time in which the other states were shifting, came early in the seventies when one of three categories subject to the property tax - personal property - was, for the most part, removed from the base. The tax was eliminated on stock in trade, livestock, mills and machinery, and most other types of personal property.

A growing professionalism in the field of assessment has resulted in more realistic land values, so that land as a part of the remaining tax base has increased in three decades from just under 20% of the total to a high of 39.7% in 1990. That high level was due, in part, to some increase in speculative investment. It was prompted by a growing prosperity which started with the removal of personal property from the base, coupled with the fact that, despite the steady improvement in property tax administration, only part of the growing land rent was being collected. The result was a short-term downturn, which has since been reversed, and land values started climbing again.

The employment "problem" in New Hampshire since the effects of eliminating taxation on personal property began to show up has not been a shortage of jobs, but a shortage of people to fill them. The unemployment rate had remained, during most of the past two decades, at least two points below that of the nation. And the availability of jobs, in turn, attracted people to the state, which encouraged growth.

Stability - as a basic characteristic of the state - is to be seen in the fact that a return to both full employment and steady population growth began to emerge in the numbers within two years of the speculative "bust" of 1990. The downturn was brief.

New Hampshire's place in this study, based primarily on the 1992 figures used in the Advisory Commission's SFFF for 1994, was eighth, measured by personal income *per capita*.

The state led all the rest of New England in income growth from 1993 to 1995 (Economic and Labor Market Information Bureau, NH Employment Security: Jan. 1997). But more revealing for purposes of this study, it had the tenth highest percentage gain for the country as a whole. (That agency's annual report, *Vital Signs* reports that in 1995 New Hampshire "leapfrogged over Maryland to have the sixth highest *per capita* disposable income in the nation.")

The most recent income rankings from the U.S. Commerce Department in its monthly "Survey of Current Business" (Vol. 76, No. 10, October, 1996) move New Hampshire up to seventh place for personal income *per capita*, but to fifth place for disposal income, a two-place difference which can be explained by the low total state/local tax burden *per capita*.

4. Why some high-income states are exceptions

FOUR of the Top Ten states listed in Table 8: 4 seem different than the other six in that they have low property tax to all tax ratios. They need to be examined if our hypothesis is to remain valid. The four are Maryland (.28), Hawaii (.16), Alaska (.28) and Nevada (.24).

Hawaii is the most glaring anomaly. There are at least four factors involved in that case:

First, the cost of living is very high, especially due to housing values and rents. Income data are not adjusted for this, even though Federal pay scales have long contained a cost-of-living allowance for location there.

Median values of owner-occupied homes in Hawaii, according to the

1990 census, were the highest in the nation, at $245,000 as compared with $79,000 for the country overall.

Second, the 1993 data is for the end-of-boom phase. Hawaii is marked by high instability, based on the inrush and outrush of outside speculators.

When Japan crashed, Hawaii crashed, too. It is very likely that its personal income *per capita* is now lower.

Hawaiian prosperity was just a shadow of Japanese prosperity. Now, Japanese lenders are foreclosing or taking properties back. Hawaii was hardest hit; it received a quarter of all Japanese investment in the United States in 1985-90, about $16 billion. Japanese speculators have lost one-third of that: their timing was terrible. Hawaii has a history of boom/bust cycles, based on first mainland, then Canadian investors, most recently Japanese (and some Korean, and probably Taiwanese). The Pacific rim problems which exploded late in 1997 are factors which should be looked at carefully when things settle down again.

Third, the balmy climate and long coastline of Hawaii attract wealthy retirees whose incomes, derived from property elsewhere, are credited to Hawaii in the 1992 numbers. This would even include many Japanese billionaires, whose penchant for buying Hawaiian shorefront homes is famous.

Fourth, Hawaii feeds heavily on United States naval base spending.

Turning to Alaska, it even more than Hawaii has high local cost of living. Coupled with the harsh interior climate and gloomy, rainy coastal climate, it results in premium salaries required to keep workers in the state. These reflect payment for hardship, rather than being true higher incomes in the welfare sense.

Maryland, like the District of Columbia and Hawaii, feeds off Federal spending. Being suburban to the District, it attracts the more highly paid federal workers, lobbyists and others unusual enough from the ordinary to affect the comparisons being made.

Nevada depends on gambling. It feeds off neighboring states where gambling is outlawed.

5. Verdict

OUR ANALYSIS of the statistical evidence supports this hypothesis: *There is a correlation between the relatively heavy use of property taxes, as a part of the state/local tax mix, and high* per capita *incomes.*

This invites one final question: How much larger would these differences be, and how much better the results, if one end of the fiscal spectrum were socially-created land rents alone, clearly distinguished from the other end - the labor and industry of individuals?

Appendix 1

An Inventory of Rent-yielding Resources

Mason Gaffney

MANY NATURAL resources of great value are not comprehended in the simple colloquial concept of land as platted or surveyed land surfaces. These natural resources yield rents that are part of the proposed land tax base.

Resource rents may be classified into three categories: the major, the minor, and the huge aggregate. (Overlap among classes is minimized but unavoidable in certain cases.) Bibliographical sources used in this appendix appear at the bottom of this inventory.

The Major Sources of Rent

1. Energy
a. Hydrocarbons
In 1959, Alfred E. Kahn (1959) put the fraction of rent in oil and gas firms at 32-38% of sales. Paul Davidson (1963, 1964) put it even higher. Of course this fraction varies from field to field, and firm to firm, and is hard to summarize in a single figure. Oil firms studiously conceal as much of it as they can, to avoid taxation. Still, this was before the OPEC price revolution and the oil price shocks, a time when you could fill your tank, have your glass cleaned, oil, water, battery and air pressure checked, use a clean restroom and get a free map, for $3.25 or so, indicating rent must be a higher fraction today. This and other material is summarized in Gaffney (1967: 409-15. *See also Gaffney 1977, 1981, 1982*).

We know that oil and gas rents support all or most of government spending in various oil-rich nations, as in the Persian Gulf and Caspian Sea areas. Dmitri Lvov (1994) estimates that Russian oil and gas revenues alone could support the entire national government budget. In Norway, in several years the mere *change* in the value of petroleum reserves has exceeded the entire GDP of Norway (Aaheim and Nyborg 1995: 65).

Appreciation is a form of rent, on top of unit-of-production rent charges. Oil deposits normally appreciate many times over between when claims are first established and actual extraction begins, and more yet before it ends. A large fraction of industry "profit" is taken this way, but not usually declared for tax purposes. In 1980 the American Financial Accounting Standards Board (FASB) required oil firms (for the first and only time) to report the change in the value of their reserves. In that year the Getty Oil Co. reserves, for example, rose by 3.8 times as much as the profit they showed otherwise (Gaffney 1982, from Getty Annual Report). These gains now receive at worst preferential "capital gains" treatment, and at best become the basis for depletion allowances such that they are never taxed, but become a tax shelter. For this and other reasons, rent from oil and gas deposits has long enjoyed a high degree of immunity to present tax systems. Some of those nations that have found ways to tap this rent for public revenues are notoriously prosperous (although others have corruptly squandered their riches).

By 1980, in developing countries, host country shares of oil profits sometimes exceeded 80%. Conrad and Gillis (1985: 27) cite Colombia, Malaysia, and Indonesia. Oil taxes were 50%-66% of total revenues in Ecuador, Mexico, Trinidad and Tobago; and two-thirds of taxes in Indonesia, Nigeria, Venezuela, Gabon, and Congo.

b. Uranium.
With China turning to nuclear energy, we may expect rising demand for this scarce mineral.

c. Hydro.
Most American jurisdictions prodigally give away this cleanest, cheapest source of power to private firms. Canada sets a better example of how provinces and the nation can tap these rents for the public.

2. Minerals
Hardrock, sulfur, sand, clay and gravel, misc. After 1965, hardrock minerals produced 10%-20% of total public revenues in Chile, Thailand and Malaysia; and over 25% in Bolivia, Gabon, Jamaica, Liberia, New Caledonia, Papua New Guinea, Zaire, and Zambia (Conrad and Gillis 1985). These are mostly

naive people dealing with highly sophisticated and even ruthless foreign firms, so it is reasonable to infer that the true rents are higher than the figures given.

3. Fresh water and adjunct resources

In arid lands, like the western half of the U.S.A., dry land surface *per se* has only low value. The scarce, limiting resource is water. Yet, claims to water resources are not on the tax rolls and are not counted when we add up all tax valuations. Water is not held by title deeds, but by a complex system of licenses, customs and legal precedents. Thus there is a great deal of rent and value here above and beyond that counted in other ways (Gaffney 1992, 1997). Some of the valuable items are listed below.

a. Licenses to withdraw (for farming, domestic, industrial, recreational, lacustrine uses);
b. Aquifers and recharge beds;
c. Dam and reservoir sites;
d. Power drops (cross-ref. 1,c);
e. Fish (fin and shell), fishing banks, waterfowl, other wildlife (high value of quotas);
f. Scenic use (from bays to tarns to waterfalls);
g. Right-of-way, navigation servitude and priority and exemption from liability;
h. Riparian values (also apply to salt water): beaches, foreshores, water lots, frontage on water, access to water, views, fresh air;
i. Eminent domain for access to divert and "wheel" water;
j. Watersheds (water blotters, for storage and regulation of flow);
k. (Formerly) source of ice;
l. Recreation use (flatwater, whitewater);
m. salinity repulsion;
n. Waste disposal.

Waters almost all belong to the Crown, the states, or the federal government (depending on the jurisdiction), in trust for the people. Levying proper public charges on some or all of the above resources would fulfill that trust in the most efficient, equitable way.

4. Timberlands

The area is vast - one-third, in the case of the U.S.A. Unit values are low, but even low values add up to a lot over such an area. The annual value (rent) for growing wood is a fraction of the harvest value. The fraction varies with the time period and the discount rate, but if the time period is

20 years, and the real discount rate (inflation-adjusted) is 5%, the annual value (rent) is 3.0% of the net harvest value (applying a standard financial formula, "the sinking fund factor"). As a very rough cut, *if* the harvest value were $20,000 per acre, every 20 years, the rent would come to $600 per acre per year. One-third of the U.S.A. comprises 771 million acres. At $600 per acre per year, that would come to $462 billions annually. This is probably too high an estimate, since many lands classified as "forest" are less productive than the example; but it is a hundred or more times higher than taxes actually levied, for timberland enjoys virtual tax-exemption, even compared with other properties that are lightly taxed (like all California real estate after 1978). In Mendocino County, California, taxes on timberland are at about 1/36 of its annualized rent value from timber culture alone (Gaffney 1995).

Land uses declared by law to be "compatible" with timber go completely unrecognized in the legislated low valuations for property tax. These include grazing, resorts, vacation (but not retirement) homes, campsites, fishing, hunting, watershed protection, tourism, rifle ranges, rights-of-way, mining, log storage, landings, roads, logging camps, etc. There is also marijuana, possibly California's most valuable crop, but unrecorded: officially it does not exist.

Some timberland also has high ripening values for "incompatible uses" like urban subdivisions that require formal changes of zoning. These growing values go completely untaxed until conversion actually occurs - by which time the accrual of value, which is part of rent, will have gone completely untaxed.

Mature trees contain a lot of stored-up rent, most of which was never taxed. It is not too late to tap this store, with interest, by using yield taxes that the industry itself has lobbied through to displace the property tax on standing timber. In general, yield taxes are not an efficient way to tap timberland rents, but there is a place for them during a transition period towards a tax-free economy, and they are popular with preservationists because they tend to slow cutting cycles. Currently legislated levels of yield tax rates are much too low to compensate for the revenues previously lost, but raising the rate is a simple matter. Revenue-neutral rates may be calculated by formula, coupled with some judgment calls (Gaffney 1997).

5. Radio spectrum

Almost everyone now recognizes that radio spectrum is a natural resource, of enormous value, and part of the public domain. The uses of spectrum are many and growing: radio, TV, cellular phones, telephones, satellite linkages, fax, email, internet, and who knows what future forms of transmission. Nationwide, there are 16m radio dispatch units (RDUs) in use; and 14m cellular phones. In Los Angeles alone, there are 550,000 RDUs.

Assignments of licenses to use spectrum are territorial, like most natural resources. Values differ widely with the territory covered, like all rents. The next big thing may be Personal Communications Services (PCS), low-power cellular, mobile phones for the masses. Construction costs are half those of cellular. Licenses are expected to go for $100-$150 per potential customer. With 250 million potential customers in the U.S.A., that comes to $15.6 billions for PCS uses alone.

Past assignments have been based on a giveaway policy. The Federal Communications Commission, charged with meting out these rights, in 1993 began pricing new assignments by auction, which helps raise the value of old ones. As economists would predict, the result has included much "rent-seeking" effort, with resulting premature acquisitions of spectrum. Licenses are now going for about double the maximum value at which a firm could break even in the first years. The rest is "rent-seeking": wasting capital today to secure rents for tomorrow.

Public service obligations, anti-merger restrictions, and regulatory control, never adequate, are now being relaxed and sloughed off, raising spectrum values. On February 18, 1993, President Clinton created a small stir when he estimated that the airwaves would sell for $4.1 bn. In the event, the 1993 auction fetched $9 billions, but it was like selling off the badlands after giving away the beachfront properties. The truth is much more stirring. AT&T paid $12.6 billions for McCaw Cellular, a smallish regional firm, whose assets consisted of spectrum licenses (*Los Angeles Times*, Aug.17, 1993, p.1). In 1995, Disney Co. paid $19 billions for Capital Cities/ABC Inc., comprising 30 TV stations and the ABC network. On this deal Warren Buffett, the second richest American, made over $2 billions, an unearned increment, a form of resource rent that we include in the proposed tax base. These were, of course, only a tiny fraction of all the outstanding licenses. Like other untaxed natural resources, spectrum is being concentrated in a few strong hands. At the auction of March, 1995, a few deep-pocket firms dominated the bidding: these were AT&T, the Baby Bells, and The Wireless Co. (Sprint, Tele-comm Inc., Cox Cable, & Comsat). Westinghouse and CBS together own 15 TV and 39 radio stations that reach one-third of the U.S. population.

These values are based mostly on economic rents, almost as though the assets traded were bare carparks. At Westinghouse, profit margins are 45% of revenues; at ABC the rent fraction is higher; at CBS, somewhat lower (*Los Angeles Times*, 2 August 1995, p.1). Rents show up as above-average rates of return on capital. In cellular phones, rates of return have ranged from 40-100% per year (Morgan Stanley Inc., 1994). During the long giveaway period before 1993, many applied for licenses "and then sat on them until they could resell them for a large profit." From 1985-94, 85% of cellular licenses turned over. In such sales, the license "accounts for approximately 60% of the sale price..." (Cohen 1995).

In addition to basic spectrum, high values attach to ancillary sites like hilltops for transmission relay stations. Even orbits like the geosynchronous orbital band and LEO (Low Elevation Orbits) are assuming a value. Many of these hilltops are on public lands, and are generally given away in what are essentially "sweetheart deals."

Teledesic (Bill Gates and Craig McCaw) next plans to link the whole globe with phone, video, and data services, using 840 satellites. Each one, of course, requires spectrum assignments from the public domain of various nations. These are Low Earth Orbit (LEO) satellites, at 435 mi. up, the cheapest kind, with the shortest life. Gravity pulls each one out of orbit every eight years or so - but the spectrum assignment remains, and spectrum lasts forever, rising in value (*Los Angeles Times*, 22 March, 1994, p.D1).

A few other major firms are aggressively expanding worldwide, seizing spectrum and orbital positions as they go, vying for the needed political influence. One of their vehicles is the ITU (International Telecommunications Union, a U.N. body with 182 members), dominated by U.S. money and national power, by which the firms exploit national power for private gain. Vice- President Al Gore, U.S. Government point man on this matter, is pushing hard, using U.S. power. "Gore said the U.S. will throw its weight behind the global network project" (speech in Buenos Aires to the ITU (*Los Angeles Times*, 22 March, 1994, p.D1).

Is it feasible for the public to collect spectrum rents? It is a simple matter of adapting classical economic theory to modern technology. Techniques and venues change; principles perdure. Professor Harvey Levin worked out feasible methods 25 years ago (Levin 1971). It only remains to apply them.

6. Rights of way, easements, etc.

Rights-of-way (ROW) occupy enormous areas. In cities, especially, streets occupy from one quarter to one half of the entire improved area. Right-of-ways have strategic monopoly bargaining power limited only by what the traffic will bear or what regulation permits. When privately owned they owe their very existence to the state, which not only granted the original land surface, but in almost every case loaned its power of eminent domain to cobble the ROW together. The power to extract rents from taxing and rating ROWs is almost limitless (Gaffney 1988). It is limited prudentially by the case for economical (marginal cost) pricing to maximize use, but this can be provided via various forms of price discrimination (declining block rates) that are compatible with extracting rent from customers on high-rent lands.

Some basic ROWs are streets, rails, highways, canals, navigation servitude with priority and subsidy and freedom from liability, air corridors with overflight privileges, ROW for power lines, phone lines, cable lines, gas lines, water lines, storm sewers, sanitary sewers, flood-control channels, drainage lines, etc.

When ROWs are congested, direct use has high marginal social cost, and could and should be used to raise revenues. Peak load tolls on ferries, bridges, and controlled highways are obvious cases. Parking fees for downtown streets are another: think what revenues New York could raise from the street parking it now gives away on land worth up to $2,000 per square foot, or about $600,000 per parking space. Moving vehicles also take up scarce space: electronic means of measuring vehicle space usage are now technologically and economically feasible and in actual use in several stretches of congested space, like California #91 in Orange County. Taxi medallions in Manhattan now trade for over $200,000 apiece, values that could easily be socialized. Oversized, space-hogging vehicles can and should pay more.

Utility ROWs are the essence of the franchise's monopoly power. Through the common devices of price discrimination they can be and are used to extract rents from consumers, limited only by regulation. A public agency might easily use such discrimination to tap rents from customers with high land values (Gaffney 1988).

ROW monopolists are often required to provide "common carrier" service to all applicants. In practice, some of them comply with the letter, but not the spirit of the law by giving outsiders and interlopers low priorities of usage, reserving the prime times for themselves. This results in monopoly profits, a form of rent, that should be taxed away, if it cannot be prevented altogether.

The common tax practice is to value utility lands on the same basis as ordinary private lands adjacent thereto - lands lacking the eminent domain premium. This results in ignoring the eminent domain premium in ROWs - in effect, valuing it at zero. A proper tax on rents would assess its monopoly value and tax it accordingly.

Many ROWs were granted, and accepted, subject to heavy public obligations, like the rails duty to carry the mails free, and carry troops in wartime, and maintain passenger service. Private beneficiaries have become expert at sloughing off these public obligations, and brainwashing the public into accepting it as being in their interest. Deregulation; privatization

Backup lands with special access and/or integration: parking, railyards, power-plant sites, tank farms, fuel stations, moorings, truckyards, rest stops, sales yards for autos, trucks, driveways, laterals, container lots, aircraft parking, billboard sites, etc.

7. Aircraft time-slots, landing rights, gates, airlanes, etc.

a.   Busy airports: congestion-relieving landing fees are rent charges.
b.   Redundant airports: high unit cost from underuse. Here, user cost equals zero, so users as such should not be charged, leaving benefited landowners to pay it all. Desired economic result: abort such airports, release vast lands for higher uses.

8. Pollution easements, *de facto* and *de jure*.

These include contingent easement (Price-Anderson Act), and subsidized waste-disposal. The alternative is "polluter pays," a "green tax," which is a rent charge (principle of "Tax bads, not goods.")

9. Farm soils

10. Recreation lands

11. Privileged use of congested commons (user charges on commons are rent taxes.)

a.   City streets: taxi permits; curb parking; access to congested times and areas; preferential traffic controls; vending licenses, *de jure* and *de facto*, mobile and stationary; licenses for oversized vehicles; surface mass transit; emergency vehicles; cortege right-of-ways; right-of-ways for utilities, with rights to stop traffic for digging, etc.
b.   Highways: peakload use; exclusive rights to serve, e.g. trucking, busing; accident investigation and clearance;
c.   Parks, beaches
d.   Air
e.   Common waters
f.   Open range (grazing, hunting)
g.   Pre-leasing exploration

12. Territorial franchises

a.   Publicly granted: bank charters; concessions at parks; utility franchises; liquor licenses; gambling licenses; etc.

b.   Privately granted: dealerships; leases that bar competition; etc.

13. Salt water

The Minor sources

1. Privileged access

2. Wildlife habitat zones

3. Misc. energy sources: geothermal, wind, solar sites, firewood, adiabatic sites, tides, currents

4. Zoning

a.   Unaccounted-for zoning losses

b.   Exclusive use zones, e.g. foreign trade; tax-preferred zones, e.g. urban redevelopment zones (clear case of All Taxes Come Out of Rent); dumpsites; commercial zoning; locally undesirable land use (nuisance) zones;

c.   Variances with grandfather protection

5. The gene pool: seed patents; natural herbs, medications; breeding stock

6. Quotas, allotments to produce or import or sell.
Generally, such quotas should simply be stricken, transferring their rents to other lands; but, if not, they are taxable property.

7. Some patents which are indirect means of dominion over natural resources. Shale oil extraction techniques; coal liquefaction; sulfur extraction; etc.

8. Licenses to produce or dispense goods or services that are generally prohibited: nuclear materials; medicinal drugs; pharmacies; alcohol; undertaking & burial; barbering; gambling, liquor, prostitution.

9. Monopoly, with or without government support.
Monopoly or market power may be recognized wherever price discrimination is practiced, or might be.

10. Aspects of advertising
Intruding without leave on public's limited attention span, downgrading associated experiences. Billboards, commercials on media, phone solicitations, junk mail, roadside lights, newspaper ads, skywriting, sound trucks, etc.

11. Easements for views, air rights, etc.
Also the converse: permission to build or maintain eyesores, like the transmission tower on Twin Peaks, San Francisco; overhead wires;

12. Moorings
Riparian and foreshore land has high premium value from water access, but in addition, space on the water itself has another value.

Falsified land values

ECONOMISTS and government statisticians trivialize values and rents of ordinary or "standard" land. To recap the high points, here are some of the devices of false measurement that make land and rent vanish.
1.   Narrow meaning of "land" to farmland.
2.   Making land and rent the "residual" when allocating value between land and extant buildings. This has its *reductio ad absurdum* when buildings are demolished, indicating a net value of zero, and the tax valuer is still valuing the building higher than the site.
3.   Understating building depreciation; ignoring building obsolescence.
4.   Granting low assessments based on current use; or current restrictive zoning that market prices ignore; or historical cost; or capitalized cash income.
5.   Valuing "acreage" as though it were farmland, regardless of location. *Reductio ad absurdum* comes to light when condemnation values are found to be many times assessed values.
6.   Subsidizing some activities by exempting their land from taxation, even though salaries earned thereon are taxed; and neglecting to value the land at market.
7.   Omitting the option value of favorable zoning until it is exercised. Likewise, omitting other option values like potential mineral leasing.
8.   Omitting the value of grandfather privileges of old buildings.

9. Omitting the value of land and resources outside state and local tax jurisdictions (e.g. the Outer Continental Shelf).
10. "Cashflow bias": overlooking noncash and other less obvious and less easily measurable non-standard values of land. Overlooking or understating imputed income and unrealized gains.
11. Treating corporate values as "intangibles," ignoring the land assets of corporations, thus treating corporate income as though it contained no land income. Ditto for other profits.
12. Valuing ROWs only in lower uses; putting no value on result of using eminent domain.
13. Ignoring the ruse of shifting income to foreign-flag vessels, thus concealing the rents taken by businesses that are vertically integrated.
14. Overlooking the rents taken by extraterritorial assets that enjoy national flag protection, for which payment should be due.
15. Maladministration of public lands, concealing their latent rents.
16. Overlooking the value of *de facto* tenures without formal fee simple titles, e.g. licenses to divert water.
17. Overlooking unrealized gains in value, a form of rent.
18. Overlooking latent strata values ("air rights").
19. Overlooking the value of reservations held back by sellers and lessors.
20. Omitting latent plottage values of wrongly sized or shaped parcels.
21. Omitting the value of favorable leaseholds.
22. Omitting the value of privileged exemption from public liability, e.g. nuclear power sites, old plants with grandfather licenses to pollute, shipping licenses, etc.
23. Omitting the premium value of lands held by firms with superior market power. Adjusting the values of "ordinary" lands (land surfaces that are surveyed and platted) for the above factors results in rent values much higher than anything conventionally measured or reported today. Yet, when we propose taxing rents, those elements of value are all part of the tax base.

It seems reasonable to conclude that aggregate resource rents, in a tax-free economy, would be adequate to replace all present taxes. That conclusion is subject to a comprehensive definition of rent, as explained above.

Bibliography

Asbjorn Aaheim and Karine Nyborg, 1995. "On the Interpretation and Applicability of a 'Green Nat. Product.'" *The Review of Income and Wealth* 1(41):57-72, March.

Warren Cohen, 1995. "Halting the Air Raid." *The Washington Monthly*, June, pp.30-32.

Robert Conrad and Malcolm Gillis, 1985. "Progress and Poverty in Developing Countries." In Stephen R. Lewis Jr. (ed.) 1985. *Henry George and Contemporary Economic Development*. Williamstown, MA: Williams College, pp.25-48.

Paul Davidson, 1964, "Reply to Comments on Public Policy Problems of the Domestic Crude Oil Industry," *American Economic Review*, 54 (March 1964), 125-34).

"   1963, "Public Policy Problems of the Domestic Crude Oil Industry," *American Economic Review*, 53 (March 1963), 85-108.

Mason Gaffney, 1997a, "A Simple General Test for Tax Bias," MS submitted for review to *National Tax Journal*.

"   1997b, "What Price Water Marketing? California's New Frontier." *Am. J. of Ecs. and Soc.* 56(4):475-520 (October, 1997).

"   1995, "Property Tax Reform in the Big Picture." A Paper Delivered at the Conference on Land, Wealth, and Poverty, Annandale, NY: The Jerome Levy Institute, November 3.

"   1992, "The Taxable Surplus in Water Resources," *Contemporary Policy Issues* 10(4): 74-82, October.

"   1988, "Tapping Land Rents after Prop. 13." *Western Tax Review* (annual), pp. 1-55.

"   1982, "Oil and Gas: the Unfinished Tax Reform." Paper delivered at 20th Annual Conference of TRED, The Committee on Taxation, Resources and Economic Development, Cambridge, MA, 1982.

"   1981, "Effects of Severance Taxation on Industrial Efficiency and State Revenues." Invited Testimony, California State Assembly Committee on Revenue and Taxation, Hearings on Oil Severance Taxation and AB 1597, 15 October.

"   1977, *Oil and Gas Leasing Policy: Alternatives for Alaska in 1977*. A Report to The State of Alaska, Jay S. Hammond, Governor, *et al.* Juneau: Interim Committee on Oil and Gas Taxation and Leasing Policy.

"   (ed.), 1967, *Extractive Resources and Taxation*, Madison: University of Wisconsin Press

Alfred Kahn and Melvin De Chazeau, 1959, *Integration and Competition in the Petroleum Industry*, New Haven: Yale University Press, 1959.

Harvey Levin, 1988 (Title not available), in *Telecommunications Policy*, March.

"   1980, "Economic Rents in Broadcasting," in *Facts and Fancy in TV Regulation*, New York: Basic Books.

"   1971, *The Invisible Resource*. Baltimore: Johns Hopkins University Press.

Dmitri Lvov, 1994, *Practicable Course of Economic Reforms in Russia*. Moscow: Russian Academy of Sciences, Central Economics and Mathematics Institute.

Morgan Stanley Inc., *cit*. Cliff Cobb, 1994. "Auctioning the Radio Spectrum." *Groundswell*, Jan/Feb, p.7.

Appendix 2

Land values for selected countries

A CENTRAL hypothesis of the study in this volume is that taxes on wages and the income flowing to capital depress the net income that owners can claim as the rent of land and natural resources. Thus, we find that the higher the tax-take, the lower the proportion of national income represented by the visible (directly measurable) net income that remains to be claimed as rent.

In Europe, Denmark is important for two reasons: it has the highest tax-take (with Finland close behind), and its land values are accurately measured for tax purposes. Our hypothesis is therefor open to testing by economists who wish to modify their models to incorporate a rent-based equation.

Data on land values on a country-wide basis is extremely poor except for a few countries such as Japan and New Zealand. A compilation of estimates for a selected number of countries is offered by Professor Frederic Jones (1997).

The estimate for Denmark used in Chapter 5 was provided by Anders Muller of the Inland Revenue Directorate, Copenhagen. For a comprehensive review of the land valuation process in Denmark see Muller & Mørch-Lassen in Banks (1989). In 1996 land was valued at 455 milliard DKK. Total value was 1,919 milliard DKK. Total taxes were 315 milliard DKK out of national income of 607 milliard DKK.

These values convert, using December 1997 exchange rates, to the following:

Land	455 milliard DKr	£40.8 bn	$67.4 bn
Property	1,919 milliard DKr	£172bn	$284 bn
Taxes	315 milliard DKr	£28.25bn	$46.7 bn
N Income	607 milliard DKr	£54.4bn	$89.9bn

Estimate of total land value, Finland (1995)

	Area (Hectares)	Average value (FinnMarks)	Billion (FMK)
RURAL AREAS			
Agricultural land	2,220.000	10.000	22.2
Forest land (without trees)	26,100.000	1.000	26.1
Sites for houses	108.000	150.000	16.2
Sites for summer cottages	142.000	200.000	28.4
Other (military,nature,prot.etc.)	1,536.000	1.500	2.3
URBAN AREAS			
Building sites	177.000		172.2
Non-building land	177.000	50.000	8.8
Total	30,460.000		276.2

These values convert (using exchange rates for December 1997) to the following:

RURAL AREAS			
Agriculture	22.2bn FMK	£2.51bn	$4.15bn
Forest w/o Trees	26.1bn FMK	£2.96bn	$4.88bn
Sites for houses	16.2bn FMK	£1.83bn	$3.03bn
Sites for cottages	28.4bn FMK	£3.22bn	$5.31bn
Other (Military etc)	2.3bn FMK	£0.26bn	$0.43bn

URBAN AREAS			
Building sites	172.2bn FMK	£19.5bn	$32.19bn
Non-building land	8.8bn FMK	£0.99bn	$1.64bn

Total	276.2bn FMK	£31.28bn	$51.63bn

The value of forests and trees was about 167bn FMK, equivalent to £18.91bn ($31.21bn).

Estimates for the value of land in Finland were provided by Pekka V. Virtanen, who as a professor at Helsinki University of Technology had specialized in the economics of real estate. The data, for 1995, does not include some parts of the 300,000 sq kms of a country which are deemed to be inaccessible for valuation purposes. In Finland, the taxable values of land are never real market values. The forest (87% of total) and agricultural lands (8%) are under-assessed for political reasons, reports Prof. Virtanen (personal communication to present authors). For fiscal purposes, the tax authorities target 70% of the market value of urban land. Prof. Virtanen has accordingly adjusted the values to bring the estimates as close to market value as possible.

Bibliography

Aaron, Henry, and Harvey Galper (1985), *Assessing Tax Reform*, Washington: The Brookings Institute.

Ballard, Charles L., John B. Shoven and John Whalley (1985), "General Equilibrium Computations of the Marginal Welfare Costs of Taxes in the United States", *American Economic Rev.*, 75.

Banks, Ronald (1989), ed., *Costing the Earth*, London: Shepheard-Walwyn.

" (1998: forthcoming), *Life, Liberty & Estate*, London: Othila Press.

Barloch, Lord Douglas of (1936), *Land-Value Rating*, London: Christopher Johnson.

Blondal, Sveinbjorn, & Stefano Scarpetta (1997), "The OECD Jobs Strategy under Scrutiny", *The OECD Observer*, No. 209, December

Brennan, Geoffrey, & James Buchanan (1980), *The Power to Tax: Analytical foundations of a fiscal constitution,* Cambridge: Cambridge University Press.

Brittan, Samuel (1997), "Redistributive Market Liberalism", The John Stuart Mill Lecture, J.S. Mill Institute, London, Nov. 10.

Broë, Williams de (1997), Market Notes, London, Dec.16.

Brown, Gordon (1997), "No quick fixes on jobs", *The Financial Times*, London: November 17.

Brown, H. James (1997), ed., *Land Use & Taxation,* Cambridge, Mass.: Lincoln Institute of Land Policy.

Buchanan, James (1993), "The Political Efficiency of General Taxation", *National Tax Journal*, XLVI(4).

Byrus, Ralph T., and Gerald W. Stone (1989), *Economics,* 4th edn., London: Scott, Foresman.

Case, Fred (1960), *Los Angeles Real Estate; A Study of Investment Experience*, Los Angeles: Real Estate Research Program, Graduate School of Business Administration, Division of Research, University of California.

Cheng, Chen (1961), *Land Reform in Taiwan*, Taipei: China Publishing Co.

Coleman, Brian (1997), "EU Picks Another Fight with US over Trade", *The Wall Street Journal Europe*, Nov. 19.

Confederation of British Industry (1997), *Fit for the Future*, London.

Crovitz, L. Gordon (1997), "Economic Freedom: Asian Lessons for the West", *Wall Street Journal Europe*, Dec.3.

Daveri, Francesco and Guido Tabellini (1997), *Unemployment, Growth and Taxation in Industrial Countries*, London: Centre for Economic Policy Research.

Douglas, Roy (1976), *Land, People & Politics*, London: Alison & Busby.

237

Elliott, Larry, and Victoria Brittain, "Seven richest could end want", London: *The Guardian*, June 12.

Etzioni, Amitai (1995), *The Spirit of Community*, London: Fontana.

European Commission (1994), *Growth, Competitiveness, Employment: The Challanges and Ways Forward into the 21st Century*, Luxembourg: EC.

Feinstein, C.H. (1968), "Changes in the Distribution of the National Income in the UK since 1860", in Jean Marchal and Bernard Ducros (eds.), *The Distribution of National Income*, London: Macmillan.

Feldstein, Martin S., and Robert P. Inman (1977), *The Economics of Public Services*, London: Macmillan.

Feldstein, Martin (1977), "The Surprising Incidents of a Tax on Pure Rent: A New Answer to an Old Question", *J. of Political Economy*, 85.

"   (1996), *How Big Should Government Be?*, Cambridge, Mass.: National Bureau of Economic Research.

"   (1997a), "Japan's Folly Drags Asia Down", *The Wall Street Journal* Europe, November 26.

"   (1997b), "EMU and International Conflict", *Foreign Affairs* 76(6), Nov-Dec.

Field, Frank (1997), *Welfare to Work, Lessons from America*, London: Institue of Economic Affairs.

Foldvary, Fred (1994), *Public Goods and Private Communities*, Aldershot, UK: Edward Elgar Publishing, 1994.

"   (1997), "The Business Cycle: A Georgist-Austrian Synthesis", *The American Journal of Economics and Sociology*, Vol 56 (4).

Friend, Andrew, & Andy Metcalf (1981), *Slump City: The Politics of Mass Unemployment*, London: Pluto Press.

Gaffney, Mason (1962), "Ground Rent and the Allocation of Land among Firms," in F. Miller (ed.), *Rent Theory*, University of Missouri Research Bulletin 810, Columbia, Mo.: Missouri Agricultural Experiment Station.

"   (1992), "Rising Concentration and Falling Property Tax Rates", in Gene Wunderlich (ed.), *Land Ownership and Taxation in American Agriculture*, Boulder: Westview Press.

"   (1994a), "Land as a Distinctive Factor of Production", in Tideman (1994).

"   (1994b), *The Corruption of Economics*, London: Shepheard-Walwyn.

Galbraith, J.K. (1987), *The Affluent Society*, Harmondsworth: Penguin.

George, Henry (1879) *Progress and Poverty*, centenary edn., Robert Schalkenbach Foundation, New York, 1979.

Goldsmith, Raymond (1962), *The National Wealth of the U.S. in the Postwar Period*, Princeton: Princeton Univ. Press.

"   (1955), *A Study of Savings in the U.S.*, Vol. 3, Princeton: Princeton University Press.

Grahl, John (1997), *After Maastricht*, London: Lawrence and Wishart.

Grebler, Leo (1955), *Experience in Urban Real Estate Investment,* New York: Columbia University Press.

Hall, Robert, and Alvin Rabushka (1995), *The Flat Tax*, 2nd edn., Stanford

University, CA: Hoover Institution Press.

Harrison, Fred (1983), *The Power in the Land*, London: Shepheard-Walwyn.

"   (1997), "The Coming 'Housing' Crash", in Frederic J. Jones (1997)

"   and Galina Titova (1997), *Land Rent Dynamics & Sustainable Development*, Boston, Mass.: Lincoln Institute of Land Policy.

Harriss, C. Lowell (1977), "Land Taxation in Taiwan", in *Property Tax Reform: Foreign and US Experience with Site Value Taxation*, Cambridge, Mass.: Lincoln Institute of Land Policy.

"   (1979), "Rothbard's Anarcho-Capitalist Critique", in R.V. Andelson (ed.), *Critics of Henry George*, Rutherford: Fairleigh Dickinson University Press.

Harvey, Robert (1988), editor, *Blueprint 2000: The Conservative Policy Towards Employment and Technology in the Next Century*, London: Macmillan.

Hayek, Friedrich von (1960), *The Constitution of Liberty*, London: Routledge & Kegan Paul.

"   (1962), *The Road to Serfdom*, London: Routledge & Kegan Paul.

Heilbroner, Robert (1983), *The Wordly Philosophers*, Harmondsworth: Pelican.

"   (1996), "Reflections on a Sad State of Affairs", in Robert Eatwell, *Gobal Unemployment: Loss of Jobs in the '90s*, Armonk, NY: M.E. Sharpe.

Hill, Christopher (1996), *Liberty Against the Law*, London: Penguin.

Holland, Daniel (1966), "The Taxation of Unimproved Value in Jamaica," in Walter J. Kress (ed.), 1965 Proceedings of the Fifty-Eighth Annual Conference on Taxation, National Tax Association, Harrisburg, Pa.

Hong Kong (1997), *Hong Kong Annual Report*, Hong Kong: Government.

Hudson, Michael (1997), "Where Did All the Land Go? The Fed's New Balance Sheet Calculations", unpublished manuscript, New York: Robert Schalkenbach Foundation.

"   and Kris Feder (1997), Real Estate and the Capital Gains Debate, Working Paper No. 187, Annandale-on-Hudson, New York: The Jerome Levy Economics Institute, Bard College.

"   and Baruch A. Levine (1996), *Privatization in the Ancient Near East and Classical World*, Cambridge, Mass.: Peabody Museum of Archaeology and Ethnology, Harvard University.

Hunter, Laurence C., & G.L. Reid (1968), *Urban Worker Mobility*, Paris: OECD.

Husain, Aasim. M (1997), "Hong Kong, China in Transition", *Finance & Development*, Washington, DC: IMF/World Bank, September.

Jacobs, Jane (1969), *The Economy of Cities*, New York: Random House.

Jefferson, Thomas (1905), *Notes on Virginia*, Washington DC: Thomas Jefferson Memorial Association.

Johnson, Bryan T., Kim R. Holmes and Melanie Kirkpatrick (1997), "Freedom's Steady March", *Wall Street Journal Europe*, Dec.1.

Jones, Frederic J. (1997), *The Chaos Makers*, London: Othila Press.

Jones, Randall S. (1997), "Japan: Population Aging", *The OECD Observer*, No. 209, December.

Jupp, Kenneth (1997), *Stealing Our Land*, London: Othila Press.

Kang, Heung Sup (1994), "A Study on the Desirable Land System in the Unified Korea", MPA Thesis, The Graduate Institute of Peace Studies, Kyung Hee University, Seoul, October.

Kay, J.A. & M. A. King (1990), *The British Tax System*, Oxford: Oxford University Press, fifth edn.

Kelsey, Jane (1995), *Economic Fundamentalism*, London: Pluto Press.

Keynes. J.M. (1920), *The Economic Consequences of the Peace*, New york: Harcourt Brace.

"   1936), *The General Theory of Employment Interest and Money*, London: Macmillan.

Kurnow, Ernest (1961), "Distribution and Growth of Land Values," in Joseph Keiper, Ernest Kurnow, Clifford Clark, and Harvey Segal, *Theory and Measurement of Rent*, Philadelphia: Chilton

"   (1960), "Land Value Trends in the U.S.," *Land Economics* 36(4

"   (1959), "Measurement of Land Rent and the Single Taxers," *Commercial and Financial Chronicle*, 190

Leggassick, Martin, and Francine de Clercq (1984), "Capitalism and Migrant Labour in Southern Africa: The Origins and nature of the System", in Shula Marks & Peter Richardson, *International Labour Migration*, Hounslow: Maurice Temple Smith.

Lincoln, John C. (1957), *Ground Rent not Taxes: The Natural Source of Revenue for the Government*, New York: Exposition Press.

MacKerron, Gordon, and Mike Sadnicki (1997), *Managing Nuclear Liabilities,* Brighton: Science Policy Research Unit, Susex University.

Marx, Karl (1887), *Capital*, Vol. 1.

McLure, Charles, and George Zodrow (1994), "The Study and Practice of Income Tax Policy", in John Quigley and Gene Smolensky (eds.), *Modern Public Finance*, Cambridge, Mass: Harvard University Press, 1994.

Meyers, Harold B. (1969), "Tax-Exempt Property", *Fortune*, May 1.

Millar, Jane, Steven Webb and Martin Kemp (1997), *Combining work and welfare*, York: Joseph Rowntree Foundation.

Miller, G.J. (1998), *Born to Die*, London: Othila Press: forthcoming.

Ministry of Construction (1992), *White Paper on Construction*, Tokyo.

Muller. Anders, & Gregors Morch-Lassen (1989), "Land Valuation and Fiscal Policy in Denmark", in Banks (1989).

Netzer, Dick (1997), "What Do We Need to know about Land Value Taxation?", Cambridge, Mass.: Lincoln Institute of Land Policy (Founder's Day Lecture, Sept. 22).

"   (1983), "Does the Property Tax Have a Future," in *The Property Tax and Local Finance*, New York: The Academy of Political Science.

OECD (1992), *Urban Land Markets: Policies for the 1990s*, Paris: OECD.

"   (1988), *Japan*, Paris: OECD.

"   (1989), *Japan*, Paris: OECD.

"   (1991), *Japan*, Paris: OECD.

Ogilvie, William (1997), *Birthright in Land*, London: Othila Press.

ONS (1996), *Public Finance Trends 96*, London: Office for National Statistics.

"   (1997), *Financial Statistics*, London: Office for National Statistics.

Pareto, Vilfredo (1971), *Manual of Political Economy* (Translator: Ann S. Schwier), New York: Augustus M. Kelley.

Piachaud, David (1998), "Million more face poverty under Labour", *The Guardian* (London), Jan.5.

Potts, Lydia (1990), *The World Labour Market: A History of Migration* (translator: Terry Bond), London: Zed Books.

Ranis, Gustav (1958-59), "The Financing of Japanese Economic Development," *The Economic History Review*, Vol. 11, 1958-59.

Reid, Margaret (1962), *Housing and Income*, Chicago: University of Chicago Press.

Ricardo, David (1821), *Principles of Political Economy and Taxation*.

Robertson, James (1997), Briefing for Policy Makers on the New Economics of Sustainable Development, Brussels: European Commission (unpublished).

Rothbard, Murray (1962), *Power and Market: Government and the Economy*, Princeton, NJ: Van Nostrand.

Samuelson, Paul (1967), *Economics*, 7th edn., New York: McGraw Hill.

"   and William D. Nordhaus (1985), *Economics*, 12th edn., New York: McGraw Hill.

Schumpeter, Joseph (1954), *History of Economic Analysis*, London: Routledge.

Seligman, E.R.A. (1913), *Essays in Taxation*, 8th edn., New York: Macmillan.

Shishido, Toshio (1992), *White Paper on Construction*, Tokyo: Ministry of Construction.

Smith, Adam (1776), *The Wealth of Nations*.

Solow, Robert. M. (1997), "How to Treat Intellectual Ancestors", in H.James Brown (1997) *Land Use & Taxation,* edited by H. James Brown, Cambridge, Mass.: Lincoln Institute of Land Policy.

"   and William S. Vickrey (1971), "Land Use in a Long Narrow City", *J. of Economic Theory*, 3(4).

Soros, George (1997), "Avoiding a breakdown", *The Fiancial Times* (London), December 31.

Stamp, Josiah (1922), *Wealth and Taxable Capacity*, London: P.S. King.

Staunton, Dennis (1997), "Fraudster Tycoon Tumbles, *The Guardian* (London), December 24.

Steinbeck, John (1939), *The Grapes of Wrath*, London: Heinemann.

Tabellini, Guido (1997), "Labor Taxes and Unemployment, *Wall Street Journal Europe*, November 21-22.

Tanzi, Vito (1995), *Taxation in an Integrating World*, Washington, DC, The Brookings Institution.

Tett, Gillian, and Bethan Hutton (1997), "Economic Hopes Boost Nikkei", *The Financial Times*, November 18.

Thatcher, Margaret (1993), *The Downing Street Years*, London: HarperCollins.

"   (1995), *The Path to Power*, London: HarperCollins.

Tideman, Nicolaus (1994), "The Economics of Efficient Taxes on Land", in Nicolaus Tideman (ed.), *Land and Taxation,* London: Shepheard-Walwyn.

Treasury, HM (1997a), *Securing Britain's Long-Term Economic Future*, London: Stationery Office CM 3804.

"   (1997b), *A Code for Fiscal Stability*, London: HM Treasury.

"   (1997c), Fiscal policy: lessons from the last economic cycle, London: Treasury, November.

United Nations (1968), *Manual of Land Tax Administration*, New York: UN.

"   (1997), *The Human Development Report*, Oxford: Oxford University Press.

Vickrey, William (1977), "The City as a Firm", in M. Feldstein & R. Inman (1977).

"   (1995), "Simplification, Progress, and a Level Playing Field, April 2, 1995, and "Propositions relating to Site Value Taxation", August 13, 1995, Columbia University (unpublished manuscripts).

Walker, Martin (1998), "Brussels mandarin dampens job hopes", *The Guardian* (London), Jan. 6.

Weizsacker, Ernst von, & Jochen Jesinghaus (1992), *Ecological Tax Reform*, London: Z Books.

Welsh, Frank (1997), *A History of Hong Kong*, London: HarperCollins.

Wessel, David (1998), "Greenspan Addresses Stock Prices," *Wall Street Journal Europe*, Jan.5.

Wicksell, Knut (1901), *Lectures on Political Economy*, transl. E. Classen , New York: Macmillan.

"   (1893), *Value, Capital and Rent*, trans. R. Frowein, London: George Allen and Unwin.

Winnick, Louis (1958), *Rental Housing:Opportunities for Private Investment*, New York: McGraw-Hill.

Young, M.D. (1992), *Sustainable Investment and Resource Use*, Paris: UNESCO.

Recommended Reading

Adams, Charles (1993), *For Good and Evil: The Impact of Taxes on the Course of Civilization*, London: Madison Books.

Barlett, Donald, and James Steele (1992), *America: What Went Wrong?*, Kansas City: Andrews and McMeel.

Barlett, Donald, and James Steele (1994), *America: Who Really Pays the Taxes?* New York: Simon and Schuster.

Phillips, Kevin, (1990), *The politics of rich and poor : wealth and the American electorate in the Reagan aftermath*, New York : Random House.

" (1993), *Boiling Point*, NY: Random House

Miller, G.J. (1998), *Born to Die*, London: Othila Press: forthcoming.

Wenzer, Kenneth C. (1997), *An Anthology of Single Land Tax Thought*, Rochester: University of Rochester Press.

About the Authors

Ronald Banks
As Chairman of the Land Policy Council, London, and of the Land & Public Welfare Foundation, St. Petersburg, Mr. Banks advises a number of Russian Federal government ministries, and regional and city administrations. He is the UK property investment adviser to Interforex Corporation, Geneva, and is a registered psychotherapist.

Mason Gaffney PhD
Dr. Gaffney received his doctorate from the University of California (Berkeley). He is Professor of Economics, University of California (Riverside). He is a foremost authority on the economics of natural resources, on which he was an adviser to ministers of the government of Vancouver, BC. He is author of *The Corruption of Economics* (1994).

Fred Harrison Msc
Fred Harrison read Philosophy, Politics and Economics at the University of Oxford, and received his MSc from the University of London. In *The Power in the Land* (1983) he correctly predicted the global recession of 1992. He is consultant to a long-range study of the Russian economy undertaken by the Russian Academy of Sciences in 1998.

Richard Noyes
Richard Noyes, a former newspaper proprietor and editor, is a member of New Hampshire's House of Representative, where he is Division Chief for Local Revenue on the Local and Regulated Revenue Committee. He is editor of *Now the Synthesis: Capitalism, Socialism & the New Social Contract* (1991, New York: Holmes & Meier).

Florenz Plassmann PhD

Dr. Plassmann received his PhD from Virginia Polytechnic Institute and State University in June 1997, where he is employed as a research associate. In his dissertation he provided statistical evidence that a shift of the property tax base from structures to land has a significantly positive effect on the construction industry.

Nicolaus Tideman PhD

Dr. Tideman received his doctorate from the University of Chicago. He was Senior Staff Economist at the President's Council of Economic Advisers before moving to Virginia Polytechnic Institute & State University, where he is Professor of Economics. He is editor of *Land & Taxation* (1994).

Robert Schalkenbach Foundation

OTHILA PRESS thanks the Robert Schalkenbach Foundation and Dr. Michael Hudson, a Research Fellow in Babylonian economic archaeology at Harvard's Peabody Museum, for permission to publish extensive extracts from unpublished reports on the US national income accounts.

The publication of this volume was assisted by a grant from the Robert Schalkenbach Foundation, 41 East 72nd St., New York, New York 10021, from whom a catalogue of publications in stock can be obtained. Telephone: (212) 988 1680.

Index